CONNECTICUT
COOKS III

Designed by
Gretchen L. vanHoosier Associates

For the benefit of
THE AMERICAN CANCER SOCIETY
Connecticut Division, Inc.

For your convenience
Connecticut Cooks III
may be purchased
at all Unit offices of the
American Cancer Society
in Connecticut.
Copies may also be obtained by
using the order forms
in the back of the book.

Connecticut historical facts from *Connecticut Firsts*
by Wilson H. Faude and Joan W. Friedland, © 1978, 1985.
Peregrine Press, Publishers, Old Saybrook, Connecticut.
Used by permission.

WIMMER BROTHERS
Memphis   Dallas

Dedication

Connecticut Cooks III is being published in 1988...the 75th anniversary of our American Cancer Society. This year's theme is "Commemorating 75 Years of Life...We are Winning." When the Society was founded in 1913, only 1 in 10 cancer patients survived. Today, 1 in 2 survive. This book is dedicated to the more than 60,000 volunteers of the Connecticut Division of the American Cancer Society whose hard work has made this progress possible.

The recipes in Connecticut Cooks III, were selected from nearly 1200 submitted by our volunteers and other friends of the American Cancer Society. They were chosen by a panel of home economists and tested enthusiastically by friends of our volunteers.

The proceeds from this book will be used to support our Research, Education, and Service and Rehabilitation programs as we strive toward our ultimate goal of eliminating cancer in our lifetime. If you are not currently a volunteer, please consider calling your local Unit to learn how you can join the fight. Opportunities range from driving cancer patients to and from their treatments to helping with simple record-keeping, filing, and light office work. There is something for everyone.

We proudly present this book and are confident that you will enjoy the wide variety of recipes. Bon appetit!

Cookbook Committee

Chairman: Mary Lou Mack
Vice Chairman: Mary Ellen Rivers

Danbury Unit: Cathy Martin
Eastern Fairfield (Bridgeport): Mollie Schuette
Hartford: Elayne Perlstein
Manchester – North: Dorothy Roberts
Meriden/Middletown/Wallingford: Phyliss Lehet, Louise Pronovest
New Britain: Marilyn Wido
New London: Jeanne Martin
Northwestern: Barbara Denza, Kathleen Svetz
Norwich/Quinebaug: Marguerite Dumaine
South Central – Nancy Manger
Southern Fairfield: Shag Kinelski
Waterbury: Mary Jay Shea
Windham: Nina Whalen, Mari Shooks

TABLE OF CONTENTS

In Mother Tenney's kitchen was a gold-edged, leather-bound book inscribed "Cooking Recipes," with her maiden name and the date "1917," a gift for her hope chest. The book was divided into categories, including Fish, Compotes, "Joints" (no entries here!), and "Various," "How to Cook Husbands," written in old-fashioned Spencerian Script, was the first entry.

How to Cook Husbands

A good many husbands are utterly spoiled by mismanagement in cooking and so are not tender and good. Some women go about it as if their husbands were bladders and blow them up. Others keep them constantly in hot water. Others let them freeze by their carelessness and indifference. Some keep them in a stew by irritating ways and words. Others roast them. Some keep them in a pickle all their lives.

It cannot be supposed that any husband will be tender and good managed in this way, but they are really delicious when properly treated.

In selecting your husband, you should not be guided by the silvery appearance as in buying mackerel, nor by the golden tint as if you wanted salmon. Be sure and select him yourself, as tastes differ. Do not go to the market for him, as the best are always brought to the door. It is far better to have none, unless you will patiently learn how to cook him. A preserving kettle of the finest porcelain is best, but if you have nothing but an earthenware pipkin it will do with care.

See that the linens in which you wrap him are nicely washed and mended, with the required number of buttons and strings nicely sewed on. Tie him in the kettle with a strong silken cord called comfort, as the one called duty is apt to be weak. They are apt to fly out of the kettle and be burned and crusty on the edges, since like crabs and lobsters you have to cook them while alive.

Make a clear, steady fire out of love, neatness, and cheerfulness. Set him as near this as seems to agree with him. Should he sputter and fizz do not be anxious, as some husbands do this till they are quite done. Add a little sugar, in the form of what confectioners call kisses, but no vinegar or pepper on any account. A little spice improves them, but it must be used with judgment.

Do not stick any sharp instrument into him to see if he is becoming tender. Stir him gently, watch the while lest he lie too flat and close to the kettle and so become useless. You cannot fail to know when he is done.

If thus treated you will find him very digestible, agreeing nicely with you and the children. And he will keep as long as you want, unless you become careless and set him in too cold a place.

Appetizers & Beverages

Antipasto

Yields 12 to 13 pints
Best made in the summer when markets have plenty of fresh produce.

1 small head cauliflower flowerets, cut into bite-sized pieces	3 cups vinegar
	3 cups water
	1½ cup olive oil
1 pound small white onions, peeled	2 (12-ounce) can Italian tuna, drained
6 green peppers, sliced	1 (10-ounce) jar green olives, drained
6 red peppers, sliced	
5 large carrots, sliced	1 (16-ounce) can ripe olives, drained
1 rib celery, cut into chunks	
1 quart string beans, cut into 1-inch pieces Mushrooms, sliced	1 (10-ounce) jar stuffed olives, drained
1 (32-ounce) bottle catsup	12 mixed sweet pickles
1½ quarts thin tomato puree	Salt and pepper to taste
Juice of 2 lemons	

Par-boil all vegetables, drain and cool; set aside. Combine catsup, puree, lemon juice, vinegar, water and olive oil in a large kettle. Bring to a boil over medium-high heat. Pour over vegetables and boil for 15 minutes. Add tuna, olives, peppers and pickles. Return to boiling. Put into sterilized pint jars, secure lids and place in a hot water bath. Steam jars for 8 minutes. Tighten jar lids while hot when removed from canner. Invert jars onto lids while cooling.

Note: Mushrooms do not need to be par-boiled as long as other vegetables. Inverting jars onto lids for cooling helps seal tightly.

In 1977, Michael and Ann Coburn became the first husband and wife team ever to enter the priesthood in the same ceremony. Ann Coburn was ordained as Connecticut's first woman priest in ceremonies at St. James Episcopal Church in Danbury on December 17, 1977.

Pickled Eggs

Yields 24 eggs
Great for game parties

6 cups water
2 cups vinegar
¼ cup vegetable oil
2 tablespoons Worcestershire
   sauce
¼ cup salt

¼ cup pickling spices
2 teaspoons ground pepper
1 tablespoon English mustard
Dash of hot pepper sauce
2 dozen small hard boiled eggs

Combine first 9 ingredients in a large mixing bowl. Mix until well blended. Remove shells from boiled eggs and place in a large jar with a tight fitting lid. Pour water-vinegar mixture over eggs to cover. Cover tightly and allow to marinate for at least 2 weeks.

In 1789, the first law reports ever published were in Litch-field, Ct.

5 Onion Confit

Yields 3 quarts

5 garlic bulbs, peeled and left
   whole
4 pounds Spanish onions, thinly
   sliced
3 pounds red onions, sliced and
   separated into rings
5 bunches scallions, cut into
   1-inch pieces

1 pound shallots, peeled and
   halved
2 tablespoons mustard seed
1 tablespoon celery seed
4 cups cider vinegar
2 cups brown sugar

Combine ingredients in a large non-aluminum pot. Bring to a boil over a medium-high heat, reduce heat and simmer for 1 hour, stirring occasionally. Cool, place in container with cover and refrigerate overnight before serving.

Marinated Greek Olives

Serves 6 to 8
Good on the buffet table

¾ cup fresh lime juice
¾ cup orange juice
⅓ cup water
3 garlic cloves, halved
1½ to 2 tablespoons fennel seed

Peels of 1 lime and 1 orange, cut
   into thin strips
1 (16-ounce) can ripe olives,
   drained
Avocado slices for garnish

Combine first 6 ingredients in a 1-quart jar. Cover with lid and shake until well blended. Refrigerate overnight. Remove peels, add olives and marinate overnight. To serve, place in bowl and garnish with avocado slices.

Note: If refrigerated, these will keep for several weeks. Dip avocado slices in lemon juice to prevent browning.

In 1792, Zephaniah Swift. LL.D., of Windham, published his "Systems of the Laws of Connecticut," which were the first of its kind in the country.

Seasoned Oyster Cracker Snack

Yields about 3 cups

1 cup vegetable oil
1 (1.75-ounce) envelope
   buttermilk salad dressing mix
½ teaspoon garlic salt

½ teaspoon dill weed
½ teaspoon lemon pepper
1 (24-ounce) box or bag oyster
   crackers

Combine first 5 ingredients in 2 cup measure. Place crackers in plastic bag or glass container with lid. Pour oil mixture over crackers. Shake well. Let set overnight before eating to allow flavors to blend.

Spinach Layered in Phyllo

Yields 24 (2-inch) squares

12 phyllo leaves
2 (10-ounce) packages frozen
   chopped spinach
1½ cups chopped onion
½ cup butter
5 eggs, well beaten

½ cup scallions, chopped
8 ounces feta cheese
½ teaspoon dill weed or 1
   tablespoon dried dillweed
½ cup chopped parsley
Melted butter

Thaw phyllo. Thaw spinach and drain thoroughly. Saute onion in butter over medium-high heat until tender. Add spinach, eggs, scallions, cheese, dill and parsley. (Do not add any salt.) Grease a 13x9x2-inch baking pan. Cut phyllo leaves to fit the pan. Place 1 leaf into dish, brush with butter and continue layering until 6 leaves are used. Spread with spinach mixture. Top with layer of phyllo leaves brushed with butter. Score the top with a sharp knife making 2-inch squares. Bake at 350° for 1 hour or until brown and puffy. Cut through scoring to serve.

Note: Phyllo leaves can be found in frozen food sections of most supermarkets. It is very delicate to work with. To prevent leaves from drying out cover with a damp cloth until used.

Alpine Cups

Yields 24 cups

24 medium-sized fresh
   mushrooms
¼ cup plus 2 tablespoons melted
   butter, divided
1 (1.75-ounce) envelope dry onion
   soup mix

¾ cup dry breadcrumbs
½ cup chopped blanched
   almonds
⅓ cup sherry
¼ cup grated Parmesan cheese

Remove stems from mushrooms. Set caps aside and chop stems until fine. In medium-sized skillet, saute chopped stems in ¼ cup butter, stirring constantly, until tender. Add onion soup mix, breadcrumbs and almonds. Mix until evenly distributed. Stir in sherry. Fill caps with onion mixture. Place cap side up on well-greased pan, brush with remaining butter and sprinkle with Parmesan cheese. Broil for 5 minutes or until stuffing is bubbly.

Cheese/Nut Balls

Yields 4 dozen
Good hors d'oeuvres to keep in the freezer!

½ cup butter, softened
⅓ cup sugar
2 cups all-purpose flour

1 teaspoon salt
2 cups grated Cheddar cheese
1 cup chopped walnuts

Combine butter and sugar in mixing bowl. Cream until smooth. Add remaining ingredients, mix until well blended and roll into 1-inch balls. Place on ungreased baking sheet. Bake at 350° for 12 to 15 minutes or until browned.

Note: Can be made ahead and frozen on trays. After frozen, place in freezer bags until ready to use. To heat place on baking sheets and bake at 350° until heated through.

Mini-Blintzes

Yield 60 blintzes
A must for every party

1 (2-pound) loaf fresh white
  bread
2 (8-ounce) packages cream
  cheese, softened
1 egg

1 teaspoon vanilla
1 cup sugar
Butter
Sugar and cinnamon mix

Trim crusts from bread and roll each slice until very thin. Combine next 4 ingredients. Mix until well blended. Spread mixture on bread slices and roll jelly roll fashion. Roll in melted butter, sprinkle with sugar and cinnamon. Cut each slice into 2 pieces; place on baking sheets. Bake at 350° for 15 minutes.

Note: These can be prepared ahead and frozen. Defrost completely before baking. Serve hot.

Italian Cheese Turnovers

Yields 3 tarts
Just delicious!

1 pound Italian sausage, casing
    removed
2 cups ricotta cheese
3 tablespoons grated Italian
    cheese
4 eggs, divided

1 teaspoon parsley
2 cups all-purpose flour
1 teaspoon baking powder
½ cup milk
6 tablespoons sausage drippings

Fry sausage until evenly browned. Drain, reserving drippings; set aside
to cool. Combine, ricotta, Italian cheese, 3 eggs and parsley. Add sausage
and mix until well blended. Combine next 4 ingredients in mixing bowl.
If drippings do not equal 6 tablespoons add enough oil to make up dif-
ference. Mix until resembles pie crust. Roll out in pie crust shape. Fill half
of 1 side of dough with ricotta-sausage mixture. Fold over unfilled portion
of dough and seal edges with milk or water. Slit tops in about 3 places.
Place tarts on baking sheets at 400° for 20 minutes. To make crust darker,
brush with milk or egg wash. Cool, slice and enjoy!

Note: These can be made up to 5 days ahead and refrigerated.

Cheese Puffs

Yields 36 puffs
Freezes well. Keep on hand for unexpected company!

1 cup sharp cheese
3 tablespoons butter, softened
½ cup sifted all-purpose flour

¼ teaspoon salt
½ teaspoon paprika
Olives

Combine cheese and butter. Mix well. Stir in flour, salt and paprika. Mix
until well blended. Wrap approximately 1 tablespoon around an olive.
Place on baking sheet. Bake at 400° for 10 to 15 minutes or until golden
brown. Serve warm.

*Note: These can be frozen for 6 months without change in flavor. Small anchovies
or other small items may be substituted for the olives.*

Mushroom-Bacon Roll-Ups

Yields 30 roll-ups
All ages love these!

10 slices white bread
1 (10¾-ounce) can cream of
   mushroom soup

1 pound bacon

Trim crusts from bread and cut each slice into 3 strips. Spread undiluted soup onto strips. Cut bacon strips in half. Place bread strip on ½ bacon slice soup side up. Tightly wrap bacon around bread strip and secure with a toothpick. Place on baking sheet. bake at 300° for 1 hour.

Note: These can be made the night before. Low calorie!

In 1736, Dr. Norman Morrison, who came to Hartford from Scotland, was the first man to separate the practice of medicine from pharmacy.

Marinated Chicken Livers

Serves 18

9 water chestnuts, halved
9 chicken livers, halved
9 slices bacon, halved

¼ cup soy sauce
2 teaspoons brown sugar
2 teaspoons bourbon

Wrap water chestnut halves in liver, then bacon and secure with toothpicks. Combine remaining ingredients. Pour over the water chestnuts and marinate in refrigerator overnight. Shortly before serving, put chestnuts on baking sheet and place under broiler for approximately 6 minutes per side or until bacon is crisp.

Chicken Wings

Serves 10
Easy and delicious

1 pound chicken wings	1 (8-ounce) bottle French dressing
1 (10-ounce) jar apricot jelly	1 (1.75-ounce) envelope onion
or jam	soup mix

Cut chicken wings into pieces. Combine jelly, dressing and onion soup. Mix until well blended. Place wings in a 13x9x2-inch baking dish. Pour dressing mixture over wings. Bake at 325° for 1 hour. Place wings under broiler for about 10 minutes to brown. Watch this carefully, so you avoid burning.

In 1785, in South Windsor, Ct., the steam boat was born, and it was John Fitch not Robert Fulton who invented and completed the first model.

Pepperoni Puffs

Yields 60 puffs
Very easy and freeze beautifully!

1 cup all-purpose flour	1 egg
1 teaspoon baking powder	¼ cup grated Cheddar cheese
1 cup milk	1 cup diced pepperoni

Combine first 5 ingredients and mix thoroughly. Add pepperoni and mix until evenly distributed throughout the mixture. Allow batter to stand for 15 minutes. Grease mini muffin pans or spray with non-stick vegetable spray. Fill each cup ¾ full. Bake at 350° for 25 to 35 minutes or until browned.

Pepperoni Squares

Serves 16 to 20

1 (10-ounce) package refrigerated
  crescent dinner rolls
1 stick pepperoni, thinly sliced
1 (8-ounce) package Swiss cheese
  grated

½ cup milk
4 eggs

Place dinner rolls in the bottom of a buttered 13x9x2-inch baking dish. Press seams together. Top with pepperoni slices. Sprinkle with Swiss cheese. Combine milk and eggs; beat until well blended. Pour milk and egg mixture evenly over the cheese. Bake at 350° for 30 to 45 minutes or until bubbly.

In 1796, the Old State House in Hartford, the oldest state house in America, was designed and built.

Layered Hors d'Oeuvres

Yields 16 (2-inch) squares

1 (10-ounce) package refrigerated
  crescent rolls
½ pound boiled ham, thinly
  sliced
½ pound provolone cheese,
  thinly sliced

½ pound hard salami, thinly
  sliced
1 (7-ounce) jar red roasted
  peppers, diced
1 egg yolk

Press ½ of crescent rolls into the bottom of an 8x8x2-inch baking pan. Layer ½ remaining ingredients in order listed. Repeat layers with remaining ingredients. Press remaining dough over top and gently press down to eliminate air pockets. Brush with beaten egg yolk. Bake at 350° for 25 to 30 minutes or until heated through and golden brown. Cool slightly and cut into squares using serrated knife. Serve warm.

Sausage Balls

Yields 48 balls

1 pound hot sausage
1 cup shredded mozzarella cheese

1 cup buttermilk biscuit baking
  mix

Combine all ingredients in large mixing bowl. Mix until ingredients are evenly distributed. Roll into walnut-sized balls. Place on baking sheet. Bake at 350° for 30 minutes.

Note: These freeze well. Bake at 350° until heated through before serving.

In 1770, the first chocolate mill in America was founded by Christopher Leffingwell in Norwich.

Sausage en Croute

Serves 8

1 sheet frozen puff pastry
1 pound pork sausage
½ cup chopped onion
½ cup chopped green or red
  pepper

1 large tomato, diced
1 cup shredded Swiss cheese
3 tablespoons chopped fresh
  parsley

Thaw pastry for 20 minutes. Meanwhile, brown sausage in a skillet over a medium-high heat, breaking into bits as it cooks. Add onion and green pepper. Continue to cook until vegetables are tender. Add tomato, cheese and parsley. Mix until well blended; set aside. Roll pastry on a floured surface to a 14x10-inch rectangle. Transfer pastry to a baking sheet which has been lightly greased. Bake at 350° for 10 to 15 minutes or until browned.

Clams in Shells or Dish

Serves 10 to 12

2 dozen clams
6 slices bacon, broken into pieces
1 small onion, minced
½ green pepper, minced
2 teaspoons chopped chives
2 teaspoons grated Parmesan
  cheese

1 teaspoon paprika
¼ teaspoon pepper
2 to 3 dashes seafood seasoning
Melted butter

Thoroughly wash clams; open, mince clam and return to shells; set aside. Saute bacon in skillet until crisp, remove, crumble and set aside to drain. Pour off fat, add onion and green pepper. Saute for 5 minutes or until tender. Mix chives, cheese, paprika, pepper and seafood seasoning in small bowl. Blend in sauteed vegetables and reserved bacon. Place 1 teaspoon bacon mixture on each clam shell. Place in a shallow baking pan and bake at 400° for 10 minutes. Serve with melted butter.

Lobster Rolls

Serves 8 to 10
Lots of raves!

1 (16-ounce) box pasteurized
  processed cheese spread
1 cup sweet butter

1 (14-ounce) can lobster, drained
2 (20-ounce) loaves thin sandwich
  bread

Melt cheese and butter in the top of a double boiler, stirring occasionally. Remove from fire and add lobster which has been finely chopped. Cool until thick enough to spread. Remove crust from bread and roll each slice until thin. Spread lobster mixture liberally on each slice and roll. Wrap well in waxed paper and refrigerate. (May be frozen at this point.) To serve, slice into halves or thirds, brush with melted butter and place on buttered baking sheet. Bake at 450° for 10 minutes or until brown and bubbly. Serve immediately.

Oysters Briguglio

Serves 8
Easy but elegant hor d'oeuvres with ingredients that can be kept on hand for "Surprise Guests"!

1 (5¾-ounce) can smoked oysters	Mayonnaise
1 (5¼-ounce) box melba toast rounds	Parmesan cheese

Place 1 smoked oyster on a melba round and cover with a dollop of mayonnaise. Sprinkle with Parmesan cheese. Broil until lightly brown and serve hot. Great with champagne.

In 1860, the first American sailing ship to beat the "Flying Cloud's" record on the New York to San Francisco run was built at Mystic.

Shrimp Canapes

Yields 2 to 3 dozen canapes
Great to have on hand in the freezer

1 (8-ounce) package shredded Swiss cheese	½ teaspoon salt
1 medium-sized onion, diced	½ teaspoon dry mustard
1 (6-ounce) can shrimp	¼ teaspoon pepper
¾ cup mayonnaise	Dash of hot pepper sauce
1 teaspoon lemon juice	1 loaf party rye bread slices

Combine all ingredients except bread in mixing bowl. Mix until well blended. Heap mixture onto bread slices. Freeze, uncovered, on baking sheet. Pack in freezer bags until ready to use. To serve, place canapes on baking sheet and broil about 10 minutes or until bubbly.

Shrimp and Clam Pizza

Yields 1 pizza

Olive oil
1 (12-inch) frozen pizza crust
2 (10-ounce) cans minced clams,
  drained
1 (5-ounce) package frozen
  shrimp

Parsley
Fresh chopped garlic
1 (4-ounce) package shredded
  mozzarella cheese

Spread olive oil on pizza crust. Drain clams and spread evenly over crust. Spread shrimp among clams. Sprinkle small amount of parsley and garlic to taste over mixture. Top with shredded cheese. Bake at 400° for 20 to 25 minutes or until golden brown and cheese melts.

Note: this pizza DOES NOT freeze well.

In 1877, Professor Asaph Hall of Goshen discovered the outer and the inner satellites of Mars.

Hot Broccoli Dip

Yields about 3 cups

4 sticks celery
2 small onions
1 (4-ounce) can mushrooms,
  drained
4 tablespoons butter

1 (6-ounce) roll garlic cheese
1 (10¾-ounce) can cream of
  mushroom soup
1 (10-ounce) package frozen
  chopped broccoli

Chop and saute celery, onions and mushrooms in butter over medium-high heat, stirring constantly. Reduce heat and add garlic cheese and soup. Continue to cook, stirring constantly, until cheese melts. Add broccoli. Simmer until broccoli is warm. Serve hot with an assortment of crackers.

Salad Dip

Serves 8 to 12
This is a family favorite!

1 cup sour cream
1 cup mayonnaise
1 cup coconut
¼ cup diced onion

¼ teaspoon curry powder
2 tablespoons minced parsley
Whole pineapple

Combine ingredients in medium-size mixing bowl. Mix until well blended. Chill. Serve in a pineapple halved lengthwise with fruit removed.

In 1947, the first helicopter with a fully servo-controlled intermeshing rotor was built in Bloomfield.

Polly's Goodie

Serves 10 to 12
Easy!

2 (8-ounce) packages cream
cheese, softened
2 cups sour cream

Chopped scallions
Cherry tomatoes, quartered
1 (8-ounce) jar picante sauce

Combine cream cheese and sour cream. Mix until smooth and creamy. Spread evenly on the bottom of a 11x8x2-inch baking dish. Layer remaining ingredients over cream cheese mixture in order listed. Serve with taco flavored or regular corn chips.

Note: Make in the morning and serve in the evening.

Crabmeat Dip

Serves 12

1 (8-ounce) package cream cheese, softened
1 teaspoon minced onion
1 tablespoon mayonnaise

½ teaspoon Worcestershire sauce
1 (3-ounce) bottle cocktail sauce or to taste
1 (6-ounce) can crabmeat, drained

Combine first 4 ingredients in mixing bowl. Mix until well blended. Flatten mixture on a serving platter. Spread a thin layer of cocktail sauce on cheese layer. Top with layer of crabmeat. Serve at room temperature with assorted crackers.

Shrimp Dip

Yields 2 to 2½ cups
Quick and easy

1 (6-ounce) can shrimp, drained
1 cup finely grated Cheddar cheese

1 cup mayonnaise
1 teaspoon Worcestershire sauce

Mash shrimp in small mixing bowl. Add all other ingredients and mix until well blended. Serve chilled with crackers.

Shrimp Butter Dip

Yields about 2½ cups
Addictive and takes only 5 minutes to make!

1 (8-ounce) package cream cheese, softened
¾ cup butter, softened
Juice of 1 lemon

2 tablespoons minced onion
4 tablespoons mayonnaise
3 (4½-ounce) cans tiny shrimp, drained

Combine first 5 ingredients. Mix until well blended. Add shrimp and mix until evenly distributed throughout the mixture. Serve with round butter crackers or thinly sliced French bread.

Tex-Mex-Dip

Serves 10 to 12
A weekend must for football games

1 (8-ounce) package cream cheese, softened
1 (16-ounce) can hot chili with beans
½ (1.25-ounce) envelope taco seasoning

1 (4-ounce) can black olives, chopped
1 (8-ounce) package Monterey Jack cheese, shredded
1 (16-ounce) bag nacho corn chips

Layer ingredients in order listed in a 1-quart casserole. Make layers as even as possible. Bake at 350° for 15 to 20 minutes or until hot and bubbly. Serve with nacho flavored corn chips, dipping down to bottom to get all flavors.

Hot "Pizza" Dip

Serves 10 to 12

1 pound American cheese, shredded
1 pound Cheddar cheese, shredded
2 pounds tomatoes, drained and finely chopped

2 (10-ounce) cans chili peppers, chopped
1½ teaspoons chili powder

Combine American and Cheddar cheese and mix until thoroughly blended. Mix remaining 3 ingredients in separate bowl and mix until well blended. Layer in a 2-quart casserole which has been sprayed with non-stick vegetable spray. Begin with tomato-chili pepper mixture and end with cheese mixture. Repeat layers. Bake at 350° for 30 minutes. Serve with corn chips.

Note: Half of this recipe still makes plenty of dip.

Fiesta Cheese Dip

Serves 20 to 25
A taste of South of the border!

2 tablespoons vegetable oil
1 cup chopped onion
2 cloves garlic, minced
1 (2-pound) box mild Mexican flavored pasteurized processed cheese, cubed

1 (8-ounce) package longhorn cheese, cubed
1 (4-ounce) can jalapeno peppers, finely chopped (optional)
1 (18-ounce) can stewed tomatoes

1 hour before serving: heat oil in crock pot or slow cooker. Add onion and garlic and saute until onion is tender. Add cheeses; heat until melted, stirring constantly. Add tomatoes and peppers, stirring frequently. Serve hot with tortilla chips or nacho flavored corn chips. Absolutely delicious!

Almond Pinecones

Yields 1½ cups

1¼ cups whole almonds
1 (8-ounce) package cream cheese, softened
½ cup mayonnaise
4 slices bacon, fried, drained and crumbled

1 tablespoon chopped green onions
½ teaspoon dillweed
⅛ teaspoon pepper

Spread almonds in a single layer on a baking sheet. Bake at 300° for 15 minutes, stirring often, until almonds just begin to color. Combine cream cheese and mayonnaise. Mix until well blended. Add remaining ingredients except almonds; mix until ingredients are evenly distributed throughout the mixture. Cover and chill overnight. Form cheese mixture into shape of 2 pinecones. Place on serving platter. Beginning at narrow end of pinecone, press almonds into cheese in slightly angled rows. Continue overlapping rows until cheese is covered. Garnish with artificial pine sprigs. Serve with crackers.

Apricot/Cream Cheese Spread

Serves 10 to 12
Easy appetizer

2 (8-ounce) packages cream
  cheese, softened
½ (10-ounce) jar apricot preserves

1 cup chopped slivered almonds
¾ teaspoon celery powder
1 cup flaked coconut

Combine cream cheese and preserves. Mix with electric mixer until well blended. Place mixture on a large piece of waxed paper. Form into a roll and place in freezer for 30 minutes or longer until the roll hardens. Combine almonds, celery powder and coconut. Pour onto baking sheet and bake at 300° for 15 minutes or until brown. Watch carefully, since this will burn easily. Remove roll from freezer, roll in almond mixture and replace waxed paper. Allow to refrigerate for 4 hours or overnight for blending of flavors. Serve with crackers.

Boursin Cheese

Yields 3 cups
Great to wrap in small packages, freeze and use as last minute hostess gifts

1 cup butter at room temperature
2 (8-ounce) packages cream
  cheese, softened
1 teaspoon oregano
1 teaspoon garlic powder
¼ teaspoon marjoram

¼ teaspoon dill
¼ teaspoon pepper
¼ teaspoon basil
¼ teaspoon rosemary
½ to 1 cup coarsely ground
  pepper

Cream butter and cheese. Add next 7 ingredients increasing or decreasing to suit individual tastes. Mix until well blended. Roll in coarse black pepper. Cover, chill and age for at least 24 hours before serving. Serve at room temperature.

German Beer-Cheese

Yields about 3½ cups
May be frozen

1 pound sharp Cheddar cheese
2 (8-ounce) packages cream
   cheese, softened
Few drops hot sauce
½ to ¾ cup beer at room
   temperature

2 teaspoons Worcestershire sauce
2 cloves garlic, minced
Salt and pepper to taste

Grate Cheddar cheese and allow to set until room temperature. Combine with cream cheese and mix until well blended. Add remaining ingredients. Beat until ingredients are evenly distributed throughout the mixture. Chill. Before serving, sprinkle with paprika, chopped parsley or ground nuts. Serve with hearty crackers and party rye bread.

Brie Wrapped in Phyllo

Serves 20
Good for a wine and cheese party!

12 sheets phyllo leaves
2 cups sweet butter, melted

1 whole (about 5 pounds) brie

Butter baking sheet large enough to hold brie. Lay 5 sheets phyllo on baking sheet. Brush each sheet with melted butter. Set brie on phyllo and fold the edges of phyllo up around the brie. Cover the top of the brie with 6 sheets of phyllo. Brush with butter. Tuck the ends securely under the brie. Brush the entire package with the remaining butter. Bake at 350° for 20 to 30 minutes or until golden brown. Remove from oven and allow to stand for at least 30 minutes before serving. Serve with crackers or small party-sized bread slices.

Blue Cheese Butter Log

Yields 1 roll

1 cup butter, softened
¼ pound blue cheese, crumbled

1 tablespoon chopped green onion
Chopped parsley

Place ingredients in mixing bowl and blend until evenly distributed. Place on sheet of waxed paper. Shape into a log; roll in chopped parsley and wrap. Refrigerate until firm. Serve with crackers.

Chutney Spread

Serves 8 to 12
Makes a nice Christmas gift

1 (8-ounce) package cream cheese, softened
½ (8-ounce) jar chutney
1 teaspoon curry powder

½ cup coconut
Dash of Worcestershire sauce
1 (4-ounce) package sliced almonds

Combine all ingredients except almonds in mixing bowl. Mix until well blended. Add almonds and blend until evenly distributed throughout the mixture. Serve with wheat crackers or round, buttery crackers.

Liver Pate Appetizers

Yields 32 appetizers

1 (10-ounce) package refrigerated crescent rolls
1 (4¾-ounce) can liverwurst spread

5 slices crisply cooked bacon, drained and crumbled
¼ cup thinly sliced scallions

Separate roll dough at perforations. Generously cover each triangle with liverwurst spread. Cut each triangle into 4 small triangles. Sprinkle bacon and onion over liverwurst. Roll each triangle into crescent. Place on ungreased baking sheet. Bake at 375° for 10 minutes.

Country Pate with Pistachio Nuts

Yields 2 loaves
A wonderful country pate flavor with the nutty texture of the pistachios

2 pounds pork butt or shoulder,
  diced into ½-inch cubes
½ pound pork fat or fat back,
  diced into ¼-inch cubes,
  divided
6 ounces chicken liver
6 cloves garlic
¼ cup heavy cream
3 eggs
⅓ cup brandy or cognac

½ cup all-purpose flour
4 teaspoons salt
2 teaspoons white pepper
½ teaspoon allspice
½ teaspoon cinnamon
2 cups pistachio nuts
1 pound ham, diced into ¼-inch
  cubes
bacon

Grind all of the pork and ½ of the pork fat using fine grind meat grinder blade. Combine next 10 ingredients in a food processor and puree. Add to ground pork mixture. Mix until well blended. Add the pistachio nuts, ham and remaining pork fat. Mix thoroughly. Line 2 (9x5x3-inch) glass loaf pans with bacon. Spoon pate mixture into the pans dividing the mixture evenly between the 2 pans. Top with bacon. Bake at 300° in a waterbath filled halfway up the sides of the loaf pans for 1 hour to 1 hour 15 minutes or until a meat thermometer inserted in the center of the pate reads 130. Remove pans from waterbath and cool slightly. For best results, weight the top of each pate with a brick wrapped in plastic wrap. Refrigerate overnight. (Turn onto plate, garnish with sprigs of parsley and serve with assorted crackers.)

Note: We serve this pate as an appetizer course with a serving of 5-onion confit on the side.

Freshfield's
West Cornwall, CT

In 1985, Denise L. Matthews of Old Saybrook became the first woman to graduate at the head of the class of a military academy.

Crabmeat Mold

Yields about 4 cups

1 tablespoon unflavored gelatin
3 tablespoons cold water
1 (10¾-ounce) can cream of
  mushroom soup
2 (3-ounce) packages cream
  cheese, softened

1 (7-ounce) can crabmeat
1 small onion, finely chopped
1 cup finely chopped celery
1 cup mayonnaise

Place gelatin in a small bowl. Add water and allow to soften. Heat soup in medium-sized saucepan over low heat. Stir gelatin mixture into warm soup. Remove from heat and cool slightly. Add remaining ingredients; mix until well blended. Pour mixture into a lightly oiled 1½-quart mold. Cover and refrigerate overnight.

In 1816, the first fanning mill for the separating of chaff from grain was patented by Benjamin D. Beecher of Cheshire.

Lobster Spread

Yields about 3 cups

2 envelopes unflavored gelatin
½ cup water
2 tablespoons lemon juice
1 (16-ounce) carton sour cream
1 (12-ounce) bottle chili sauce

2 tablespoons horseradish
1½ cups finely chopped cooked
  shrimp or lobster or imitation
  crabmeat

Sprinkle gelatin over water and lemon juice in a small saucepan. Let stand for 1 minute. Stir over low heat until gelatin is completely dissolved, about 5 minutes. With a wire whip or rotary beater, blend in sour cream, chili sauce and horseradish; fold in lobster. Pour mixture into a well-oiled 3½ cup mold. Cover and chill until firm.

Salmon Pate

Yields 2 cups

1 (7¾-ounce) can salmon
1 (1.75-ounce) envelope Italian
    salad dressing mix

1 (8-ounce) package cream cheese,
    softened
⅓ cup chopped cucumber

Line a 2-cup bowl or mini-loaf pan with plastic wrap. Combine ingredients in mixing bowl and mix until evenly distributed. Press into bowl and chill at least 1 hour before serving. Unmold, serve with crackers or cucumber slices.

In 1930, the first radio broadcast from a submerged submarine was successfully accomplished and broadcast on December 7, at New London.

Cranberry Cooler

Serves 6
This is a refreshing summer drink!

1 (16-ounce) can jellied cranberry
    sauce, chilled
2¼ cups cold water, divided
½ cup fresh or bottled lemon
    juice

¾ cup chilled orange juice
1 teaspoon almond extract
1 cup chilled ginger ale

Combine cranberry juice and 1 cup water in blender container. Cover and blend on high speed until mixture is smooth. Combine remaining ingredients in a large bowl, add cranberry mixture and stir until well blended. Serve over ice.

Note: This recipe may be doubled and served in a punch bowl.

Summertime Tea

Yields 3½ quarts

1½ cups sugar
6 small tea bags
1 quart boiling water
1 (6-ounce) can frozen lemonade
concentrate, thawed and
undiluted

1 (6-ounce) can frozen orange
juice concentrate, thawed and
undiluted
2 quarts cold water

Add sugar and tea bags to boiling water; stir well. Cover and steep for 5 minutes. Remove tea bags, squeezing gently. Stir in remaining ingredients. Cool slightly. Serve over ice.

Ginger Tea

Serves 1
Soothes sore throats and helps relieve cold symptoms, but tastes good

1 (¾-inch) piece fresh ginger
1½ cups water

Few drops of lemon juice
2 teaspoons honey

Cut the ginger into ¼-inch slices. Place in water in saucepan and bring to a boil. Boil for 5 minutes. Stir in lemon juice and honey. Strain the tea into a mug and serve immediately!

Mexican Chocolate

Serves 20 to 25

5 quarts milk
25 ounces semi-sweet chocolate
squares, cut into small pieces

15 cinnamon sticks
1 tablespoon plus 1 teaspoon
vanilla

Combine milk, chocolate and cinnamon sticks in saucepan. Cook over a medium heat, stirring constantly, until chocolate melts. Remove from heat. Remove cinnamon and stir in vanilla. Beat with electric beater until frothy. Serve immediately. Pour chocolate into mugs. Add cinnamon stick to each mug for stirring.

Champagne Blossom Punch

Yields 2 quarts

⅓ cup frozen orange juice concentrate, thawed and undiluted

⅓ cup frozen lemonade concentrate, thawed and undiluted

1 (25.4-ounce) bottle Riesling, chilled

1 (25.4-ounce) bottle champagne, chilled

Lime, lemon or orange slices

Combine first 3 ingredients, stirring well. Gradually add champagne. DO NOT STIR. Garnish each serving with a fruit slice, if desired.

Anniversary Punch

Yields 1 gallon

3 (10-ounce) packages frozen strawberries

Juice of 2 limes

3 teaspoons grated lime peel

1 (25.4-ounce) bottle dry champagne

1 (25.4-ounce) bottle cold duck

1 (25.4-ounce) bottle Riesling

Place strawberries, lime juice and peel in saucepan. Bring to a boil over medium-high heat. Reduce heat and simmer for 10 minutes. Strain mixture, cool and pour over ice block. Add chilled wines just before serving.

Pink Lady Punch

Yields 1 gallon

1 (32-ounce) bottle cranberry juice cocktail, chilled

1 (32-ounce) bottle pineapple juice, chilled

1 to 1½ cups sugar

2 quarts ginger ale, chilled

Combine all ingredients in a large pitcher or container; stir until well blended. Pour over ice to serve.

Foamy Lime Punch

Yields 4 quarts

2 (0.25-ounce) packages lemon-lime flavored, unsweetened soft drink mix
2 quarts water
2 cups sugar

1 (46-ounce) can unsweetened pineapple juice
1 quart ginger ale, chilled
1 quart lime sherbet

Combine first 4 ingredients in large container. Mix until well blended; chill. To serve, combine chilled mixture and ginger ale in a punch bowl. Drop sherbet by scoops into punch.

Note: Punch can be made ahead and stored. Add ginger ale and sherbet just before serving.

In 1840, the first American shaving soap was made by James B. Williams of Glastonbury.

Apricot Stone Sour Slush

Serves 24 to 30

8 cups water
¾ cup sugar
2 (12-ounce) cans frozen lemonade concentrate
1 (12-ounce) can frozen orange juice concentrate

½ of a fifth of apricot brandy
50/50 or lemon-lime carbonated beverage

Bring water to a boil in a large saucepan. Add sugar and stir until sugar is completely dissolved. Place mixture in container with a tight fitting lid and freeze until solid. To serve, add enough 50/50 or lemon-lime carbonated beverage to make a slushy mixture. Recipe doubles well.

Wooden Shoe

Serves 1
A great after dinner drink!

2 ounces choclair liqueur **1 ounce vodka**

Fill "on the rocks" glass with crushed ice. Gently pour liqueur and vodka over ice and swirl to stir.

Fuzzy Navel

Serves 1
A real winner from Florida!

1 to 1½ jiggers peach Schnapps **Ice**
Orange juice

Pour Schnapps into an "on the rocks" glass. Fill remainder of glass with orange juice and ice. Stir until well mixed.

Tequila Sunrise

Serves 1

1½ ounces (1 jigger) tequila **1 teaspoon grenadine or**
½ cup chilled fresh orange juice   **to taste**
1 tablespoon fresh lime juice or to **½ lime slice for garnish**
  taste

Half fill an 8-ounce stemmed glass with ice cubes. Combine the first 3 ingredients and stir until well blended. Add the grenadine letting it sink to the bottom of the glass. Garnish with lime slice.

Mexicali Maria

Serves 1

1½ ounces (1 jigger) vodka or
  tequila
¾ cup chilled tomato-vegetable
  juice
2 teaspoons fresh lime juice or to
  taste
½ teaspoon Worcestershire sauce
  or to taste

¼ teaspoon ground cumin or to
  taste
¼ teaspoon pickled jalapeño
  pepper juice, if desired
Hot pepper sauce to taste

Half fill a tall glass with ice cubes. Combine ingredients in order listed in the ice filled glass. Stir gently until ingredients are well blended.

In 1881, Phineas Taylor Barnum of Bethel was the "American Impresario" without equal and invented the two and the three ring circus, where before only one had existed.

"The Brethren's Cider"

Serves 8
This spirited Thanksgiving or Christmas pre-dinner drink comes, it is said, from the Sabbathday Lake Shaker Community in Maine.

4 cups apple cider
1½ cups apple brandy

Ice cubes
Lemon peel slivers for garnish

Mix cider and brandy in a large pitcher. Chill thoroughly. Pour over ice cubes and add lemon peel to serve.

Note: Serve the children well-chilled plain cider.

Yankee Style Eggnog

Yields 1 quart

4 eggs	**Dash of nutmeg**
1½ cups sugar	**1 quart apple cider**
5 shot glasses bacardi white rum	

Combine eggs and sugar in a large mixing bowl. Beat with rotary beater until mixture is foamy. Add rum, nutmeg and apple cider. Beat until well blended.

In 1975, Ella Tambussi Grasso was sworn in as the Governor of Connecticut and was the first woman in America to assume that office without having inherited it from her husband.

Salads & Salad Dressings

Cranberry Cream Cheese Ring

Serves 10

1 (3-ounce) package cherry or
strawberry flavored gelatin
2½ cups boiling water, divided
1 (16-ounce) can whole cranberry
sauce
1 (3-ounce) package lemon
flavored gelatin

1 (8-ounce) package cream cheese,
softened and cut into cubes
1 cup crushed pineapple with
juice
¼ cup nuts

Dissolve cherry gelatin in 1¼ cups boiling water. Add cranberry sauce and mix until well blended. Pour mixture into a lightly oiled 4-cup mold. Chill until firmly set. Dissolve lemon flavored gelatin in remaining boiling water. Blend in cream cheese cubes, pineapple and nuts. Pour into mold over cranberry layer, cover and refrigerate overnight. Unmold onto platter before serving.

Cranberry-Horseradish Mousse

Serves 6 to 8
Good with roasts, ham or turkey

1 cup sugar
½ cup water
2 cups whole cranberries, washed
and stemmed
1 cup sour cream

4 tablespoons prepared
horseradish
1 tablespoon lemon juice
1 envelope unflavored gelatin
½ cup cold water

Combine sugar and water in saucepan. Bring to a boil over high heat. Boil for 5 minutes, stirring briefly, just until sugar is dissolved. Add cranberries and cook an additional 5 minutes or until berries pop. Remove from heat and cool slightly. Place berries in a mixing bowl, add next 3 ingredients and blend until well mixed; set aside. Combine gelatin and water in small saucepan. Let stand until gelatin softens. Cook over medium heat, stirring constantly, until gelatin is dissolved. Add to berry mixture and gently blend until ingredients are thoroughly mixed. Pour into a lightly oiled 4-cup mold, cover and refrigerate for about 6 hours or until firm. Loosen with a dull-edged knife and unmold on platter before serving.

Yogurt Fruit Salad

Serves 6

2 tablespoons honey
1 tablespoon lemon juice
3 oranges, peeled and sectioned
1 medium-sized apple, unpeeled
  and diced

2 bananas, sliced
1 cup chopped pecans
1 (8-ounce) carton plain yogurt

Combine honey and lemon juice in a large bowl; stir well. Add fruit and pecans, tossing gently to coat. Chill thoroughly. Fold in yogurt just before serving; toss gently.

Muffin Cup Frozen Salad

Serves 10 to 12
A great summer salad

1 (16-ounce) carton sour cream
⅛ tablespoon lemon juice
⅛ teaspoon salt
½ cup sugar
1 (8-ounce) can crushed
  pineapple, drained

Drop of red food coloring
1 (16-ounce) can pitted bing
  cherries, drained
¼ cup chopped pecans

Combine sour cream, lemon juice, sugar and pineapple in mixing bowl. Add just enough red food coloring to tint the mixture a delicate pink color. Mix until well blended. Fold in pecans and cherries. Pour into 12 paper lined muffin cups, cover and freeze overnight. Defrost about 15 minutes before serving. If preferred, the salad may be spooned into a 9x5x3-inch loaf pan lined with aluminum foil and frozen instead of making individual salads. To serve loaf, slice and place on lettuce leaves.

Note: Individual salads may be wrapped in aluminum foil and frozen for up to 2 weeks in advance.

Champagne Orange Salad

Serves 6 to 8

3 cups butter lettuce
¾ cup pecans
1 (6-ounce) jar artichoke hearts,
  sliced
¼ cup champagne
½ teaspoon orange rind
¼ cup olive oil

¼ cup freshly squeezed orange
  juice
¼ cup white wine vinegar
1 navel orange
¼ teaspoon salt
White pepper to taste

Combine lettuce, pecans and artichoke hearts in large salad bowl. In a small bowl, whisk together the next 5 ingredients. Peel orange, remove membrane, chop and add to champagne mixture. Pour over ingredients in salad bowl; toss. Add salt and pepper to taste.

In 1796, Amelia Simmons wrote the first American cookbook. It was published in Hartford under the title, "American Cookery or the art of dressing viands, fish, poultry and vegetables."

Colorful, Flavorful Salad

Serves 8 to 10
Can make ahead and freeze

1 (21-ounce) can pie filling,
  any flavor
1 (21-ounce) can chunk
  pineapple, drained
1 (14-ounce) can sweetened
  condensed milk

1 (8-ounce) container frozen, non-
  dairy whipped topping
1 cup miniature marshmallows
1 (8-ounce) package cream cheese
½ cup nuts

Combine ingredients in a large mixing bowl; mix until well blended. Cover and refrigerate until ready to serve.

Holiday Fruit Salad

Serves 10 to 12
Keeps well because of dressing which also adds texture to the salad

1 (15½-ounce) can pineapple
  chunks
½ cup sugar
2 tablespoons all-purpose flour
1 egg, beaten
1 cup pecans, chopped
3 bananas, sliced

2 (11-ounce) cans mandarin
  oranges, drained
3 medium-sized, unpeeled
  apples, chopped
½ pound red seedless grapes,
  halved

Drain pineapple, reserving juice. Measure sugar and flour into a small saucepan; stir until well blended. Slowly, add juice and egg. Cook over low heat, stirring constantly, for 8 to 10 minutes or until mixture is thick and smooth. Remove from heat and cool. Combine pecans and fruits. Add dressing and gently stir until all ingredients are well coated with dressing. Cover and thoroughly chill before serving.

Grape and Cheese Salad

Serves 8
Excellent!

3 heads butter bib lettuce, torn
  into bite-sized pieces
1 cup seedless grapes, halved

½ cup chopped pecans
1½ cups grated Monterey Jack
  cheese

Combine ingredients in salad bowl; toss to mix. Pour dressing over mixture and toss to coat ingredients with dressing just before serving.

Dressing:
1 clove garlic
¼ cup lemon juice
½ cup safflower oil

2 tablespoons sour cream
1 tablespoon sugar

Combine ingredients in small mixing bowl. Mix until well blended.

Easy Green Salad

Serves 8 to 10
So good!

2 (3¾-ounce) boxes instant
    pistachio pudding mix
1 (16-ounce) container sour cream
½ cup chopped nuts

1 (20-ounce) can crushed
    pineapple, drained
½ cup flaked coconut

Combine ingredients in mixing bowl; mix until thoroughly blended. Pour into crystal serving dish, cover and refrigerate until chilled.

In 1985, the Griswold Inn in Essex, which opened in 1776 and still in operation today, is the oldest inn in continual use in the country.

Curried Chicken Salad

Serves 4

1 (3-pound) broiler-fryer chicken
1 cup water
1 teaspoon curry powder
¼ teaspoon pepper
1 tablespoon lemon juice
1 cup diced cantaloupe

1 cup seedless grapes, halved
½ cup walnut pieces
1 tablespoon grated fresh ginger
½ cup mayonnaise
¼ cup sour cream

Place chicken in large, deep saucepan. Add water, cover pan and steam for 45 minutes or until fork can be inserted into chicken with ease. Cool. Bone chicken reserving broth for other uses. Cut boned chicken into bite-sized pieces. Add curry powder, pepper and lemon juice. Toss until ingredients are evenly distributed. Refrigerate until chilled. Add remaining ingredients, toss to mix and chill before serving.

Oriental Chicken Salad

Serves 4
Good on a hot summer day

1 whole, boneless chicken breast, cooked and cut into bite-sized pieces
2 (¼-inch thick) slices baked ham, cubed
1 rib celery, chopped
1 carrot, peeled and chopped
6 large mushrooms, sliced
12 snowpeas
½ cup beansprouts
1 head lettuce of your choice, broken into bite-sized pieces

Combine ingredients in large salad bowl; toss to blend. Add dressing and toss until ingredients are coated.

Dressing:
½ cup peanut oil
¼ cup tarragon vinegar
1 teaspoon soy sauce
1 tablespoon sesame oil
1 tablespoon sesame seed

Combine ingredients in a jar with lid. Cover and shake until well blended.

Hot Chicken Salad

Serves 6

2 cups cooked and chopped chicken
½ cup slivered almonds
1 cup slivered water chestnuts
Pepper
1 cup cut up pimiento
¼ teaspoon celery salt
2 tablespoons lemon juice
1 cup mayonnaise
½ cup crumbled French fried onion rings
¾ cup grated American cheese

Combine ingredients in order listed in large mixing bowl except for onion rings and cheese. Pour mixture into a greased 1½-quart casserole. Mix onion rings and cheese. Sprinkle over top of casserole. Bake, uncovered, at 350° for 30 minutes.

Chicken Tortilla Chip Salad

Serves 6 to 8
Light, yet spicy!

2 whole chicken breasts, boiled, boned and shredded
1 cup shredded Monterey Jack cheese
2 medium-sized tomatoes, chopped into bite-sized pieces
½ red onion, thinly sliced
1 ripe avocado, cut into small cubes
½ cup ripe olives, sliced
1 large head lettuce, torn into bite-sized pieces
2 cups tortilla chips, broken into bite-sized pieces

Combine first 6 ingredients in mixing bowl. Mix until well blended and chill. To serve, break lettuce into salad bowl. Add chicken mixture, dressing and tortilla chips; toss. Serve immediately.

Dressing:
½ cup oil-vinegar type Italian dressing
½ cup medium picante salsa
1 teaspoon chili powder

Combine ingredients in container with lid. Shake until well blended.

Jellied Corned Beef Loaf

Serves 6
Good for summertime luncheon

1 envelope unflavored gelatin
1¾ cups boiling water
1 (7-ounce) can corned beef
1 tablespoon Worcestershire sauce
1 tablespoon minced onion
1 tablespoon green pepper
½ tablespoon dry mustard
½ cup mayonnaise

Sprinkle gelatin over water. Stir until dissolved; cool slightly. Add remaining ingredients in order listed and stir until well blended. Spoon into a lightly oiled 9x5x3-inch loaf pan. Cover and refrigerate until firm.

Shrimp and Avocado Salad

Serves 4
Nice for ladies' luncheon

1 pound shrimp, cleaned and
   cooked
¼ cup French style dressing
2 medium-sized ripe tomatoes,
   cut into bite-sized pieces
1 ripe avocado, cut into bite-sized
   pieces

2 hard boiled eggs, quartered
Salt and pepper to taste
Mayonnaise
Lettuce

Marinate shrimp in dressing for 2 to 4 hours. Add next 4 ingredients; mix well. Add mayonnaise to taste; mix until well blended. Serve on lettuce leaves.

In 1878, the wall type telephone was first used in Meriden.

Shrimp and Cauliflower in Dill Mayonnaise

Serves 4 to 6
Serve as a first course or as a main dish for a light summer meal

1 small head cauliflower, cut into
   flowerets
2 tablespoons lemon juice,
   divided
1 cup diced celery

1 cup small cooked shrimp
½ cup mayonnaise
2 tablespoons fresh dill or
   1 teaspoon dried dillweed
Salt and pepper to taste

Cook cauliflower in large pot of boiling water with 1 tablespoon lemon juice for 7 to 10 minutes or until tender-crisp. Cool under cold water; drain thoroughly. Combine cauliflower, celery and shrimp. Mix until well blended. Combine mayonnaise, remaining 1 tablespoon lemon juice and dill. Pour over cauliflower mixture; toss gently until all ingredients are coated. Cover and refrigerate until serving.

Shrimp and Rice Salad

Serves 6
Great Summer Salad

1 cup raw rice
½ cup chopped chives
½ small onion, minced
1 small green pepper, chopped
1½ cups small shrimp, cleaned
    and cooked

1 cup mayonnaise
Pinch ginger
Salt or lemon juice to taste
Lettuce
Toasted sesame seeds

Cook rice according to package directions and cool. Snip chives and add to cooled rice along with onions and peppers. Mix until well blended. Add shrimp and mayonnaise. Season to taste with ginger, salt and lemon juice. Mix until ingredients and seasonings are evenly distributed. Cover and refrigerate until serving time. To serve, scoop on top of bed of lettuce or a lettuce leaf and top with sesame seeds.

Italian Sausage Salad

Serves 6 to 8
Good served warm or chilled

6 sweet or hot Italian sausages
1 (8-ounce) package macaroni
    twists
1 green pepper, julienned
1 red onion, thinly sliced
3 hard boiled eggs, quartered

2 tablespoons chopped parsley
½ cup black olives, halved
1½ cups broccoli flowerets,
    blanched
10 cherry tomatoes, halved

Place sausages in skillet, prick skins and cover with water. Cook over medium-high heat until water boils, reduce heat, cover and simmer for 10 minutes or until thoroughly cooked. Drain and cut into small bite-sized pieces. Cook macaroni following package directions, drain. Place sausage, macaroni and remaining ingredients in salad bowl. Toss gently. Pour your favorite Italian dressing over salad. Toss and serve.

Irish Pasta Salad

Serves 12 to 16

½ (12-ounce) box spaghetti
1 (8-ounce) package spinach
   noodles or rotini primavera
   colored twists
½ Bermuda onion, diced
2 to 3 tomatoes, diced

1 to 2 green peppers, diced
1 (2-ounce) jar pimiento
1 (1.75-ounce) envelope zesty
   Italian dressing
1 (8-ounce) bottle Caesar salad
   dressing

Cook pasta according to package directions. Drain, rinse and set aside to cool. When cooled, add next 4 ingredients. Toss until well blended. Sprinkle Italian dressing mix and Caesar dressing over mixture. Toss until ingredients are well coated with dressings. Chill before serving.

Note: Black olives, strips of salami or ham, mushrooms or whatever you have on hand can be added.

Nikki O'Neill
Governor's Mansion
Hartford, CT

Broccoli Salad

Serves 6 to 8
Delicious, different, easy company salad

1 large bunch fresh broccoli
½ medium-sized onion, chopped
6 to 8 slices bacon, cooked and
   crumbled
½ cup raisins

½ cup mayonnaise
2 teaspoon sugar
1 teaspoon vinegar
½ cup roasted, sliced almonds
   (optional)

Combine ingredients in order listed. Toss until ingredients are evenly distributed and coated with mayonnaise. Enjoy!

Note: This can be made ahead. Leftovers may be stored in a covered container in the refrigerator. If stored in this manner, it will remain fresh and tasty for several days.

Black-Eyed Pea Salad

Serves 6
High in protein and low in fat: quick, easy and colorful

1 (16-ounce) can black-eyed peas, drained
1 cup finely chopped celery
¼ cup sweet or green chopped onions
½ cup sweet green pepper, chopped
1 medium-sized tomato, chopped
2 cups lettuce, cut into long thin strips
1 cup coleslaw dressing

Combine ingredients in a mixing bowl; toss slightly to distribute ingredients. Serve immediately.

Sweet and Sour Cabbage Slaw

Serves 20

1 (3-pound) head of cabbage, shredded
1 green pepper, diced
2 medium-sized onions, diced
1½ cups sugar

Combine ingredients in large mixing or salad bowl. Pour dressing over cabbage and stir. Cover and refrigerate for 3 days, stirring occasionally, before serving.

Dressing:
1 cup oil
1 cup vinegar
1 teaspoon salt

Measure ingredients into saucepan. Heat over medium heat until mixture boils, stirring occasionally.

Chinese Cabbage Salad

Serves 6 to 8
Great for dinner or buffet

½ head cabbage, finely sliced
2 green onions, slivered
2 tablespoons sesame seeds,
   toasted

2 tablespoons slivered almonds,
   toasted
1 (3-ounce) package ramen
   (flavored noodles), uncooked

Combine first 3 ingredients in a mixing bowl; mix until blended. Pour dressing over mixture; toss until ingredients are coated with dressing. Cover and refrigerate until chilled. Just before serving, add nuts and ramen noodles; toss.

Note: Amounts of sesame seeds and almonds can be increased if desired. To toast sesame seeds, bake at 300° for 10 minutes. For toasting almonds, bake at 300° for 20 minutes.

Dressing:
2 tablespoons sugar
3 tablespoons vegetable oil
3 tablespoons sesame oil
½ teaspoon monosodium
   glutamate

½ teaspoon pepper
3 tablespoons white vinegar

Combine ingredients in small bowl or jar. Whisk or mix until well blended.

In 1777, the first Chirstmas tree, trimmed and illuminated, was the work of Hendrick Rodemore and he set the tree up in his cabin behind the Denslow Farm In Windsor Locks.

Carrot and Pineapple Salad

Serves 10
Excellent "make ahead" summer salad

1 (20-ounce) can crushed
  pineapple
1 (3-ounce) package lemon
  flavored gelatin
1 cup boiling water
3 teaspoons vinegar

½ teaspoon salt
1 teaspoon prepared horseradish
1 teaspoon minced onion
¾ cup chopped celery
2 large carrots, grated

Drain pineapple, reserving juice; set aside. Dissolve gelatin in boiling water. Add pineapple juice, vinegar, salt, horseradish and onion. Chill until partially set. Add pineapple, celery and carrots. Pour into lightly oiled 4-cup mold, cover and chill until set. Unmold onto platter before serving.

Caesar Salad

Serves 2
Piquant salad dressing

2 cloves garlic, mashed
4 anchovy fillets, mashed
Juice of 1 lemon
3 to 4 dashes Worcestershire sauce
2 teaspoons Dijon mustard
1 coddled egg
3 ounces olive oil

1 head romaine lettuce, washed,
  dried and torn into pieces
Freshly ground black pepper
4 tablespoons grated Parmesan
  cheese
Plain or garlic croutons

Mix garlic and anchovies in a large salad bowl. Add next 3 ingredients and mix until well blended. Add egg and oil. Beat with wire whisk until mixture thickens. Add romaine and toss until greens are coated with dressing. Add freshly ground pepper and cheese. Toss. Garnish with croutons or toss into salad before serving.

Julienne of Celery and Red Onion with Blue Cheese Vinaigrette

Serves 4

6 ribs celery, each trimmed to a
   length of 9 inches
1 small red onion, cut into thin
   slivers
6 tablespoons light olive oil
2 tablespoons white wine vinegar

½ teaspoon salt
Pinch of dried thyme, crumbled
Freshly ground pepper
2 ounces blue cheese, crumbled
2 scallions with tops, chopped

Cut each celery rib into 3 pieces. Cut each of these pieces into julienne strips; place in small bowl. Add onion slivers and toss. Place next 5 ingredients in a medium-sized mixing bowl and beat with wire whisk until thoroughly blended. Stir in blue cheese. Add celery-onion mixture and scallions; toss to coat ingredients with dressing. Refrigerate, covered, until ready to serve.

Sweet Potato Salad Bangkok

Serves 6
Great "variation" on potato salad

¼ cup lemon juice
2 teaspoons ground coriander
¾ teaspoon hot red pepper flakes
1 teaspoon salt
¼ teaspoon pepper
½ cup vegetable oil (scant ½ cup)
¾ cup chopped onion

1½ cups diced green pepper
⅔ cup roasted peanuts
⅓ cup chopped cilantro
3 pounds fresh sweet potatoes,
   cooked, peeled and cut into
   bite-size cubes

Combine all ingredients except sweet potatoes in a large mixing bowl. Mix until well blended. Add sweet potatoes and gently mix until potatoes are evenly coated with dressing. Cover, chill thoroughly and serve.

Blue Cheese Salad Dressing

Yields 1 to 1½ pints
Great as a salad dressing or as a dip for fresh vegetables

1 (8-ounce) carton sour cream
1 cup cottage cheese
4 ounces blue cheese, crumbled

1 cup mayonnaise
1 teaspoon seasoned salt
½ teaspoon garlic powder

Combine ingredients; mix to blend. Place in covered container and refrigerate.

Note: Best if made 1 to 2 days in advance to allow flavors to blend.

In 1685, Dr. John Durand brought the first lilacs to America, to his home. "Brownie Castle," in the town of Derby.

Club Salad Dressing

Yields 1½ pints
Delicious! You'll get great raves!

2 teaspoons flavor enhancer
1½ teaspoons dry mustard
3 teaspoons Spanish paprika
1½ teaspoons white pepper
1½ tablespoons sugar

2½ teaspoons salt
½ ounce garlic cloves
2 egg yolks
¼ cup cider vinegar
3 cups vegetable oil

Place first 6 ingredients in a sifter; sift into mixing bowl. Slice garlic. Place in blender container with egg yolks and vinegar; puree. Add pureed mixture to spices and mix at medium speed of electric mixer until a smooth paste is formed. Do Not Use Blender for this! Gradually add oil, a little at a time, until all oil has been added. Mix for 4 to 5 minutes or until mixture is smooth.

Chunky French Dressing

Yields 3½ cups

1 cup catsup
1 cup vegetable oil
½ cup white vinegar
½ cup red wine vinegar
1 tablespoon Worcestershire sauce
1 tablespoon soy sauce
1 tablespoon dry mustard
1 tablespoon paprika

1 tablespoon sugar
1 teaspoon salt
2 cloves garlic, minced
2 plum tomatoes, peeled, seeded
  and diced
1 rib celery, diced
½ small Bermuda onion, diced

Combine first 11 ingredients in mixing bowl. Whisk until well blended. Add tomatoes, celery and onion; stir until incorporated. Cover or pour into a container with a tight fitting lid. Refrigerate at least 1 day allowing flavors to blend. Whisk or shake well before serving.

Note: Goes well with mixed green salads such as kale, chicory, romaine, escarole, etc.

Randy Nichols, Chef
Freshfield's
Rt. 128
West Cornwall, CT

In 1800, James Lamb of Middletown invented and patented the Lamb Cooking Stove, which was the first stove to evenly distribute heat around the oven.

Boursin Cheese

Yields 4 to 5 margarine tubs of cheese

3 (8-ounce) packages cream
   cheese, softened
¾ cup butter, softened
1 (8-ounce) bottle green goddess
   type salad dressing

3 cloves garlic, minced, or ½
   teaspoon garlic powder
Chives and/or freshly ground
   pepper

Combine ingredients in large mixing bowl. Beat with electric mixer until butter disappears. Place in containers, cover and refrigerate.

Note: Can be frozen.

In 1858, the first United States patent for a can opener was issued January 5, to Ezra J. Warner of Waterbury.

Raspberry Vinegar

Yields 1 pint
It's delectable used in a French dressing for salads

1½ cups white wine vinegar

½ cup French raspberry liqueur

Combine ingredients in a 3-cup container with a tight fitting, non-corrosive lid. Cover and shake well to mix ingredients. Let stand 24 hours to mellow. Store, tightly covered, at room temperature.

Note: To make French dressing, mix vegetable oil, raspberry vinegar, salt and pepper in the proportions which suit your taste. Excellent served with a platter of lettuce, avocado and seafood.

Herb Wine Salad Dressing

Yields about 1½ cups
Good on hardy chef salads

½ cup sauterne wine
½ cup olive oil
¼ cup white wine vinegar
1 teaspoon sugar

½ teaspoon dry mustard
½ teaspoon onion salt
¼ teaspoon celery salt
1 teaspoon grated onion

Combine ingredients and stir until well blended. Place in a jar with a tight fitting lid. Cover and store in refrigerator until ready to use. Shake vigorously before serving.

In 1928, the first woman to win the U.S.A. Women's Squash Raquets Singles Championship was E.R. Sears of Greenwich.

Great Cole Slaw Dressing

Yields ¾ to 1 cup

3 tablespoons evaporated milk
3½ tablespoons cider vinegar
1 white portion of a leek, minced
3 sprigs parsley, minced

Sprinkle of sugar
Juice of ¼ lemon
1 small solid head cabbage
Dash paprika

Combine first 6 ingredients in a jar with a tight fitting lid. Cover and shake to mix ingredients. Refrigerate for several hours. Soak cabbage in ice cold salted water for at least 20 minutes. Slice or shave cabbage or finely shred in food processor. Shake dressing well before pouring over cabbage. Sprinkle with paprika before serving.

Note: The colder this is when served, the crispier and better it will be.

Vinaigrette Salad Dressing

Yields about ½ cup

2 tablespoons mustard with wine   6 tablespoons olive oil
2 tablespoons good red wine
    vinegar

Mix mustard with vinegar, whisking constantly. Slowly, add olive oil. Continue to beat with whisk until dressing becomes thick and creamy.

In 1856, while living in Torrington, Gail Borden perfected his experiments and successfully produced, for the first time in the world, commercially available condensed milk.

Breads, Whole Grains & Rice

Apple-Orange Bread

Yields 1 loaf
The orange flavor makes this special

2 cups unsifted all-purpose flour
1 cup sugar
½ cup wheat germ
2 teaspoons baking powder
½ teaspoon baking soda
1½ teaspoon salt
1 to 1½ cups chopped apples,
    peels included

3 tablespoons grated orange rind
½ cup orange juice
¼ cup warm water
1 egg
2 tablespoons vegetable oil

Mix first 6 ingredients in mixing bowl. Stir in apples and orange rind until incorporated into the mixture. Combine the remaining ingredients in a separate bowl. Mix until well blended. Add orange juice mixture to dry ingredients all at once. Stir only until the dry ingredients are all moistened. Pour batter into a well greased 9x5x3-inch loaf pan. Bake at 350° for 50 minutes to 1 hour or until a toothpick inserted in the center of the loaf comes out clean. Remove from pans immediately; cool on racks. Top with glaze before serving, if desired. Best if served warm.

Glaze:
½ cup confectioners' sugar
2 tablespoons melted butter

1 tablespoon water

Combine ingredients; mix until well blended. Pour over slightly cooled bread.

In 1810, in Mansfield, Rodney Hanks invented machinery for spinning silk by water power and on Hanks Hill erected the first silk mill in the United States.

Apple Bread

Yields 3 loaves

3 cups all-purpose flour
1¼ cups sugar
2 teaspoons baking soda
1 teaspoon cinnamon
¼ teaspoon ground cloves
1 cup raisins

4 medium-sized apples
½ cup margarine
½ cup vegetable oil
1 tablespoon vanilla
2 large eggs

Combine first 6 ingredients in a large mixing bowl; stir until blended. Peel and core apples. Cut apples into small pieces and mix into the flour mixture. In a saucepan, melt margarine over a low heat. Remove from heat and stir in oil, vanilla and eggs. Stir butter mixture into dry ingredients. Spoon batter into 3 well greased 1-pound coffee cans. Bake at 350° for 1 hour 15 minutes or until tester inserted into the center of loaf comes out clean. Cool in cans on wire rack for 10 minutes. Remove from cans and allow bread to cool completely. Wrap bread and store overnight before slicing.

Note: Bread freezes well. After you clean your cans, place in the oven to dry. This will prevent rusting.

Date Nut Bread

Yields 1 loaf

1 (8-ounce) package chopped
  dates
¾ cup boiling water
2 teaspoons butter, softened
¾ cup dark brown sugar
1 egg, beaten

1½ cups all-purpose flour
1 teaspoon salt
1 teaspoon baking soda
1 teaspoon vanilla or rum extract
1 cup chopped walnuts

Place dates in mixing bowl, add water and allow to set for 15 to 20 minutes to soften. Add next 4 ingredients and mix until well blended. Sift dry ingredients into bowl and add to date mixture. Stir in nuts. Pour into a greased 8x4x3-inch loaf pan. Bake at 325° for 1 hour or until tester inserted in the center of the loaf comes out clean.

Apricot Date Bread

Yields 3 (6x3x3-inch) loaves, 2 (8x4x3-inch) loaves or 1 (9x5x3-inch) loaf
Wonderful for brunch with whipped cream cheese

1 cup pitted dates, halved
1 cup dried apricots, halved
1½ cups sugar
2 teaspoons baking soda
¼ cup margarine

1¾ cups boiling water
2 eggs
2½ cups sifted all-purpose flour
2 cup walnut halves

Combine dates, apricots, sugar, baking soda and margarine in mixing bowl. Cover with boiling water, stir and allow mixture to cool for 15 to 20 minutes. Drain liquid into another bowl; set fruit aside. Add eggs, flour and nuts to liquid. Mix until well blended. Add fruit mixture and stir until evenly distributed throughout the batter. Pour into greased loaf pans. Bake at 350° for 1 hour 10 minutes or until cake tester inserted in the center of the loaf comes out clean.

Note: Reduce baking time for smaller loaves.

Banana Pineapple Bread

Yields 1 load

2 cups all-purpose flour
¾ cup sugar
1 teaspoon baking powder
1 teaspoon baking soda
½ teaspoon salt
1 egg, beaten
1 teaspoon vanilla

¼ cup vegetable oil
1 cup mashed bananas
1 cup crushed pineapple with
   juice
½ cup nuts
1 cup dates or raisins (optional)

Measure first 4 ingredients into large mixing bowl, mix and set aside. Combine next 5 ingredients into a separate bowl. Mix until well blended. Add egg mixture to dry ingredients. Mix until dry ingredients are moistened. Batter will not be smooth. Stir in nuts and dates or raisins, if desired. Pour batter into a greased 9x5x3-inch loaf pan. Bake at 350° for 1 hour or until tester inserted into the center of the loaf comes out clean. Cool on racks.

Cranberry Nut Bread

Yields 1 loaf
Tasty company dessert for the holidays or any day

2 cups sifted all-purpose flour	3 tablespoons white vinegar plus
1 teaspoon baking soda	water to make ⅔ cup
1 teaspoon salt	1 teaspoon grated orange rind
¾ cup sugar	¼ cup melted shortening
1 egg	1 cup cranberries, cut in quarters
⅓ cup orange juice	1 cup chopped nuts

Sift first 4 ingredients into a large mixing bowl. In another mixing bowl, beat egg; add liquids, orange rind and melted shortening. Mix until blended. Add all at once to flour mixture; stir until flour is just dampened. Batter will not be smooth. Add cranberries and nuts; stir just until evenly distributed among other ingredients. Pour into a greased 9x5x3-inch loaf pan. Bake at 350° for 1 hour to 1 hour 10 minutes. Remove from pan and cool several hours or overnight before slicing.

Note: Freezes well. Wrap in aluminum foil or air-tight plastic bags before freezing.

Orange Cranberry Pecan Loaf

Yields 1 loaf
Makes a great quick and easy holiday gift

¾ cup orange juice	1½ teaspoons baking powder
Zest of 3 oranges	1 teaspoon salt
2 tablespoons vegetable oil	½ teaspoon baking soda
1 egg, beaten	1 cup cranberries, chopped
2 cups all-purpose flour	½ cup pecans, chopped
¾ cup sugar	

Combine juice, zest, oil and egg; mix and set aside. Combine next 5 ingredients in large mixing bowl; mix. Add liquid to dry ingredients. Mix until dry ingredients are moistened. Do Not Overmix! Add cranberries and pecans. Mix to evenly distribute these throughout the batter. Pour batter into an ungreased 8x4x3-inch loaf pan. Decorate with pecans and berries. Bake at 350° for 40 minutes to 1 hour or until tester inserted in the center of the loaf comes out clean. Remove from pan and cool on a wire rack.

Fresh Pear Bread

Yields 1 loaf
Moist and delicious

2 eggs
1 cup sugar
¾ cup sour cream
¼ cup vegetable oil
1 teaspoon lemon peel
2 cups all-purpose flour
2 teaspoons baking powder

½ teaspoon baking soda
¼ teaspoon salt
½ teaspoon cinnamon
1½ cups peeled and chopped
    fresh pears or 1 (16-ounce) can
    pears, drained and chopped
1 cup pecans

Place eggs in a large mixing bowl. Beat until fluffy and lemon colored. Add next 4 ingredients; beat until well blended. Measure flour into mixing bowl. Add remaining dry ingredients. Add dry ingredients to egg mixture and stir until moistened. Stir in pears and pecans. Pour into a greased and floured 9x5x3-inch loaf pan. Bake at 350° for 1 hour or 1 hour 10 minutes or until a toothpick inserted in the center of the loaf comes out clean. Cool for 10 minutes in the pans; remove from pan and cool completely. Wrap tightly and store in refrigerator.

Cider Pumpkin Bread

Yields 1 loaf

1 cup brown sugar, firmly packed
1 cup canned pumpkin
½ cup vegetable oil
½ cup apple cider or juice
1 egg
1¾ cups all-purpose flour

½ cup wheat flour
3 teaspoons baking powder
1½ teaspoons cinnamon
½ cup chopped nuts
½ cup raisins

Combine first 5 ingredients in a large mixing bowl; mix until well blended. Measure dry ingredients into a separate mixing bowl; stir until evenly distributed. Add dry ingredients to pumpkin mixture, stirring just until dry ingredients are moistened. Stir in nuts and raisins. Grease and flour the bottom only of a 9x5x3-inch loaf pan. Pour batter into pan and bake at 350° for 55 minutes to 1 hour 5 minutes or until toothpick inserted in the center of the loaf comes out clean. Cool in pan for 10 minutes; remove from pan and allow to cool completely. Store in refrigerator.

Orange Cream Cheese Loaf

Yields 2 (8x4x3-inch) loaves
Great for breakfast or company

2¼ cups all-purpose flour
3 teaspoons baking powder
1 teaspoon salt
½ cup shortening
1⅔ cups sugar, divided
2 eggs
1 cup milk

1 (8-ounce) package cream cheese,
    softened and cut into ½-inch
    cubes
½ cup chopped walnuts
¼ cup orange juice
2 teaspoons orange peel

Sift first 3 ingredients into large mixing bowl; set aside. Place shortening in mixing bowl. Cream with electric mixer until smooth and fluffy. Add eggs; mix until blended. Add dry ingredients alternately with milk, beginning and ending with dry ingredients. Mix well after each addition. Fold cream cheese cubes into batter. Add walnuts and orange juice. Stir until incorporated into batter. Pour into 2 greased 8x4x3-inch loaf pans. Bake at 375° for 50 to 55 minutes or until tester inserted in the center of the loaves comes out clean. Combine remaining ⅓ cup sugar and orange peel. Brush on hot loaves.

Moppy's Cornbread

Yields 1 (9-inch) round
A family favorite

1 cup sifted all-purpose flour
¼ cup sugar
4 teaspoons baking powder
¾ teaspoon salt

1 cup yellow cornmeal
2 eggs
1 cup milk
¼ cup vegetable oil

Sift first 4 ingredients into a large mixer bowl. Stir in cornmeal. Combine eggs, milk and oil, mixing until well blended. Add to flour mixture and beat for 1 minute or until smooth with wire whisk or electric mixer. Pour into a 9-inch round baking pan which has been greased with bacon grease or fat. Bake at 425° for 20 to 25 minutes. Remove from oven, cool slightly and serve warm.

Beer Bread

Yields 1 loaf

3 cups self-rising flour　　　　**1 (12-ounce) can or bottle beer**
2 tablespoons sugar

Combine ingredients in order listed and mix until well blended. Pour batter into a greased 9x5x3-inch loaf pan. Bake at 350° for 1 hour. Remove from oven, rub with butter and wrap in a wet kitchen towel. Serve hot.

Note: 3 cups all-purpose flour plus 3 teaspoons baking powder can be substituted for the self-rising flour.

Spinach Bread

Yields 3 small loaves
Great with herb butter

1 cup sugar　　　　　　　　　　**1 teaspoon baking soda**
½ cup vegetable oil　　　　　　**1 teaspoon salt**
Grated rind of 1 lemon　　　　　**2 teaspoons mixed herbs**
2 eggs　　　　　　　　　　　　**½ (10-ounce) package frozen**
1½ cups all-purpose flour　　　　**chopped spinach, thoroughly**
2 teaspoons baking powder　　　　**drained**
　　　　　　　　　　　　　　　　½ cup almonds, grated

Combine sugar, oil and lemon rind in mixing bowl. Mix until well blended. Add egg and beat until incorporated into sugar-oil mixture. Sift flour, baking powder, baking soda, salt and herb mixture into large mixing bowl. Add spinach and almonds. Mix until spinach and almonds are evenly distributed throughout the flour mixture. Add sugar-egg mixture and mix until well blended. Divide into 3 (8x4x3-inch) greased loaf pans. Bake at 400° for 28 to 30 minutes or until center of loaf tests done.

Oatmeal Bread

Yields 4 loaves

2 cups rolled oats
4 cups boiling water
1 cup molasses
4 teaspoons salt
2 tablespoons butter

2 envelopes dry yeast
1 cup lukewarm water
    (110° to 115°)
12 to 14 cups flour

Measure oats into a large mixing bowl. Add boiling water and allow to stand for 8 to 10 minutes. Add molasses, salt, butter, yeast which has been allowed to dissolve in lukewarm water and flour. Beat thoroughly. Cover and let rise for 30 minutes or until doubled. Beat and knead mixture. Divide dough, shape into loaves and place it in 4 greased 9x5x3-inch loaf pans. Cover and let rise about 45 minutes or until doubled in bulk. Bake at 375° for 50 minutes.

Pepperoni Bread

Yields 1 loaf
Easy and different

2 cups sifted all-purpose flour
2 teaspoons baking powder
Pinch of salt
2 eggs, beaten
⅔ cup milk

1 cup grated Cheddar cheese
1 medium-sized stick pepperoni,
    cut into small pieces
½ cup margarine, melted

Combine flour, baking powder and salt in mixing bowl. Combine eggs and milk. Add egg-milk mixture and remaining ingredients to flour. Mix until well blended. Pour mixture into a greased and floured 9x5x3-inch loaf pan. Bake at 350° for 45 to 50 minutes or until tester inserted in center of loaf comes out clean.

Easter Bread

Yields 1 loaf
A real family favorite

4 to 5 cups all-purpose flour,
   divided (more may be needed)
½ cup sugar
1 teaspoon salt
1 package dry yeast
½ cup warm water (110° to 115°)
¼ cup milk

½ cup margarine
3 eggs at room temperature
1 tablespoon anisette
¼ teaspoon ground nutmeg
5 colored raw eggs
Melted butter or margarine

Thoroughly mix 1 cup flour, sugar, salt and yeast in a large mixing bowl. Combine water, milk and ½ cup margarine in a saucepan. Heat over low heat until liquids are warm (110° to 115°); margarine does not need to melt. Gradually add to dry ingredients and beat for 2 minutes at medium speed of electric mixer, scraping bowl occasionally. Add eggs, anisette, nutmeg and 1 cup flour or enough to make a thick batter. Beat at high speed of mixer for 2 minutes, scraping bowl occasionally. Stir in enough additional flour to make a soft dough. Turn out onto a lightly floured board; knead for 8 to 10 minutes or until smooth and elastic. Place in a greased bowl, turning to grease top. Cover with towel, let rise in a warm place for about 1 hour or until doubled in bulk. Punch dough down, turn out onto floured board and divide into 2 equal pieces. Roll each piece of dough into a rope. Twist the ropes together like a braid and form into a ring. Place on a greased baking sheet; brush the top with melted butter. Place colored raw eggs in the center of each twist. Cover and let rise for 30 to 45 minutes or until doubled in bulk. Bake at 350° for 30 to 35 minutes or until lightly browned. Remove from baking sheet. Frost and sprinkle with colored candy bits.

Frosting:

1 cup sifted confectioners' sugar
2 to 3 tablespoons milk

1 tablespoon melted butter

Combine ingredients, mix until well blended. More milk can be added to attain consistency needed to drizzle frosting onto loaf.

Monkey Bread

Yields 1 loaf
Fun for children to make

1 cup sugar
2½ teaspoons cinnamon
5 (7-ounce) cans refrigerated
   buttermilk biscuits

½ cup butter or margarine,
   melted
1 cup brown sugar

Combine sugar and cinnamon in small bowl; set aside. Cut biscuits into quarters, roll in cinnamon-sugar mixture and place in layers in a well-greased 10-inch bundt pan. Combine butter and brown sugar. Pour over top of dough. Bake at 350° for 30 minutes. Remove bread from pan immediately by placing a plate upside down on pan and inverting bread onto plate. Serve hot, just pick it apart to eat.

James Beard's Pronto Pumpernickel Bread

Yields 1 loaf

1 (13¾-ounce) package hot roll
   mix
2 eggs, separated
¼ cup molasses

¾ cup warm water
¾ cup unsifted rye flour
1½ teaspoons caraway seeds

Prepare hot roll mix as directed on package, using 1 whole egg and 1 egg yolk. Reserve remaining egg white for glaze. Stir molasses into warm water in a large mixing bowl. Add rye flour, prepared mix and caraway seeds. Mix until dough forms. Cover and let rise in a warm place for about 45 minutes or until mixture doubles in bulk. Punch down. Turn out onto a lightly floured board, knead lightly and shape into a ball. Place on a buttered baking sheet, cover and let rise for 45 minutes or until doubled in bulk. Brush lightly with beaten egg white and sprinkle top with additional caraway seeds. Bake at 375° for 35 to 40 minutes.

Vienna Stollen

Serves 10
Original recipe from an Austrian baker for this Christmas specialty!

½ cup unsalted butter, softened
1½ cups sugar
3 eggs
5 cups all-purpose flour
5 teaspoons baking powder
1 pound pot cheese

1 teaspoon vanilla
½ teaspoon salt
1 lemon rind, grated
1½ cups raisins
1 cup sliced almonds
1 cup candied fruit peel

Combine sugar and butter in mixing bowl. Cream, using electric mixer, until smooth. Add eggs; beat with electric mixer until mixture is smooth and lemon colored. Add next 6 ingredients. Mix until well blended. Stir in raisins, almonds and fruit peel. Dough will be quite stiff. Place in a 13x9x2-inch greased baking dish. Form like loaf. Bake at 500° for 5 minutes. Reduce heat to 350° and bake for 1 hour.

Whole Wheat Breadsticks

Yields 32 to 40 breadsticks
Kids love these! A wholesome snack

¼ cup margarine
1½ cups water
1 cup cottage cheese
1 cup honey

6 cups whole wheat flour, divided
3 teaspoons salt
3 packages dry yeast
1 egg

Melt margarine in a saucepan over a low heat. Add next 3 ingredients, stir and heat to 120°. Remove from heat and combine with 2 cups flour and remaining ingredients. Beat with electric mixer for 2 minutes or until mixture is smooth. Stir in remaining flour to make stiff dough. Turn onto a floured board and knead for 2 minutes. Cover and let rise for 1 hour or until doubled in bulk. Punch dough down, divide into 4 balls and hand roll 8 to 10 breadsticks from each ball. Place on lightly greased baking sheets and bake at 300° for 8 to 10 minutes or until lightly browned on the bottom. Turn sticks and bake an additional 8 to 10 minutes or until other side is lightly browned.

Brennan Bagels

Yields 36 bagels
As fun to make as they are to eat

3 tablespoons dry yeast
½ cup warm water (110° to 115°)
9 cups sifted all-purpose flour
1 cup wheat germ
5 tablespoons dark brown sugar
2 teaspoons salt

3 teaspoons cinnamon
3 teaspoons vanilla
2 cups raisins
2 cups cold milk
1 tablespoon sugar
1 egg, well beaten

Combine yeast and warm water in bowl. Let stand for about 5 minutes or until foamy. Measure flour and wheat germ into a large mixing bowl; mix. Combine next 5 ingredients and mix. Add to wheat germ/flour mixture. Add cold milk to yeast mixture. Pour milk/yeast mixture slowly into flour mixture. Knead until dough is smooth and elastic. (If dough is too moist, add several tablespoons of flour. Transfer dough to a lightly floured plastic bag, squeeze air out, twist closed and let rise in a warm place for about 1 hour or until double in bulk. Divide the dough into 36 equal pieces. Shape each piece into a smooth 2-inch ball. Poke a finger through the center of the ball. Twirl dough around 2 fingers to make a larger hole. Bring 4 quarts of water and 1 tablespoon sugar to a boil in a large saucepan. Reduce heat until water simmers. Drop 8 bagels into simmering water; cook for 30 seconds on each side. Transfer bagels to a lightly greased baking sheet. Brush with beaten egg. Bake at 400° for 20 minutes. Remove from sheets and cool on wire racks.

In 1908, New Departure Division of General Motors Corporation, with plants in Bristol and Meriden, was an early entry in the field of automotive manufacturing.

Food Processor Dinner Rolls

Yields 8 rolls
From start to finish in 90 minutes!

2 to 2½ cups unsifted all-purpose
   flour, divided
2 tablespoons sugar
½ teaspoon salt

1 package dry yeast
½ cup milk
¼ cup water
2 tablespoons margarine

Place 1 cup flour and all other dry ingredients into processor work bowl. Combine milk, water and margarine in a saucepan and heat over low heat until 120° to 130°. Using steel processor knife and with machine running, pour liquid into work bowl through the feed tube. Immediately add remaining flour to mixture through feed tube by heaping tablespoonfuls. Process until dough forms a ball. Continue to process for 30 to 40 seconds to knead dough. Remove bowl from processor and place on a lightly floured board. Divide dough into 8 equal portions. Shape each into a ball and place in a greased 8-inch round pan. Pour 1-inch boiling water in a large pan and place on the bottom rack of a cold oven. Set pan of rolls on rack above water. Cover with a clean towel, close oven door and allow to rise for about 30 minutes. Uncover rolls, remove pan of water from lower oven rack and turn oven temperature to 325°. Bake for 20 to 25 minutes or until golden brown. Remove rolls from pan and cool slightly. Best when served warm.

In 1902, the first time a President of the United States ever rode in an automobile was August 22, 1902, when President Theodore Roosevelt took such a ride in Hartford.

Pretzels

Yields 18 pretzels
Easy and fun for children to do from start to finish

1½ cups lukewarm water (110° to 115°)	1 tablespoon sugar
	4 cups all-purpose flour
1 package dry yeast	1 egg or 1 egg white, beaten
1 teaspoon salt	Coarsely ground salt

Place water in large mixing bowl. Add yeast; allow to stand for 5 minutes. Stir to dissolve. Add salt, sugar and ½ flour. Mix well. Add enough remaining flour to form dough which can be handled. Turn dough onto lightly floured board and knead for 8 to 10 minutes or until smooth and elastic. Cut dough into 18 pieces; roll into ropes and twist into pretzel shapes. Place on lightly greased baking sheets. Brush with egg or egg white, as desired, and sprinkle with coarsely ground salt. Bake at 425° for 12 to 15 minutes.

In 1727, the first copper coins in America were minted at the Higby Mine in Simsbury by Dr. Samuel Higby between 1727 and 1737.

Miss Johnny's Hushpuppies

Serves 6
Meant to accompany fried seafood

2 cups cornmeal	1 egg
1 tablespoon all-purpose flour	6 tablespoons grated onion
1 teaspoon baking soda	2 cups buttermilk
1 tablespoon salt	Deep fat or oil for frying

Combine ingredients in order listed in a medium-sized mixing bowl; mix until well blended. Shape into walnut-sized balls and fry in deep fat or oil heated to 375° for 3 to 5 minutes or until cooked through. Drain and serve warm.

Colossal Popover

Serves 1 or 2
Great breakfast popover

2 tablespoons margarine	**3 eggs**
½ cup milk	**Confectioners' sugar, jam or**
½ cup all-purpose flour	**syrup**

Place margarine in cast iron skillet. Heat over medium heat until margarine sizzles. Turn off heat. Measure milk, flour and eggs into mixing bowl; mix until well blended. Pour into skillet and bake at 375° for 13 minutes. Remove from oven, sprinkle with confectioners' sugar, jam or light syrup before serving.

1802, the first brass rolled in this country was the work of Abel Porter and Company of Waterbury.

Dillweed Popovers

Yields 6 popovers

1 cup all-purpose flour	**2 tablespoons melted butter or**
¼ teaspoon salt	**margarine, divided**
2 eggs	**½ tablespoon of dillweed**
1 cup milk	

Combine flour and salt in mixing bowl; set aside. Combine eggs, milk and dillweed; beat until well blended. Stir in 1 tablespoon melted butter; mix. Gradually, stir egg mixture into flour mixture with remaining 1 tablespoon butter. Generously grease 6 (6-ounce) custard cups. Fill ½ full with mixture. Place on baking sheet and set in cold oven. Set oven at 425° and bake for 30 to 40 minutes or until puffed and golden.

Pecan Rolls

Yields 12 rolls
Easy to prepare, very tasty, inexpensive to make but expensive-looking!

1 cup pecans
1 (16-ounce) loaf frozen bread
   dough, cut into 10 to 12 equal
   sized pieces
½ (3¾-ounce) package instant
   butterscotch pudding mix

½ cup butter
½ cup brown sugar
1 teaspoon cinnamon

Grease a large bundt pan; sprinkle pecans evenly over the bottom. Separate the pieces of frozen bread dough and arrange on pecans. Pour dry pudding mix over rolls. Melt butter, add brown sugar and cinnamon; mix until blended. Pour over rolls. Cover pan loosely with waxed paper and allow to rise overnight. Bake at 350° for 30 minutes. Serve warm to delighted tasters!

Blueberry Dumplings

Yields 8 dumplings
A breakfast treat

1½ to 2 cups fresh blueberries
⅓ cup sugar
1 cup water
1 tablespoon lemon juice

1 buttermilk baking mix
1 tablespoon sugar
6 tablespoons milk
½ teaspoon almond extract

Combine blueberries, sugar and water in a large saucepan. Bring to a boil over a medium-high heat, stirring constantly. Reduce heat, cover and simmer for 5 minutes. Remove from heat; add lemon juice and mix. Combine remaining ingredients in a mixing bowl. Mix until well blended. Drop by spoonfuls onto the berry mixture, dividing the batter into 8 dumplings. Cover and simmer for 10 minutes. Serve with whipped cream, if desired.

Bran and Honey Muffins

Yields 9 to 12 muffins
Healthy breakfast treat

2 cups bran
1 cup all-purpose flour
¼ to ½ teaspoon baking soda
¼ teaspoon salt

1½ cups milk
½ cup honey
2 tablespoons melted butter
Raisins and/or nuts, if desired

Sift first 4 ingredients into a large mixing bowl. Pour bran which remains in sifter into another mixing bowl. Add next 3 ingredients; beat until mixed. Add to flour mixture and stir until dry ingredients are moistened. Stir in raisins and/or nuts to taste. Fill greased muffin cups or muffin cups which have been linked with papers ⅔ full of mixture. Bake at 400° for 25 to 30 minutes.

Jumbo Banana Muffins

Yields 7 to 9 muffins
These rise like popovers.

2½ cups all-purpose flour
¾ cup sugar
1 tablespoon baking powder
¾ teaspoon salt
¼ cup plus 2 tablespoons butter
    or margarine

3 ripe-bananas, mashed
2 eggs
⅓ cup milk
½ teaspoon vanilla

Measure first 4 ingredients into a large mixing bowl. Add margarine and cut in with a pastry blender until mixture resembles cornmeal; set aside. Combine bananas, eggs, milk and vanilla in blender container. Blend on high until well mixed. Add to flour mixture; mix until all dry ingredients are moistened. Pour mixture into muffin cups which have been greased or lined with paper cups, filling each cup to the top. Bake at 400° for 25 to 30 minutes.

Note: Food processor works well for making these.

Cider and Apple Muffins

Yields 12 muffins

1 egg
½ cup fresh sweet cider
¼ cup vegetable oil
1 cup grated tart apples
1½ cups sifted all-purpose flour

½ cup sugar
2 teaspoons baking powder
½ teaspoon salt
1 teaspoon cinnamon

Place egg in mixing bowl. Beat slightly with a fork. Stir in cider, oil and grated apples. In another container, sift flour, sugar, salt and baking powder to mix. Add flour mixture to egg-apple mixture and stir only until flour is moistened. Do Not Over Mix! Fill greased muffin cups or muffin cups lined with paper liners ⅔ full of batter. Bake at 400° for 25 to 30 minutes.

Note: A mixture of ⅓ cup finely chopped nuts, 2 tablespoons brown sugar and ½ teaspoon cinnamon may be sprinkled on top of muffin batter before baking, if desired.

Oat Bran Muffins

Yields 12 muffins

2½ cups uncooked oat bran cereal
2 teaspoons baking powder
½ teaspoon baking soda
¼ cup brown sugar
1 teaspoon cinnamon, nutmeg or
   vanilla

1 cup skim or lowfat milk at room
   temperature
2 tablespoons vegetable oil
1 banana, mashed

Combine first 5 ingredients into a medium-sized mixing bowl; stir to mix; Combine remaining ingredients; mix until well blended. Pour milk mixture over dry ingredients and mix only until dry ingredients are moistened. Batter will be lumpy. Pour into 12 greased muffin cups or cups lined with paper liners. Bake at 450° for 15 minutes.

Ricotta Cheese Pancakes

Yields 4 servings
Great idea for a Sunday family brunch

½ cup ricotta cheese
1½ eggs
1 tablespoon vegetable oil
2 tablespoons plus 2 teaspoons
    all-purpose flour

1 teaspoon honey
⅛ teaspoon salt
Margarine, for frying

Combine ingredients in a blender container. Cover and blend on high for
about 5 minutes or until mixture is smooth, scraping the sides of the
blender occasionally. Pour enough batter into a hot buttered skillet to
make about a 3-inch pancake. Cook over a medium heat until bubbles
appear on the top of the pancakes. Turn and cook until other side browns.
Serve at once with honey or jam.

Oatmeal Pancakes

Yields 10 to 12 pancakes
Better flavor than regular pancakes

¾ cup oats
1½ cups buttermilk
1 egg
½ cup all-purpose flour

¾ teaspoon salt
½ teaspoon baking soda
1 tablespoon sugar

Combine oats and buttermilk in a medium-sized mixing bowl. Stir until
blended; allow to stand for 10 minutes. Combine remaining ingredients
in another mixing bowl. Add oat-buttermilk mixture. Mix until blended.
Fry as for other pancakes in a lightly greased skillet.

Rice Ring

Serves 10

2 (13¾-ounce) cans chicken broth
1 cup water
¾ teaspoon salt, divided
2 cups uncooked converted long-
    grain rice
2 tablespoons butter or margarine
½ cup chopped onion
8 ounces fresh mushrooms, sliced

1 cup mayonnaise
3 tablespoons milk
2 tablespoons horseradish
1 clove garlic, minced
⅛ teaspoon pepper
⅓ cup chopped green pepper
⅓ cup chopped red pepper

Bring chicken broth, water and ½ teaspoon salt to a boil in a medium saucepan over high heat; add rice. Reduce heat, cover and simmer for about 30 minutes or until rice is tender. Remove from heat and cool to room temperature. Melt butter in a skillet over a medium-high heat. Add onion and saute, stirring constantly, for about 2 minutes. Add mushrooms and saute for about 5 minutes or until tender, stirring constantly; set aside. Combine next 5 ingredients and remaining ¼ teaspoon salt in a small mixing bowl; mix. Add to rice along with mushroom mixture and green and red peppers. Toss to coat evenly with dressing. Press mixture into a lightly greased 2-quart mold; let stand for 1 minute. Invert onto serving plate. Refrigerate until serving time.

In 1779, Samuel Huntington of Norwich was a self-made man, a lawyer, a signer of the Declaration of Independence and one of the State's most outstanding Revolutionary leaders.

St. Paul's Rice

Serves 8 to 10
A wonderful contribution to a pot luck dinner

1 pound hot pork sausage
1 large green pepper, chopped
1 large onion, chopped
3 ribs celery, chopped
2 envelopes dry chicken noodle
  soup mix

½ cup rice
4½ cups water
½ cup almonds, slivered

Cook sausage over medium heat until browned. Crumble into small pieces as cooking. Remove sausage from skillet and drain on paper towels. Pour most of the sausage drippings from pan. Saute peppers, onion and celery over medium heat, stirring constantly, for 3 to 5 minutes or until tender; set aside. Combine soup, rice and water in a saucepan. Bring to a boil and continue to boil for 7 minutes. Add sausage pieces and pepper combination to soup-rice mixture. Add almonds; stir until mixed. Pour into a greased 2-quart casserole. Bake, covered, at 350° for 1 hour.

Orzo Parsley Gratin

Serves 10
Great as a side dish with chicken or veal

1 (16-ounce) package orzo
6 garlic cloves, unpeeled
1 cup heavy cream
1 cup chicken broth

1 cup grated Parmesan cheese,
  divided
1 cup minced parsley, divided
4 tablespoons dry breadcrumbs

Boil the orzo with the garlic as directed on the package for 10 minutes or until "al dente"; drain. Rinse with cold water and thoroughly drain. Remove the garlic cloves from the orzo, peel and mash with a fork. In a large mixing bowl, whisk the mashed garlic with the cream, add the orzo, the broth and ¾ cup cheese and ¾ cup parsley; mix well. Transfer the mixture to a buttered 2-quart baking dish and smooth the top. Toss the breadcrumbs, remaining cheese and remaining parsley in a small bowl. Sprinkle over the orzo mixture and dot the top with butter. Bake at 325° for 1 hour 15 minutes or until bubbly around the edges and the top is golden.

Soups

Fruit Soup

Serves 4 to 6

3 cups orange, apple or pineapple
   juice, unsweetened
1 banana
1 apple, peeled and chopped
1 peach, peeled and chopped
Pieces of fresh cantaloupe to taste

Juice of 1 lemon
2 tablespoons honey or to taste
1 cup yogurt, sour cream or
   buttermilk
Dash of cinnamon, nutmeg or
   allspice

Combine all ingredients in a blender container. Blend on high until pureed and smooth. Additional banana or yogurt can be used to thicken, if desired, or more fruit juice can be added if a thinner soup is desired. Chill thoroughly.

Chilled Honeydew Soup

Serves 6
A refreshing no-cook summer soup

1 navel orange
1 ripe honeydew melon
1 tablespoon lime or lemon juice
1 teaspoon sugar

1 teaspoon salt
¼ teaspoon ground allspice or
   nutmeg
⅓ cup heavy cream

Using vegetable peeler, pare two long strips of the highly colored rind of the orange. Cut into strips; set aside for garnish. Squeeze orange juice and reserve 2 tablespoons. Cut melon in quarters, scoop out seeds and remove rind. Cut pulp into small pieces and puree in blender small portions at a time. Transfer puree into a large mixing bowl. Stir in remaining ingredients. Blend until well mixed. Chill. Serve in chilled soup cups. Garnish with reserved orange rind strips.

Cream of Broccoli Soup

Serves 6

3 cups water
1 bunch fresh broccoli or 2
    (10-ounce) packages frozen
    broccoli
3 tablespoons butter or margarine
¼ cup minced onion

3 tablespoons all-purpose flour
2½ cups milk
¼ teaspoon salt
Pepper to taste
½ cup heavy cream

Bring water to a boil in a large saucepan; add broccoli and cook for 5 to 8 minutes or until tender. Meanwhile, melt margarine in skillet, add onion and saute, stirring constantly, until transparent. Gradually add flour and cook until foamy, stirring constantly. Cool for an additional 1 minute. Stir in milk and continue stirring with wire whisk until mixture boils constantly. Reduce heat and continue cooking for 2 minutes. Add salt and pepper. Add drained and pureed broccoli. Bring to a boil, cover and remove from heat. Allow to cool slightly. Add cream, stir and serve while warm.

Cream of Squash Soup

Serves 6 to 10
Low in calories and great on taste!

¼ cup butter
2 tablespoons vegetable oil
1 large onion, minced
2 cloves garlic, minced
3 to 4 pounds of yellow squash,
    thinly sliced

3 (10-ounce) cans chicken broth
1 cup half and half
1½ teaspoons salt
½ teaspoon white pepper

Combine butter and oil in a large Dutch oven. Heat until melted. Add onion and garlic; saute for 5 to 8 minutes, stirring constantly, until tender. Stir in squash and chicken broth, cover and simmer for 20 minutes or until squash is tender. Spoon ⅓ mixture into blender container and process on liquify until smooth. Be careful not to splatter the hot liquid. Repeat with remaining mixture. Return to Dutch oven; stir in half and half, salt and pepper. Cook over low heat until well heated. Garnish with parsley; serve hot or cold.

Broccoli and Leek Soup

Serves 4
Easy delicious first course

4 tablespoons butter
4 leeks, white portions washed
    and chopped
1 (10-ounce) package frozen
    chopped broccoli

2 chicken bouillon cubes
1 cup water
2 cups milk
1 cup half and half

Melt butter in Dutch oven over medium-high heat. Add leeks and saute for 3 to 5 minutes or until tender, stirring constantly. Add broccoli and chicken bouillon cubes and water. Cook over medium heat for 10 minutes. Add to blender container. Blend until smooth. Return to Dutch oven, add remaining ingredients and cook over medium high heat until hot, but not boiling.

Lentil Barley Soup

Serves 10
Great on a cold day served with bread and salad. Tastes even better the following day.

1 cup lentils
1 cup barley
1 (16-ounce) can chopped
    tomatoes
1 cup onion, chopped
1 cup celery, sliced

¾ cup carrots, sliced
2 tablespoons soy sauce
½ teaspoon ground pepper
1 teaspoon dillweed
1 teaspoon garlic powder
10 cups defatted chicken broth

Combine all ingredients in a large saucepan. Bring to a boil. Cover and reduce heat. Simmer for about 1 hour. If soup is too thick, add extra water.

Note: Healthy, lowfat and low in cholesterol.

Calico Soup

Serves 8
Best if made the day before and reheated

2½ cups mixture of 7 kinds of
   beans and legumes
2 quarts water
2 tablespoons salt
Ham bone or ham hocks
   (optional)
1 large onion, chopped

1 (20-ounce) can stewed tomatoes
1 large pod red pepper or 1
   teaspoon chili powder
1 clove garlic, chopped
Juice of 1 lemon
Salt and pepper to taste

Wash beans thoroughly, place in a large soup kettle, cover with water and salt, and soak overnight. Drain water, rinse and add 2 quarts water. Bring to a boil over medium-high heat, reduce heat and simmer for 2½ to 3 hours. Add remaining ingredients. Simmer for an additional 20 minutes. Serve hot with crackers and salad.

Note: Makes a hearty vegetarian meal if ham is eliminated.

Vegetable Ham Soup

Serves 8 to 10

1 (32-ounce) can tomato juice
2 cups water
1 meaty ham bone or 1 ham slice,
   cut into chunks
4 medium potatoes, peeled and
   diced
2 cups frozen whole kernel corn
   or 2 (17-ounce) cans corn,
   drained

2 ribs celery, chopped
1 medium-sized onion, chopped
1 teaspoon pepper
2 (16-ounce) cans butter beans,
   drained

Combine all ingredients, except for beans in a large Dutch oven. Bring to a boil over a medium-high heat, reduce heat and simmer, covered, for 1 hour. Remove ham bone and cut meat from bone into chunks. Return to soup. Add beans and simmer for an additional 15 minutes.

Leek-Potato Soup

Serves 4

3 medium-sized leeks
2 tablespoons margarine
4 medium-sized potatoes, peeled
 and cut into cubes

4 cups stock or 4 cups water plus
 4 bouillon cubes

Trim green tops from leeks; cut white portion of leeks into ½-inch slices. Wash making sure there is no sand between the layers of the leaves. Set aside to drain. Melt margarine in a heavy saucepan. Add leeks and saute over high heat, stirring constantly, until slightly browned. When browned, add stock. Bring to a boil and add potatoes. Reduce heat and simmer for 25 minutes or until potatoes are tender. Serve with grated Italian style cheese and chow mein noodles or oyster crackers.

Russian Potato Soup

Serves 6
A hearty winter lunch or supper

2 leeks, chopped
2 large carrots, cut up
5 tablespoons butter, divided
6 cups chicken broth
Chicken, cooked and cut into
 bite-sized pieces, if desired
2 teaspoons dill weed

2 teaspoons salt
Dash of pepper
1 bay leaf
5 cups peeled and diced potatoes
1 pound mushrooms, sliced
1 cup half and half
2 tablespoons all-purpose flour

Saute leeks and carrots in 3 tablespoons butter in a large kettle or dutch oven for 5 minutes or until soft. Stir in chicken broth and chicken, dill, salt, pepper, bay leaf and potatoes. Bring to a boil over high heat. Reduce heat and simmer for 20 minutes or until potatoes are tender. Remove bay leaf. Saute mushrooms in remaining butter for 5 minutes or until golden. Stir half and half into flour. Stir mushrooms and half and half mixture into soup. Cook, stirring constantly, until mixture thickens and comes to a boil. Serve hot!

Note: This can be made ahead of time and frozen.

Tomato-Mushroom Soup

Serves 6
A family favorite

1 medium-sized onion, chopped
¼ teaspoon garlic powder
2 tablespoons butter
1 pound fresh mushrooms, thinly
   sliced
1 green pepper, seeded and
   chopped

2 (16-ounce) cans stewed tomatoes
4 cups chicken broth
Salt and pepper to taste
¼ teaspoon crushed dried
   tarragon leaves

Saute onion and garlic in butter for 2 minutes. Add mushrooms and pepper; saute for 5 minutes, stirring constantly, until tender. Break up tomatoes and add to pot along with broth and seasoning. Cover and simmer for 20 minutes until heated through. Serve warm.

Note: For a heartier soup, leftover rice may be added. Tomatoes with herbs can be added for additional flavor, if available.

Curried Zucchini Soup

Serves 4
Low calorie!

1 teaspoon butter
⅓ cup minced onion
2¼ cups chicken stock, divided
1½ teaspoons curry powder
4 cups coarsely chopped zucchini

½ cup evaporated skim milk
½ bay leaf
1 cup diced zucchini
1½ tablespoons whipped cream
½ teaspoon curry powder

Heat butter in a 3-quart saucepan over a medium heat. Add onion and 2 tablespoons chicken stock. Cook gently until onions are tender. Add curry and stir until incorporated into mixture. Add remaining chicken stock, zucchini, milk and bay leaf. Bring to simmer. Simmer for 30 minutes. Remove and discard bay leaf. Strain solids from soup and puree in blender. Stir puree back into soup. Strain soup once more; chill thoroughly. To prepare garnish, steam diced zucchini for about 3 minutes or until tender; cool. Ladle soup into chilled bowl, sprinkle with steamed zucchini and add small portion of cream. Top with sprinkle of curry powder.

Minestrone Soup

Yields approximately 6 quarts
A very filling meal!

½ cup olive oil
1 clove garlic
2 cups chopped onion
1 cup chopped celery
1 tablespoon chopped parsley
1 (6-ounce) can tomato paste
1 (10½-ounce) can beef broth

9 cups water
1 cup chopped cabbage
2 carrots, thinly sliced
2 teaspoons salt
¼ teaspoon pepper
⅛ teaspoon sage
1 cup uncooked macaroni

Heat oil in a large saucepan over medium heat. Add next 3 ingredients and saute, stirring constantly, for 3 to 5 minutes or until tender. Add remaining ingredients except for macaroni. Bring mixture to a boil, reduce heat and simmer for 1 hour. Cook macaroni according to package directions and add during the last 15 minutes of cooking. Viola! A meal for a cold winter day.

Note: The following ingredients may be added or substituted for other ingredients in the soup: 1 zucchini, thinly sliced, 1 (16-ounce) can green beans, 1 (16-ounce) can chick peas and/or 1 (16-ounce) can kidney beans. Bouillon cubes dissolved in water may be substituted for the beef broth in this soup. If desired, grated Parmesan cheese may be sprinkled on top of the soup when serving.

In 1684, Noadiah Russell of New Haven compiled the first printed almanac in America, "The Cambridge Almanack," by N. Russell, Astrologer.

Potato, Cheese and Chili Soup

Serves 4 to 6
Great for winter days

4 medium-sized potatoes
3 cups water
1½ cups chopped onion
1 tablespoon butter
1 tablespoon olive oil
Freshly ground pepper
1 teaspoon cumin
1¾ teaspoons salt
1 teaspoon basil

2 medium cloves garlic, crushed
1½ cups chopped green pepper
1 cup diced canned green chilis
¾ cup sour cream
1 cup milk
¾ cup grated Monterey Jack
   cheese
2 scallions, finely minced

Scrub potatoes, cube and cook, partially covered with water, until tender. Cool to room temperature. Saute onions in oil and butter 3 to 5 minutes or until tender. Add pepper, cumin, salt, basil and garlic. Add pepper and continue to saute until tender, stirring constantly. Puree potatoes in water. Return to pan and add onion-pepper saute. Stir in chilis, sour cream and milk. Heat mixture over low heat. When mixture is heated throughout, stir in cheese and scallions. Serve immediately.

Sherried Crab Soup

Serves 6
Easy and elegant!

1 (10½-ounce) can tomato soup
1 (10½-ounce) can pea soup
1 cup light cream
1 cup milk
1 cup cooked fresh or canned
   crabmeat

½ cup sherry
2 tablespoons chopped parsley
⅛ teaspoon curry powder
Salt and pepper to taste

Combine soups, cream and milk in a blender container. Blend on high until smooth. Transfer mixture to the top of a double boiler; heat over boiling water until mixture simmers, stirring occasionally. Add crab, sherry, parsley and seasonings; stir until evenly distributed. Continue to heat until soup is piping hot, but not boiling. Serve at once in heated soup bowls.

Sausage and Chick Pea Soup

Serves 4
Husband's favorite

1 tablespoon vegetable oil
1 cup chopped onion
½ cup chopped green pepper
½ pound fresh mushrooms,
   sliced
1 clove garlic, minced
Dash of black pepper
1 quart chicken broth

1 pound sausage links, cut into
   ½-inch slices
1 (19-ounce) can chick peas,
   undrained
1 medium-sized head escarole,
   torn into pieces
3 cups cooked rice
Grated Parmesan cheese

Heat oil in a 6-quart saucepan over a medium heat until it sizzles. Add onion, green pepper, mushrooms, garlic and black pepper. Saute, stirring occasionally, for 3 to 5 minutes or until onion is translucent. Add broth and bring to a boil. Add sausage, cover and simmer for 20 minutes. Add chick peas and escarole. Cover and simmer for 10 minutes or until escarole is wilted. Divide rice in heated serving bowls. Pour soup over rice; top with grated cheese. Serve with Italian bread for dunking.

Note: Sausage will cut easier if partially frozen.

Split Pea Soup

Serves 6 to 8

1 (16-ounce) package green split
   peas
3 quarts water
1 small ham shank
1 large onion, finely chopped

3 carrots, thinly sliced
1 cup chopped celery
2 chicken bouillon cubes
½ teaspoon pepper

Combine first 6 ingredients in a large, deep soup pot. Add chicken bouillon and seasonings. Bring to a boil over a high heat; reduce heat and simmer for 2 to 2½ hours or until soup reaches desired thickness.

Cream of Fresh Mushroom Soup

Serves 8 to 10
An impressive "make-ahead" soup

1 small onion, finely chopped
½ cup butter or margarine
¾ pound fresh mushrooms,
   finely chopped
¾ cup all-purpose flour

6 cups chicken stock
2 cups light cream or skim milk
½ teaspoon salt
¼ teaspoon white pepper

In a large saucepan, saute onion in ½ cup butter over medium-high heat for 3 minutes or until tender. Add flour, stirring constantly, until well-blended. Add chicken stock and simmer, stirring often, for 20 minutes. Add cream, salt and pepper and bring to a boil. Remove from heat and place in blender container. Blend until smooth. Place in serving bowl and add garnish to each.

Garnish:
¼ pound fresh mushrooms,
   sliced
2 tablespoons butter or margarine

2 tablespoons sherry

Saute mushrooms in butter and sherry for 3 to 5 minutes or until tender.

Venus de Milo Soup

Serves 8 to 10
Can be the main meal

1 (16-ounce) can tomatoes, cut up
4 cans water
2 envelopes dry onion soup mix
1 (20-ounce) package frozen
   mixed vegetables

1 pound ground beef, browned
   and drained
½ cup orzo
Parmesan cheese

Place tomatoes and water in a large saucepot. Bring to a boil. Add onion soup mix, vegetables and ground beef; simmer for 20 minutes. Cook orzo according to package directions. Add to soup mixture and simmer for an additional 10 minutes. Top with Parmesan cheese, if desired.

Cream of Carrot Soup

Serves 8 to 10
A hearty change of pace from pea soup

2 quarts water
3 to 4 vegetable bouillon cubes
1 pound carrots, peeled and
    sliced

1 medium-sized onion, chopped
2 cups heavy cream
1 teaspoon ground nutmeg

Place water, carrots, onions and bouillon cubes in a large soup pot. Bring to a boil and cook until carrots are tender. Transfer mixture to a blender container and blend until pureed. Reheat if necessary and add heavy cream to taste. Sprinkle nutmeg over the top of individual servings to taste.

Note: Food processor can be used in preparing this soup as well.

Cream of Peanut Soup

Serves 18
This recipe was created and first served at the Annual Westport Historical Society Holiday Luncheon in 1980.

4 ribs celery, finely chopped
1 onion, finely chopped
½ cup butter
2 tablespoons all-purpose flour
1 gallon chicken stock or canned
    chicken broth

1 (16-ounce) jar creamy peanut
    butter
1 quart cream

Saute celery and onion in butter in large soup pot over medium heat until tender. Do Not Burn! Add flour; cook until well blended, stirring constantly. Add broth and bring to a boil. Gradually, add peanut butter, a little at a time, blending well after each addition. Add cream; stir until blended. Heat until warmed throughout.

Note: This can be prepared in advance and reheated. Reheat slowly.

Betty's Ham Chowder

Serves 6

4 large carrots, diced
4 stalks celery, diced
2 small onions, chopped
4 large potatoes, peeled and diced
5 cups water
2 to 3 cups diced ham
2 tablespoons butter or margarine

Salt to taste
Freshly ground pepper to taste
6 tablespoons all-purpose flour
2½ cups milk
Paprika and/or chopped parsley
   for garnish

Place carrots, celery, onion and potatoes in a large Dutch oven. Add water and boil for about 20 minutes or until tender. Add ham, butter, salt and pepper. Blend flour and milk, stirring until smooth. Slowly, add to soup mixture. Heat, stirring constantly, until mixture boils. Reduce heat and allow to simmer, partially uncovered, for 10 to 20 minutes or until flavors have blended. Pour soup into a large bowl or soup tureen, sprinkle with paprika and/or parsley.

Nancy's Cape Chowder

Serves 8 to 12
You can cut quantities, but this is excellent when reheated.

2 pounds cod or flounder fillets
¼ cup butter or margarine
1 pound onions, sliced
1 quart boiling water
1 pound potatoes, thinly sliced
4 carrots, sliced
2 tablespoons Worcestershire
   sauce

2 teaspoons salt
1 bay leaf
¼ teaspoon tarragon, dill or
   thyme
2 cups milk
1 cup cream

Cut fillets into 2-inch pieces; set aside. Melt butter in a heavy soup pot. Saute onions. Add water, potatoes, carrots, Worcestershire, salt, bay leaf and tarragon. Bring mixture to a boil over a medium-high heat. Cover, reduce heat and simmer for 10 minutes. Lay fish on top of the soup, cover and simmer for an additional 15 to 20 minutes or until fish flakes and vegetables are tender. While fish is simmering, scald milk, stir in cream and gradually, add to chowder. Heat to desired temperature, but do not boil.

Meatball Chowder

Serves 8 to 10
Great on a cold day; better when reheated

1 pound ground beef	2 beef bouillon cubes
¼ teaspoon pepper	3 carrots, peeled and sliced
¼ cup crushed cracker crumbs	2 cups sliced celery
1 tablespoon milk	3 cups tomato juice
1 egg	2 potatoes, peeled and diced
⅛ cup parsley	1½ teaspoons sugar
3 tablespoons all-purpose flour	2 bay leaves
2 tablespoons vegetable oil	2 tablespoons rice
2 to 3 onions, cut into ⅛ths	½ teaspoon majoram
3 cups water	1 (10-ounce) can corn or mexicorn

Combine first 6 ingredients in a large mixing bowl; mix until well blended. Form into small balls about 1½-inches in diameter. Roll in flour and fry until browned. Drain and set aside. Place remaining ingredients except for corn into a large soup or stew kettle. Carefully, stir in meatballs. Heat on medium-high heat until mixture begins to boil. Reduce heat to low and simmer for 30 minutes. Drain corn and add to mixture. Stir until evenly distributed. Simmer for 5 minutes more. Serve with tossed salad and garlic bread for a nourishing dinner on a snowy winter evening.

In 1867, Hartford was the first city in the U.S. to erect a building designed for the use of Y.W.C.A.

Pasta, Cheese & Eggs

Stuffed Shells

Serves 8

½ pound mild goat cheese, at
   room temperature
½ pound ricotta cheese, at room
   temperature
¼ pound bleu cheese, at room
   temperature
1 (10-ounce) package frozen
   chopped spinach, thawed,
   drained and squeezed dry
½ cup heavy cream

1 egg
¼ cup packed fresh basil, minced
⅓ cup freshly grated Parmesan
   cheese, divided
Freshly ground pepper
4 cups tomato sauce
1 (12-ounce) package jumbo
   pasta shells
2 tablespoons fresh breadcrumbs

In a medium bowl, mash together the cheeses. Stir in spinach, cream, egg, basil and ¼ cup Parmesan cheese. Season with pepper to taste. Spoon half the tomato sauce over the bottom of a large baking dish. Stuff shells with filling and place in the baking dish filling side up. Drizzle remaining tomato sauce evenly over the shells. In a small bowl, combine breadcrumbs and remaining Parmesan cheese. Sprinkle mixture evenly over tomato sauce. Bake at 400° for 30 to 40 minutes until tender but still firm and filling is heated through. Let pasta cool for 10 minutes before serving.

Lazy Sunday Linguini

Serves 6 to 8

1 pound linguini
⅓ pound bacon, diced
1 medium onion, chopped
½ pound fresh mushrooms,
   sliced and sauteed in butter
   or margarine

1 (2.2-ounce) can pitted sliced
   ripe olives
3 eggs, slightly beaten
½ cup grated Romano or
   Parmesan cheese

Cook pasta in boiling salted water until tender. In skillet, saute bacon then remove from pan. Add onions and saute in bacon drippings until transparent. Remove from heat. Add bacon, mushrooms, olives to skillet. Drain pasta, reserving 1 cup cooking water. Return pasta to pan; add all, including remaining ingredients. (Heat from pasta will cook eggs.) Serve with additional cheese. If mixture is too dry, add some cooking water.

Vegetarian Lasagna

Serves 2 to 3
My favorite!

2 lasagna noodles
¾ cup carrots, peeled and finely chopped
3 tablespoons chopped onion
1 clove garlic, minced
2 tablespoons vegetable oil
¾ cup extra-thick meatless spaghetti sauce
2 tablespoons water
1 teaspoon dried oregano, crushed
1 teaspoon dried basil, crushed
½ teaspoon salt

¾ cup sliced fresh mushrooms
½ medium zucchini, cut into bite-size sticks (½ cup)
½ (10-ounce) package frozen chopped spinach, thawed and well-drained
1 cup cream-style cottage cheese
½ cup grated Parmesan cheese
1 egg, beaten
1 cup shredded mozzarella cheese
1 tablespoon sliced, pitted ripe olives
Whole chili peppers (optional)

Cook lasagna noodles in boiling water until tender, about 10 minutes. Drain; cut noodles crosswise into thirds. In skillet cook carrots, onion and garlic in hot oil, covered, about 4 minutes or until onion is tender. Stir in spaghetti sauce, water and seasonings. Simmer, covered, about 15 minutes or until carrots are tender. Reserve a few mushrooms for garnish. Stir in zucchini and remaining mushrooms.

Cheddar Cheese Noodle Pudding

Serves 6
Good any time, quick and easy

1 (8-ounce) package wide egg noodles
3 tablespoons butter or margarine
1 (8-ounce) carton cottage cheese

1 (8-ounce) carton sour cream
1 cup shredded sharp Cheddar cheese
Corn flake crumbs

Cook noodles according to package directions. Drain, then add butter, cottage cheese, sour cream and Cheddar cheese. Put in a 9-inch square pan and sprinkle corn flake crumbs on top. Bake at 350° for 1 hour until golden brown. May be reheated at any time.

Angel Hair Pasta with Sun-Dried Tomato Sauce

Serves 6
Delicious meatless sauce–best on homemade pasta

Homemade Tomato Sauce:

¼ cup olive oil
2 medium leeks (white and
   green portions)
2 (14½-ounce) cans Italian style
   tomatoes

1 teaspoon sugar
¼ teaspoon salt
Freshly ground pepper

Heat olive oil in skillet over medium-high heat. Add leeks; saute for 5 minutes or until limp. Add tomatoes which have been chopped into small pieces and juice. Stir in sugar, salt and pepper. Reduce heat and simmer for 45 minutes or until sauce is reduced to ½ original volume. Set aside.

Pasta and Pasta Sauce:

1 tablespoon olive oil
1 tablespoon butter or margarine
4 tablespoons minced shallots
1 tablespoon minced garlic
2 cups Homemade Tomato Sauce
1 pound fresh mushrooms, sliced
   or 1 pound tiny whole
   mushrooms

3 tablespoons sun-dried
   tomatoes, minced
2 tablespoons chopped parsley
½ cup heavy cream
¾ pound fresh angel hair pasta
¾ cup freshly grated Parmesan
   cheese

Combine olive oil and butter in skillet. Heat over medium-high heat until mixture foams. Add shallots and garlic; saute for 5 minutes or until lightly browned. Add about 2 cups of the tomato sauce and mushrooms. Simmer for about 10 minutes or until mixture is thick. Add sun-dried tomatoes and pepper to taste. Stir in parsley and cream; simmer for an additional 2 minutes. If sauce is too thick add a little more tomato sauce until consistency desired. Cook pasta according to package directions. Drain and add cooked pasta to sauce, stirring gently until coated with sauce. Add grated cheese and serve immediately or serve pasta on individual plates with sauce and cheese on top.

Note: Pasta Sauce can be made ahead of time and refrigerated for up to 5 days. When ready to serve; heat sauce in a large pan over low heat until it simmers and is heated through. Cook pasta and serve as directed. Leftover Homemade Tomato Sauce may be frozen for use at a later time.

Cottage Cheese and Noodle "Kugel"

Serves 6 to 8

1 (12-ounce) package wide
  egg noodles
4 eggs
½ cup plus 1 tablespoon
  sugar, divided
½ teaspoon salt

¾ cup melted butter
2 cups sour cream
2 cups small curd cottage cheese
1 (16-ounce) can crushed
  pineapple, drained
1 teaspoon cinnamon

Cook noodles according to package directions. Rinse in cold water and drain. Combine eggs, ½ cup sugar, salt, butter, sour cream and cottage cheese; mix until smooth. Pour mixture over noodles. Fold in drained pineapple. Pour all into large buttered baking dish. Sprinkle with cinnamon and remaining 1 tablespoon sugar. Bake 350° about 1 hour. Cool and serve in squares with sour cream of jam.

Broccoli Pasta

Serves 2

1 pound fresh broccoli
3 cups water
6 ounces very thin egg noodles
¼ pound fresh mushrooms,
  sliced

6 tablespoons butter or
  margarine, divided
⅓ to ½ cup grated Parmesan
  cheese
Salt and pepper to taste

Parboil broccoli in water about 3 to 4 minutes; drain and reserve water. Set broccoli aside. Cook egg noodles in reserved water. While noodles are cooking, saute mushrooms in 3 tablespoons butter. Combine all of the above with the remaining butter and Parmesan. Season to taste.

Note: Be careful not to use too much Parmesan cheese as it will change the texture. This is not good reheated and must be prepared just before serving.

Springtime Spaghettini

Serves 6
Colorful and delicious

1 pound capellini
5 quarts water
1 tablespoon olive oil
¼ cup butter or margarine
2 teaspoons minced garlic
2 large carrots, cut julienne
1 small sweet red or green
  pepper, seeded and cut
  julienne

1 medium zucchini, cut julienne
1 cup heavy cream
½ cup freshly grated Parmesan
  cheese
¼ cup chopped fresh dill
½ teaspoon salt
¼ teaspoon freshly ground
  pepper

Cook capellini al dente in 5 quarts boiling water to which olive oil has been added. Meanwhile, melt butter in large skillet over medium high heat. Add garlic and saute until garlic just begins to color, about 1 minute. Add vegetables and toss over high heat for 2 minutes. Remove pasta from heat and drain. Place vegetables over high heat. Stir in cream, Parmesan, dill, salt and pepper. Add pasta to skillet and toss gently to blend. Leftovers reheat well in microwave.

Note: Preparation time, about 40 minutes.

Cheese Souffle

Serves 6

6 slices white bread (not French
  bread), cubed
8 ounces extra sharp Cheddar
  cheese, cubed

3 eggs, well-beaten
2 cups milk
Salt and pepper to taste
Nutmeg to taste

Mix bread and cheese cubes together. Beat eggs well; add milk. Combine all ingredients and pour into a well-greased casserole. Refrigerate for at least 6 hours. Bake at 350° for 1 hour.

Never Fail Cheese Souffle

Serves 4
Main dish with vegetable and salad

¼ cup butter or margarine
3 tablespoons all-purpose flour
1 cup milk
1 cup shredded cheese
  (your choice)

3 eggs, separated
½ teaspoon salt
⅛ teaspoon paprika
2 teaspoons minced onion

Melt butter in top of double boiler; remove from heat. Add flour and blend well. Add milk. Place over boiling water, stirring until smooth. Cook, stirring, until thickened. Add cheese and stir until melted. Beat eggs separately, whites first. Add beaten yolks to cheese mixture gradually, stirring constantly. Add salt, paprika and onion. Fold in stiff egg whites. Turn into greased 1½-quart casserole. Set in a pan of warm water and bake at 375° for 40 to 50 minutes or until firm.

Note: Preheat oven 10 minutes and put pan of water in 5 minutes before soufflé. It comes up fast but cook it full 50 minutes.

80's Eggplant Parmigiana

Serves 4

2 cups well-seasoned spaghetti
  sauce
1 small eggplant, peeled and very
  thinly sliced (⅛-inch thick)
Oregano, garlic, pepper and
  Parmesan cheese to taste

4 ounces or less part-skim
  mozzarella cheese, shredded or
  thinly sliced

Pour a thin layer of spaghetti sauce into a 10-inch shallow casserole dish. Arrange a layer of eggplant slices over the sauce. Sprinkle with oregano, garlic, pepper, and Parmesan. Repeat layers until ingredients are used up, ending with mozzarella. Cover with aluminum foil, making a "tent" so cheese will not stick to foil. Bake 350° for about 45 minutes or until eggplant is tender and casserole is bubbly. Uncover for 10 to 15 minutes if desired to lightly brown cheese.

Triple Cheese Strata

Serves 4 to 6

3 tablespoons butter or
  margarine, divided
4 ounces fresh mushrooms, sliced
½ cup chopped onion
½ teaspoon marjoram
6 slices bread (day old is best)

½ cup shredded Cheddar cheese
¼ cup grated Parmesan cheese
1 teaspoon dry mustard
6 eggs, slightly beaten
1½ cups milk
Salt and pepper to taste

Melt 1 tablespoon butter in a 10-inch skillet over medium heat. Add mushrooms, onion and marjoram and cook until onion begins to turn clear; remove from heat. Spread remaining 2 tablespoons butter over side of bread. Cut bread into ½-inch cubes leaving crusts on. In a casserole dish or 10 to 12 individual custard cups, layer half the bread cubes on bottom of dish. Cover with mushroom and onion mixture. Combine all 3 cheeses and dry mustard. Sprinkle over the mixture in dish; top with remaining cubes. Mix eggs, milk, salt and pepper and pour over bread and cheese mixture. Cover and refrigerate at least 3 hours or overnight. When ready to cook, uncover, and bake at 350° for 20 minutes or until the top turns a golden brown.

Cheese Melts

Serves 6
May be made ahead and reheated 350°, 10 minutes

6 (6-inch) unsplit pita bread
1 (8-ounce) package cream cheese
12 slices provolone cheese
1 (8-ounce) package shredded
  mozzarella cheese

½ pound mushrooms, sauteed
4 ounces alfalfa sprouts

Spread each pita evenly with cream cheese. Evenly cover pita with sliced provolone and mozzarella; top with mushrooms. Broil 4 to 5 minutes until cheese is lightly browned and bubbly. Top with sprouts and enjoy.

Note: Tuna, roasted peppers or crab may be substituted for the mushrooms. For an hors d'oeuvre, cut into wedges.

Quiche Lorraine

Serves 8 to 10
May be served as an appetizer or supper with soup or salad

Crust:

2 cups all-purpose flour	**1 egg**
½ cup butter or margarine	**¼ cup cold water**
½ teaspoon salt	

Place flour, butter and salt in a large bowl and work together with hands until smooth. Add egg and water and work with hands until of rolling consistency. Place dough on floured pastry board and roll to ⅛ to ¼-inch thickness. Place in a 9-inch pie pan and crimp edges. Refrigerate for 1 hour.

Filling:

8 strips bacon	**½ teaspoon salt**
½ cup diced Swiss cheese	**¼ teaspoon white pepper**
¼ cup diced ham	**¼ teaspoon nutmeg**
1½ cups light cream	**4 eggs**

Fry bacon until crisp and drain. Crumble bacon over bottom of refrigerated pastry shell. Sprinkle cheese and ham over bacon. Place cream, seasonings and eggs in blender; cover and run on high speed until thoroughly mixed. Pour over ingredients in shell. Bake at 350° for 30 minutes or until top is golden brown and mixture is set. Serve warm.

In 1822, Moses Austin of Durham, with his son Stephen F. Austin, led 300 families into the Southwest Territory to establish, along the Brazos River, the first Anglo community in the territory.

Broccoli Egg Puff

Serves 6

1 pound broccoli
2 tablespoons all-purpose flour
½ teaspoon baking powder
5 eggs, beaten
1 cup cream-style cottage cheese

4 slices bacon, cooked crisp,
   drained and crumbled
½ cup shredded Cheddar or
   Swiss cheese

Cut off broccoli buds; set aside. Chop remaining stalks; cook, covered in a small amount of boiling, salted water for 5 minutes. Add reserved buds; cook 5 minutes. Drain and set aside. In a small mixing bowl, stir together flour and baking powder; set aside. In a medium bowl beat eggs. Beat in flour mixture. Stir in cottage cheese and bacon. Evenly spread broccoli in bottom of a greased 10x6x2-inch baking dish. Pour egg mixture over broccoli. Bake, uncovered, at 350° for 20 minutes. Sprinkle with cheese. Bake 3 minutes more or until center is almost set and cheese is melted. Let stand 5 minutes before serving.

Eggs and Clam New England

Serves 6
Keep can of clams on hand–great for "drop in" meals or Sunday supper with salad

3 slices bacon
3 cups (about 1 pound) diced
   peeled potatoes
¼ cup chopped green onions
   with tops

12 eggs
⅓ cup milk
¾ teaspoon dill weed
1 (6½-ounce) can minced clams,
   drained

In a 10-inch skillet, cook bacon until crisp. Remove from pan, drain and set aside. Pour off all but 2 tablespoons of fat. Cook potatoes and onions in drippings, stirring occasionally until potatoes are tender and lightly browned, about 15 minutes. Mix eggs, milk, dill weed until blended; stir in clams. Pour over potato mixture. As eggs begin to set, draw an inverted pancake turner across the bottom of pan, forming large, soft curds. Cook until eggs are thickened but still moist. Do not stir constantly. Sprinkle with crumbled bacon.

Baked Eggs

Serves 8 to 10
Great do-ahead brunch

½ package cheese croutons
10 eggs
3 cups milk
2 cups shredded Cheddar cheese

1 teaspoon dry mustard
Salt and pepper to taste
½ pound cooked bacon

Line the bottom of a buttered 13x9x2-inch baking dish with croutons. Mix eggs, milk, cheese, mustard, salt and pepper and pour over croutons. Break bacon into 1 to 2 inch pieces and spread over mixture. Bake, uncovered, at 325° for 45 to 50 minutes or until set. Tent with foil if top begins to overbrown.

Eggs Ann Arbor

Serves 4
Delicious! and great idea for your summer tomato harvest

4 large tomatoes
All-purpose flour
Vegetable oil
6 eggs

4 ounces Cheddar or Monterey
Jack cheese, cut into julienne
strips
⅛ cup Parmesan cheese

Slice tomatoes into ½-inch slices and dredge in flour. Arrange in round frying pan and grill in oil until golden brown. Break eggs over grilled tomatoes and immediately arrange strips of cheeses between eggs. Sprinkle with Parmesan. Cover and allow to cook until set. Serve over English muffins.

In 1783, Private Robin Starr, from Danbury, was the first black soldier to receive the nation's Purple Heart.

Meats, Poultry & Fish

Roast Fillet Of Beef

Serves 8 to 10
An elegant do ahead dinner

1 (5 to 6-pound) fillet of beef,
   trimmed
4 to 5 cloves garlic, cut into
   thin slivers
1 teaspoon salt
Freshly ground pepper
3 tablespoons hot pepper sauce

1 cup soy sauce
½ cup olive oil
1 cup port wine
1 teaspoon thyme
1 bay leaf
4 bacon strips

Make gashes in the roast and fill with garlic. Rub entire outside of roast well with salt, pepper and hot sauce. Marinate in the soy, olive oil, wine and herbs, turning several times, for about 4 or 5 hours. Place meat on rack in shallow roasting pan, top with bacon strips and roast at 425° for 30 to 35 minutes. Baste several times with marinade. Meat thermometer should register 125° for rare or 120° for very rare. If using 2 ovens, serve with baked potatoes, popovers and vegetable casseroles that can heat after the meat is removed from oven. All preparations can be completed before guests arrive. All that's needed is a robust red wine.

Beef Drumsticks

Serves 3 to 4
Great for a quick meal

1 pound ground beef
1 teaspoon salt
1 teaspoon mustard
1 teaspoon Worcestershire sauce

¼ cup chopped onion
1 egg
¾ cup breadcrumbs, divided

Combine all ingredients except ½ cup breadcrumbs. Shape into drumsticks and roll in reserved crumbs. Fry in deep fat until golden brown. Serve with tomato sauce if desired.

Beef Rouladen With Mushroom Sauce

Serves 10
For a very special dinner

3 pounds sirloin tip roast, sliced
  ¼-inch thick
1 large onion, finely chopped
10 tablespoons butter or
  margarine, divided
1½ pounds mushrooms
¾ pound ham, sliced ⅜-inch
  thick
¾ cup grated Parmesan cheese

1 cup dry red wine
1 cup regular strength beef broth
1 teaspoon salt
Freshly ground pepper
2 tablespoons cornstarch
2 tablespoons cold water
2 tablespoons finely chopped
  parsley

Place 1 slice of meat between pieces of waxed paper and pound lightly with smooth side of wooden mallet until meat is about 1/16-inch thick. Cut each pounded piece into rectangles about 4x6-inches; set aside. In a large frying pan saute onions in 2 tablespoons butter until limp and transfer to a bowl. Finely chop half the mushrooms (save the smallest ones for the sauce) and saute in 2 tablespoons butter; add to the onions. Cut ham into julienne strips about ½-inch long and ⅛-inch wide and add to stuffing mixture along with cheese; mix lightly. Place 1 heaping tablespoon filling on each meat rectangle; fold the long sides of the meat over the filling about ½-inch on each side and roll up the meat. Secure with a toothpick. Repeat until all the meat rolls are filled. In 2 large frying pans melt 2 tablespoons butter in each pan and brown meat rolls. Pour in wine and broth and season with salt and pepper. Cover and simmer gently for 10 to 15 minutes or until beef is fork tender. Remove toothpicks from meat rolls and transfer to an ovenproof serving dish. Bring the wine juices to a boil and blend in a paste of cornstarch and cold water; stirring and cooking until thickened. Saute remaining whole mushrooms in 2 tablespoons butter for about 5 minutes or until tender and add to the meat sauce. Pour the mushroom sauce over the meat rolls. If made in advance, let cool, then cover and refrigerate. If prepared continuously, cover and bake at 375° for 20 minutes. If refrigerated, cover and bake at 375° for 45 to 50 minutes; sprinkle with parsley before serving.

Pot Roast (Boeuf A La Mode)

Serves 4

4 (5-ounce) pieces rump steak
1¼ cups beef stock
½ cup plus 2 tablespoons
  red wine
1 small onion, finely chopped
1 teaspoon mixed dried herbs
2 tablespoons vegetable oil or
  drippings

8 baby onions
2 tablespoons all-purpose flour
¼ pound carrots, sliced with a
  fluted chip cutter
Salt and pepper
Few drops gravy browning
1 tablespoon chopped parsley

Put the steak in a dish with the stock, wine, onion and herbs and marinate for at least 2 hours, turning occasionally. Drain the meat, reserving the marinade. Heat the oil or drippings in a pan add the meat and baby onions and fry until browned. Transfer to an ovenproof casserole. Add the flour to the fat remaining in the pan and fry gently until browned. Stir in the marinade and bring to a boil. Add to the casserole with the carrots, seasoning and gravy browning. Cover and cook at 300° for 1½ hours or until the meat is tender. Serve the meat in a hot dish with the vegetables arranged around it. Garnish with chopped parsley just before serving.

Prairieland Pot Roast

Serves 6 to 8
A hearty meal-stick to your ribs fare

1 (3 to 4-pound) pot roast
Salt and pepper
1 (8-ounce) bottle Catalina
  French salad dressing
1 cup water, divided

8 small onions
4 medium carrots, cut into
  4-inch pieces
4 potatoes, peeled and quartered
¼ cup all-purpose flour

Season meat with salt and pepper. Brown in ¼ cup salad dressing in Dutch oven over low heat; add remaining dressing and ½ cup water. Cover and simmer 2 hours. Add vegetables. Continue to simmer, covered, for 1 hour or until meat and vegetables are tender. Remove meat and vegetables to a platter. Gradually add remaining ½ cup water to flour, stirring until well blended. Gradually add to hot liquid in pan. Cook, stirring constantly, until mixture boils and thickens. Simmer 3 minutes, stirring constantly. Serve with meat and vegetables.

Saucy Steak Skillet

Serves 4
Easy company supper

1 pound boneless beef round
  steak, cut into serving pieces
¼ cup all-purpose flour
1 tablespoon vegetable oil
1 large onion, chopped
1 (16-ounce) can whole potatoes,
  drained and liquid reserved
¼ cup catsup
1 tablespoon Worcestershire
2 teaspoons green pepper flakes

1 teaspoon instant beef bouillon
1 teaspoon salt
½ teaspoon dried marjoram
  leaves
¼ teaspoon pepper
1 (10-ounce) package frozen
  green beans
1 (2-ounce) jar sliced pimiento,
  drained

Coat beef pieces with flour; pound into beef. Brown beef in oil in 10-inch skillet; push beef to side. Cook and stir onion in oil until tender; drain. Add enough water to reserved potato liquid to measure 1 cup. Mix potato liquid, catsup, Worcestershire, pepper flakes, bouillon, and seasonings. Pour on beef and onion. Bring to a boil; reduce heat and simmer, covered, about 1¼ to 1½ hours until beef is tender. Rinse frozen beans under cold water to separate. Add potatoes, beans and pimiento to skillet. Bring to a boil; reduce heat. Cover and simmer until beans are tender, 10 to 15 minutes.

Beef Roll-Ups

Serves 6
Good, easy "gourmet" recipe

2 pounds beef sandwich steaks
Spicy brown mustard

1 pound bacon
½ cup butter or margarine

Spread each sandwich steak with mustard. Put a slice of bacon on each steak. Roll up and secure with toothpick. Brown in butter in frying pan. Serve with drippings.

Meat Pie With Potato Crust

Serves 6
Great for leftover meats and the family enjoys it

Potato Crust:

3 or 4 large potatoes
1 egg
¼ cup all-purpose flour

Salt and pepper to taste
Dash of vegetable oil

Peel and wash potatoes. Dry and grate them. Add egg and flour to potatoes; season to taste. In a deep dish pie pan, spread potato mixture as you would a pastry shell, being sure that the sides of the pan are padded more than the bottom. Glaze the potatoes very slightly with oil and bake at 350° for 15 to 20 minutes. Remove from oven.

Filling:

2 cups leftover meats, diced or
    cubed
1 (16-ounce) can peas and carrots
1 (10¾-ounce) can cream of
    mushroom soup, undiluted

1 (4-ounce) can sliced mushrooms
    (optional)
4 or 5 slices American cheese

Layer ingredients in order listed into potato crust. Return to oven and bake for 45 to 60 minutes or until cheese is brown and slightly bubbly.

Barbecue Cups

Serves 4 to 6
A treat for children and grown-ups, too

1 pound ground beef
½ cup barbecue sauce
1 tablespoon minced onion
1½ tablespoons brown sugar,
    firmly packed

1 (8-ounce) can refrigerated flaky
    biscuits
¾ cup shredded Cheddar cheese

Saute ground beef until brown; drain off fat. Stir in barbecue sauce, onion and sugar. Press each biscuit into a greased muffin cup. Spoon in meat mixture and sprinkle with cheese. Bake at 400 degrees about 12 minutes.

Stuffed Fillet Of Beef

Serves 10
Elegant for a dinner party

1 whole fillet of beef	1 cup chopped ham
3 large onions, thinly sliced	1 teaspoon pepper
3 tablespoons olive oil	1 teaspoon thyme
4 tablespoons butter or margarine	Salt to taste
2 cloves garlic, minced	2 egg yolks, beaten
1 (4-ounce) can ripe olives, chopped	2 tablespoons chopped parsley

Trim off fat from whole fillet; partially slice (¾) meat into 1-inch sections; set aside. Saute onions until limp in olive oil and butter. Add garlic and olives, ham and seasonings. Stir in egg yolks and parsley. Spoon stuffing between slices of meat. Place in pan large enough to hold meat (I use a broiler pan). Cook, uncovered, at 325° for exactly 60 minutes. Let rest for 10 minutes before slicing and serving. Cooking time is important–do not overcook.

Pizza Hamburger

Serves 4 to 6
A family favorite, especially the children

1 pound lean ground beef	Sprinkle of oregano
½ cup breadcrumbs	4 ounces shredded Cheddar cheese
1 (9-inch) pastry shell, unbaked	
1 (8-ounce) can tomato sauce	2 ounces shredded mozzarella cheese
1 (4-ounce) can mushrooms, drained	

Mix ground beef and breadcrumbs; press mixture into a 9-inch pastry shell. Spread 1 layer of each of remaining ingredients as listed. Bake at 350° for 25 minutes. Better if used following day; may be frozen.

Stuffed Beef In Wine

Serves 4
Fast and easy

2 medium onions, sliced
1 medium green pepper, sliced
½ pound fresh mushrooms,
    quartered
2 cloves garlic, minced (optional)

Olive oil
¾ pound thinly sliced prepared
    roast beef
½ cup dry red wine

Saute onion, pepper, mushrooms and garlic, if using, until tender in olive oil. Remove to a dish to cool. Place 4 double slices of roast beef on waxed paper. Evenly distribute onion mix onto each of the beef slices, roll tightly and skewer with toothpicks to hold together. Place back in fry pan and brown on all sides for several minutes. Pour wine into pan and turn to high heat (to burn off alcohol) for 2 minutes. Cover and reduce heat to simmer for 5 minutes. Serve on a bed of rice with fresh garden salad. The size of these rolls may be cut in half for a wonderful appetizer. Another option is to place a slice of mozzarella cheese inside each roll prior to cooking and add 1 can of crushed tomatoes to the wine while sauteeing. Serve over linguini with garlic bread and salad.

Kay's Chili Con Carne

Serves 4 to 6

1 pound ground beef
1 cup chopped onion
1 cup chopped green pepper
1 (16-ounce) can red kidney beans
1 (24-ounce) can cocktail
    vegetable juice

1 to 2 tablespoons chili powder
1 bay leaf
½ teaspoon paprika
1 clove garlic, minced
Few drops hot pepper sauce

In heavy skillet cook meat, onions and green pepper until meat is browned. Stir in remaining ingredients. Simmer, uncovered, for 1 hour.

Down-Right Chili

Serves 10 to 15; yields 2 gallons
Quick, easy meal for those winter get-togethers

2 pounds ground beef
5 cups diced onion
3 cups diced celery
1 teaspoon pepper
¼ teaspoon red pepper
2 tablespoons salt
¼ cup plus 1 tablespoon chili
   powder

2 teaspoons ground cumin
1 (No. 10) can small red beans
1 (51-ounce) can tomato soup
¾ cup catsup
1½ cups water

In a 2-gallon kettle brown ground beef with onion and celery until onion is transparent and celery soft. Add spices, ½ can beans, soup, catsup and water. Mash other ½ can of beans; mix all well. Bring to a boil and serve immediately or refrigerate then heat what you need, when you need it!

Sunday Biscuit Bake

Serves 6
A light dinner on Sunday—serve with a green salad

1 small onion, chopped
2 tablespoons vegetable oil
1 pound ground beef
2 teaspoons salt
½ teaspoon thyme
½ teaspoon oregano

¼ teaspoon pepper
½ cup barbecue sauce
1 (8-ounce) can refrigerated
   biscuits
10 thin slices sharp Cheddar
   cheese

Saute onion in oil until transparent. Add beef and brown, drain off oil. Add seasonings and barbecue sauce. Press biscuits into ungreased muffin tins. Fill with meat sauce and top with slice of cheese. Bake at 400° about 10 minutes or until cheese is melted. Freezeable.

Tomato And Beef Loaf

Serves 8 to 10

1½ pounds ground beef
1½ cups breadcrumbs
⅔ cup diced American cheese
1 small onion, diced
½ green pepper, diced
2 teaspoons salt

1 crumbled bay leaf
½ teaspoon garlic salt
¼ teaspoon thyme
2 eggs, beaten
1¼ cups tomato sauce

Mix ground beef, breadcrumbs, cheese, vegetables and seasonings together. Combine eggs and tomato sauce; add to meat mixture. Roll into greased loaf pans and bake at 350° for 1 hour.

Ham and Pineapple Rolls

Serves 6
Easy luncheon dish

1 (8-ounce) can crushed pineapple
1 (6-ounce) package chicken
   flavor stuffing mix

12 thin slices boiled ham
1 to 2 tablespoons butter or
   margarine

Drain pineapple, measuring syrup; add water to make 1½ cups. Prepare stuffing mix as directed on package substituting measured liquid for the water and add the pineapple with the stuffing crumbs. Spoon about ¼ cup stuffing onto each ham slice; roll up and place, seam side down, in melted butter in a skillet. Heat, uncovered, turning occasionally. Serve with Mustard Sauce.

Mustard Sauce:
1 tablespoon butter or margarine
1 tablespoon all purpose flour
2 tablespoons dry mustard
⅓ cup hot water

⅓ cup vinegar
½ cup sugar
¼ teaspoon salt
⅓ cup mayonnaise

Melt butter in saucepan over low heat. Blend in flour and dry mustard. Slowly, add hot water and vinegar, stirring constantly, until mixture is smooth.

Baked Ham

Serves a crowd
Delicious

1 whole or half ham	**1 or 2 cloves garlic**
1 cup sugar	**Firmly packed brown sugar**
1 cup vinegar	**Breadcrumbs**
2 teaspoons cinnamon	**Prepared mustard**
5 or 6 whole cloves	**Whole cloves**

Cover ham with boiling water; add next 5 ingredients. Simmer, uncovered, about 2 hours. Let stand in the liquid overnight or at least 5 hours. Drain. Mix 4 parts brown sugar to 1 part crumbs. Add mustard to make a thick paste and spread over ham. Insert whole cloves 1 inch apart all over ham. Bake at 300° allowing 10 minutes per pound.

Roast Leg Of Lamb With Herb Seasoning

Serves 8
Great Sunday or Easter dinner

⅓ cup chopped parsley	**1 small clove garlic, crushed**
¼ cup olive or vegetable oil	**1 (4 to 4½-pound) lamb leg shank**
2 teaspoons salt	**half**
2 teaspoons rosemary, crushed	**8 medium potatoes, peeled and**
½ teaspoon pepper	**cut into 1½-inch chunks**

About 2½ hours before serving, in a small bowl combine first 6 ingredients; set aside. With knife cut crosswise slits, each about 4x¼-inch, on top of lamb leg. Lightly press some parsley mixture into slits; pat remaining parsley mixture onto top of lamb. Place lamb, fat side up, on small rack in a 17x12-inch open roasting pan. Insert meat thermometer into center of lamb being careful not to touch bone or fat with thermometer. Roast lamb at 325° for 30 to 35 minutes per pound (160 on meat thermometer for medium) or until desired doneness. About 35 minutes before lamb is done add potatoes to roasting pan with meat, turning potatoes to coat on all sides with pan drippings, turn potatoes occasionally to brown all sides. When lamb is done, place on large platter, let stand 10 minutes for easier carving. Continue roasting potatoes about 10 minutes longer or until tender. Spoon potatoes around lamb.

Boneless Stuffed Leg Of Lamb

Serves 8
This is a wonderful company meal

1 (5-pound) sirloin half leg of
lamb
Salt and pepper
½ cup unsalted hazelnuts, toasted
and ground
¾ pound good quality sausage
with herb seasoning
2 tablespoons butter or margarine
1 medium leek, washed carefully
and chopped

1 pound fresh spinach, washed,
stems removed and leaves
coarsely chopped
2 tablespoons fresh sage, minced
or 2 teaspoons dried sage
2 teaspoons fresh marjoram,
minced or ½ teaspoon dried
marjoram
2 eggs, lightly beaten

Bone and butterfly a sirloin half leg of lamb. Trim any large pockets of fat from the center and skin-side of the meat. Sprinkle both sides with salt and pepper and spread the roast over a flat surface, skin side down. Spread the hazelnuts over a cookie sheet and toast at 425° about 15 minutes until the skins begin to crack. Watch carefully as nuts can burn quickly once they've started to toast. Allow to cool slightly, then rub nuts together to remove most of the skin. Finely grind the nuts and reserve. In a large skillet crumble and brown sausage over medium heat. Remove and drain. Wipe out the skillet and add the butter. Lower the heat and add the leek. Saute until soft, about 5 minutes. Add the spinach and toss about 2 minutes or until soft. Add herbs and saute for 30 seconds. Add the toasted, ground hazelnuts, salt and pepper to taste. Stir and remove from heat. Add the egg and mix well. Allow to cook briefly. Spread mixture over the entire piece of lamb, filling in pockets where bones were removed. Cut kitchen twine into 3 or 4 (1-foot) lengths and 2 (2-foot) lengths. Starting at one of the shorter ends of the roast, roll it tightly. Don't worry if some of the stuffing falls out; poke it back in or discard it. Place the short pieces of twine under the roast and tie them tightly around the meat at intervals. Use the longer pieces to tie the roast end to end. Set on a rack in a roasting pan and roast at 375° 1 to 1¼ hours for a medium rare roast or 1½ to 1¾ hours for well-done meat. Remove from oven and allow to sit for 10 minutes before cutting. Slice and serve with pan gravy and your favorite vegetables.

Gravy:
Pan juices
¼ cup vermouth
2 tablespoons butter or margarine
1 shallot, minced

1 carrot, peeled and finely
   chopped
1 cup chicken stock
Salt and pepper to taste

Discard any fat from the pan in which the roast was cooked. Add vermouth to the pan and scrape up the brown bits; reserve. In a small saucepan melt the butter and saute the shallot and carrot for 5 minutes. Add chicken stock and simmer until carrots are very soft and easy to mash. Puree the mixture and add the pan juices. Adjust seasonings, adding salt and pepper as needed. Moisten the slices of lamb with a little of the gravy and serve the remainder on the side.

Note: Stuffing may be made the night before and refrigerated; the roast may be boned the day before.

Lamb Curry With Rice

Serves 4

¾ pound boneless lamb, cut into
   1½-inch cubes
3 tablespoons vegetable oil
1 medium onion, minced
1 cooking apple, peeled and
   chopped
¼ cup butter or margarine,
   melted

3 tablespoons all-purpose flour
1 cup milk
1 tablespoon curry powder
1 tablespoon lemon juice
1½ teaspoons salt
¼ teaspoon ground ginger
Pepper
Hot cooked rice

Condiments-currants, raisins, peanuts, onion, green pepper, orange sections. Cook lamb in oil until brown; drain and set aside. Saute onion and apple in butter until tender. Add flour and cook 1 minute, stirring constantly. Gradually add milk; cook over medium heat, stirring constantly, until thickened and bubbly. Stir in next 5 ingredients. Add lamb to sauce mixture; serve over rice. Serve with several of the condiments.

Spicy Grilled Lamb

Serves 12
Great for company barbeque

1 cup Dijon mustard
½ cup vegetable oil
2 tablespoons dry red wine
2 cloves garlic, minced
1 teaspoon dried rosemary,
   crushed
1 teaspoon dried basil, crushed

½ teaspoon dried oregano,
   crushed
½ teaspoon dried thyme, crushed
¼ teaspoon pepper
1 (4-pound) leg of lamb, boned
   and butterflied

Combine mustard, oil, wine, garlic, herbs and pepper. Place lamb in shallow dish. Spread lamb with mustard mixture. Cover and marinate 1 hour at room temperature or overnight in refrigerator. Drain off marinade and reserve. To cook, grill over medium coals, for 45 minutes to 1 hour. Spread marinade over meat a few minutes before end of cooking time. Meat should be charred on outside and pink inside. To serve cut diagonally as for London broil. Heat remaining marinade; pass with meat.

Chinese Pork Roast

Serves 6 to 8
Good

1 (4 or 5-pound) boneless rolled
   pork loin
1 tablespoon vegetable oil
½ cup soy sauce
2 cups beef bouillon

4 to 6 tablespoons honey
½ to ⅔ cup sherry
1 (10¾-ounce) can condensed
   cream of celery soup

Brown meat in oil; pour off oil. Combine next 4 ingredients in pot with meat, basting occasionally. Cook on top of range for 2 to 3 hours. Spoon off oil and add soup to pan juices to make gravy.

Judy's Sauerkraut And Pork

Serves 6 to 8
A favorite on Christmas Eve

1 (3 or 4-pound) boneless pork
  roast
1 or 2 (16-ounce) cans sauerkraut,
  rinsed and drained

2 apples, pared and sliced
2 onions, peeled and sliced
Sherry
Caraway seeds to taste

Roast pork at 425° for 1 hour. Place sauerkraut in large pot; saute apples and onions in butter and add to sauerkraut. Add sherry and caraway seeds. Add pork and cover with sauerkraut. Simmer 3 to 5 hours on top of range or until sauerkraut is very tender.

In 1892, Dr. Washington Wentworth, a dentist in New London, is credited with inventing the first collapsible metal toothpaste tube.

Dutch Pork Chops

Serves 2 to 4
Busy day favorite–can be made in advance

1 to 2 tablespoons vegetable oil
4 center-cut pork chops, 1-inch
  thick
Salt and pepper
Paprika

1 small onion, thinly sliced
1 (32-ounce) can sauerkraut, well-
  drained
1 teaspoon caraway seeds
2 (10¾-ounce) cans tomato soup

In large frying pan heat oil over medium heat. Brown chops on both sides. Place in glass baking dish. Top with onions. Spread sauerkraut over onions; sprinkle caraway seeds over sauerkraut. Spoon tomato soup evenly over all. Bake, covered, at 350° for 45 minutes. Uncover and cook 5 minutes longer. Do not allow to dry.

Italian Pork Chops

Serves 4

4 pork chops
1 (11-ounce) can Cheddar cheese
   soup
1 can water
1 (6-ounce) can tomato paste

Pinch of basil
Salt and pepper to taste
Dash of hot pepper sauce
Mozzarella cheese
Hot cooked noodles

Fry pork chops; mix with next 6 ingredients in large skillet. Top with mozzarella; simmer 45 minutes. Last 5 minutes add cooked noodles and more
mozzarella.

In 1846, Arvid Dayton built his first reed organ in Torrington,
and thereby was the first to build an organ of this kind in
America.

Glazed Stuffed Pork Chops

Serves 4
Makes a drab day special

1 medium apple, chopped (about
   1 cup)
1 cup unseasoned croutons
¾ cup apple juice, divided

1 1⅜-ounce) package onion soup
   mix (not instant)
1 teaspoon ground cinnamon
4 pork chops (about 1½ pounds)

In a medium bowl mix apples, croutons, ½ cup apple juice, onion soup
mix and cinnamon. With long, sharp knife cut a deep pocket in each chop;
fill with stuffing mixture. Arrange chops in single layer in lightly greased
shallow baking dish. Brush with some of the remaining apple juice. Bake
at 400° for 35 minutes or until brown and tender, brushing with apple
juice 2 or 3 times during cooking time.

Barbequed Pork

Serves 6
Easy and delicious

¼ cup soy sauce
2 tablespoons dry red wine
1 tablespoon honey
1 tablespoon firmly packed
 brown sugar

1 clove garlic, crushed
½ teaspoon cinnamon
1½ pounds pork fillet

Combine first 5 ingredients; sprinkle cinnamon on top. Add pork and marinate for several hours; grill. Lightly baste meat with sauce while cooking; if you use too much it tends to burn. Heat remaining marinade and pour over meat to serve.

Ragout Of Pork Stroganoff

Serves 6

2 pounds boneless pork, cut into
 strips
6 tablespoons butter or
 margarine, divided
1 cup chopped onion
1 pound fresh mushrooms
1¼ cups dry white wine, divided

3 tablespoons tomato paste
½ teaspoon dried dill
1 teaspoon salt
½ teaspoon pepper
2 teaspoons all-purpose flour
1 cup sour cream
Hot buttered noodles

Cook pork in large skillet with 3 tablespoons butter until lightly browned on all sides. Remove pork from pan; to drippings in pan add onion and cook for 5 minutes. Add remaining 3 tablespoons butter and mushrooms and cook 5 minutes longer. Return pork to skillet; stir in 1 cup wine, tomato paste, and seasonings. Bring to a boil, cover and cook for 25 minutes over low heat. Mix flour with sour cream; stir into skillet. Add remaining ¼ cup wine just until thickened, stirring often. Serve with noodles.

Pork Fillet In Wine (Filet De Porc Chasseur)

Serves 6

2 pounds pork fillet (tenderloin),
   cut into 1½-inch pieces
2 tablespoons vegetable oil
¼ cup butter or margarine
½ pound onions, chopped

½ pound button mushrooms
2 tablespoons all-purpose flour
1 cup beef stock
½ cup white wine
Salt and pepper

Brown pork quickly in hot oil then remove from pan. Heat butter in pan, add onions and cook slowly until soft. Add mushrooms. Blend in flour, stock and wine. Bring to a boil then simmer 2 to 3 minutes. Return pork to pan and season with salt and pepper. Cover and simmer for 40 to 50 minutes until pork is tender.

Quick And Easy Sausage And/Or Veal And Peppers

Serves 8 to 10
A crowd pleaser–great for a buffet

16 to 18 large green peppers or a
   combination of red and green
   peppers
2½ to 3 pounds veal stew meat or
   Italian sausage (may combine
   sweet and hot sausage or veal
   and sausage)

1 pound fresh mushrooms
1½ cups spaghetti sauce

Rinse and cut up peppers; cut veal or sausage into bite-size pieces. Combine in a 15x10-inch baking pan. Cover loosely with aluminum foil; do not add any liquid. Bake at 350° for 2½ hours. During last half hour, remove foil and add sliced mushrooms and spaghetti sauce. May be served as main dish with spaghetti or plain as a side dish. Prepare a day ahead and reheat before serving if desired.

Wyoming Milk Can Dinner

Serves 30
Serve when corn is plentiful, great Labor Day dinner

30 ears of corn, shucked	**4 large heads of cabbage,**
30 potatoes, scrubbed, not peeled	**quartered**
4 pounds carrots, peeled	**60 polish sausages**
6 large onions, quartered	**½ gallon water**

Secure a 10-gallon milk can in good condition–no rust spots; clean well. Prepare a fire pit with cement blocks or large bricks. Have available small pieces of firewood. Place corn standing on end in milk can; add remaining ingredients. Loosely set the lid on the can or cover loosely with 2 layers of foil. Never put the lid on tight–it can become a missile! Place the can on the fireplace; start a small fire under the can. Continue to keep the fire going. When you see steam and smell your dinner, begin to time the cooking process. In Wyoming, we cook it 45 minutes. Water boils at a lower temperature here so you may want to cook your dinner a few minutes longer. Serving is tricky. Two people with padded mitts are needed to remove the can from the fire. Turn the can upside down, have the contents fall into a large metal or plastic container. Use tongs to serve 30 amazed folks.

Note: I use a tea towel lined plastic milk case to pour the contents into. The juice runs off onto the ground that way. Have lots of butter and napkins available. Rolls and a light salad complete a wonderful Wyoming style meal. Enjoy!!!

Sausage Ring

Serves 6

3 tablespoons corn flakes	**¾ cup breadcrumbs**
1 pound sausage	**2 tablespoons chopped parsley**
1 tablespoon minced onion	**1 egg, beaten**

Press corn flakes onto bottom of a slightly greased 7-inch ring mold. Combine remaining ingredients; put into mold and bake at 350° for 15 minutes. Drain fat; bake 15 minutes longer or until done. Invert ring onto platter and fill center with scrambled eggs.

Pepperoni Pie

Serves 4 to 6
A big hit at parties

3 (8-roll) packages refrigerated
  crescent rolls
2 large sticks of pepperoni,
  chopped
1 pound sweet Italian sausage,
  cooked
1 pound mozzarella cheese,
  shredded

3 eggs
Dash of salt
1 teaspoon garlic powder
½ cup grated Parmesan cheese
1 large green pepper, chopped

Line 2 (8x5-inch) ungreased pans with 6 rolls each. Combine remaining ingredients in a large bowl. Fill the 2 pans with the mixture and cover with remaining rolls. Bake at 350° for 30 minutes.

Note: Hot sausage may be substituted for sweet; hot peppers may also be added. This is very versatile—add any extras that appeal to you.

Stuffed Italian Peppers

Serves 5, yields 7 peppers

7 large Italian frying peppers
1½ cups (¾ pound) Italian
  sausages
5 cloves garlic, diced
1 small onion, diced
4 large eggs

½ cup seasoned breadcrumbs
⅓ cup shredded cheese
1 teaspoon oregano
¼ teaspoon pepper
4 packages chicken broth
  seasoning, divided

Preboil washed peppers that have been seeded for 4 minutes in boiling water. Remove sausage from casing and cook with garlic and onion. Mix together eggs, breadcrumbs, cheese, oregano, pepper, 2 packages chicken broth and sausage mixture; drain and reserve liquid. Stuff peppers when cool. Place in baking dish, cover with 2 cups water (including reserved liquid) to which remaining 2 packages of chicken broth has been added. Bake at 350° for 30 minutes. Serve with tossed salad and Italian bread.

Veal Pecke

Serves 6

1 pound veal scallops, lightly
 pounded to ¼-inch thickness
Salt and freshly ground white
 pepper
4 eggs, beaten
2 cups fine dry breadcrumbs,
 from French or Italian bread
½ cup clarified butter
2 tablespoons butter or margarine

2 medium shallots, minced
3 medium ripe peaches, peeled
 and thinly sliced
1 cup Madeira
2 cups heavy cream
1 teaspoon dry mustard
½ teaspoon salt
¼ teaspoon freshly ground
 pepper

Season veal with salt and white pepper. Dip in egg, allowing excess to drip back into bowl. Dredge in breadcrumbs, pressing gently so crumbs adhere to meat. Heat about 1 teaspoon clarified butter in heavy large skillet over medium-high heat until hot but not smoking. Add veal in batches and cook until golden brown, about 1 minute per side. Add more clarified butter to skillet as necessary. Transfer to platter. Cover with foil and keep warm in low oven. Wipe out skillet. Add 2 tablespoons butter and melt over medium heat. Add shallots and stir 1 minute. Add peaches and cook 30 seconds, stirring gently. Add Madeira, increase heat and boil until liquid is reduced to ¼ cup. Add cream, mustard, salt and pepper. Boil until sauce is reduced by almost half. Adjust seasoning. Arrange veal on warm platter; remove peaches with slotted spoon and arrange down center of veal. Surround with sauce and serve.

Veal Mustard

Serves 4

4 veal rib, loin or sirloin chops,
 ¾-inch thick
1 teaspoon salt
½ teaspoon pepper

3 tablespoons prepared mustard
½ cup diced bacon
¾ cup light cream

Season chops with salt and pepper; spread both sides with mustard. Place in ungreased 9-inch square baking pan. Sprinkle bacon on and around chops; add cream to pan. Bake at 350° for 1¼ hours. Place chops on warm platter; keep warm.

Veal Veronique

Serves 6 to 8

2 pounds thin veal cutlets
¼ cup all-purpose flour
¾ teaspoon sugar
⅛ teaspoon pepper
⅓ cup butter or margarine

2 tablespoons thinly sliced white
  onions or scallions
¼ cup chopped parsley
½ cup chicken broth
2 cups halved and pitted white
  grapes

Pound veal thin; roll up and fasten with toothpick. Combine flour, salt and pepper. Dust veal with mixture. Heat butter in skillet; brown veal. Sprinkle with onion and parsley. Add chicken broth. Cover and simmer over low heat 10 minutes or until tender. Add grapes; cook 2 minutes. Arrange veal and grapes in serving dish. Stir pan juices and pour over veal and serve.

Veal Piccata *Easy—but not as good as Art Museum Chicken Piccata.*

Serves 4
Can be prepared quickly

1½ pounds thin slices of veal
  scallopini
½ cup all-purpose flour
¼ cup butter or margarine,
  divided
2 tablespoons olive oil
Salt to taste

Few twists freshly ground pepper
3 tablespoons lemon juice
½ cup dry white wine
½ cup chicken broth
2 tablespoons finely chopped
  parsley
Thin slices of lemon

Coat veal slices with flour; shake off excess. In large skillet heat 2 tablespoons butter and olive oil until hot. Add veal slices and cook over high heat to brown 1 side, about 2 minutes. Turn and brown other side. When browned, transfer to hot platter and keep warm. Sprinkle with salt and pepper. Leave pan drippings in skillet and add lemon juice, wine and broth. Bring to a boil and boil 2 to 3 minutes, stirring to loosen all browned particles. Add parsley and remaining 2 tablespoons butter. Place scallopini in skillet and heat, turning each in the sauce. Arrange scallopini on warm serving platter and pour sauce over. Garnish with lemon slices. May substitute chicken scallopini or turkey for veal.

Veal In Pecan Sauce

Serves 4
Wonderful company dish

1½ pounds veal, cubed
½ cup water
½ cup chopped onion, divided
1 teaspoon chicken bouillon
   granules
1 clove garlic, minced
½ teaspoon salt

¼ teaspoon thyme
¼ teaspoon oregano
1 tablespoon butter or margarine
½ cup chopped pecans
3 tablespoons all-purpose flour
½ cup sour cream

Combine veal, water, ¼ cup chopped onion, bouillon, garlic, salt, thyme and oregano in large pot. Simmer 60 minutes, drain and reserve broth. Add water to broth to make 1½ cups. Saute remaining onions in butter; add pecans. Blend flour in sour cream; stir in broth. Combine with onion mixture; add veal. Return to heat to thicken but do not boil. Serve with rice or noodles.

Hot Dogs And Noodles

Serves 4 to 6
Also good for outings

¼ cup vegetable oil
¼ cup chopped onion
1 tablespoon Worcestershire sauce
4 tablespoons firmly packed
   brown sugar
½ teaspoon salt

¼ teaspoon paprika
2 tablespoons lemon juice
1 (12-ounce) bottle chili sauce
½ cup warm water
4 cups cooked wide noodles
1 pound frankfurters

Put all ingredients except noodles and frankfurters in a saucepan and simmer for 15 to 20 minutes. Place noodles in a rectangular baking dish; arrange hot dogs over noodles. Cover with sauce and bake at 350° for 30 minutes. May be reheated.

Hot Dog Hash

Serves 4
Children and the young-at-heart enjoy this hash

4 cups finely diced cold cooked
  potatoes
1 medium onion, chopped
3 tablespoons all-purpose flour
Salt and pepper to taste

¼ cup milk
½ pound hot dogs, thinly sliced
3 tablespoons butter or margarine
½ cup shredded Cheddar cheese

Combine potatoes and onion. Sprinkle with flour and season to taste.
Add milk and hot dogs. Put in shallow baking dish; dot with butter. Bake
at 425° for 30 minutes. Top with cheese. Bake for 5 minutes longer or until
cheese is melted. Serve with buttered corn, carrot and celery sticks.

Frankfurter And Kraut Tahitian

Serves 6

½ cup chopped onion
½ cup green pepper strips
2 tablespoons vegetable oil
2 tablespoons all-purpose flour
1 (20-ounce) can pineapple slices,
  drained and 1 cup syrup
  reserved
½ cup water
1 beef bouillon cube
¼ cup brown sugar, firmly
  packed

1 teaspoon salt
½ teaspoon pepper
1 teaspoon soy sauce
1 teaspoon ground ginger
2 (16-ounce) cans sauerkraut,
  drained
2 pounds frankfurters, cut into
  2-inch pieces

Saute onion and green pepper in oil until tender-crisp. Stir in flour; gradually blend in reserved pineapple juice and water. Stir in beef cube, sugar,
salt, pepper, soy sauce and ginger. Bring to a boil, stirring constantly.
Arrange layers of sauerkraut and halved pineapple slices around sides of
a 3 or 4-quart baking dish. Pile frankfurters in center. Pour sauce over all.
Bake at 350° for 30 minutes or in microwave oven on high power for 4 to
5 minutes.

Chicken Breasts Stuffed With Duxelle In Phyllo Pastry

Serves 10 to 12

6 whole chicken breasts, split,
   boned and skinned
1 cup unsalted butter or
   margarine, divided
¼ cup olive oil
⅓ cup cognac
12 sheets phyllo pastry
Duxelles

Saute breasts in ½ cup butter and oil in a heavy skillet for 1 to 2 minutes on each side until lightly browned. Remove to a plate reserving butter and juices. Heat and ignite cognac and pour over chicken breasts. When flames are extinguished, pour liquid into skillet and set aside. Melt remaining butter in a small saucepan. Spread a sheet of phyllo on a damp cloth, brush with butter, fold in half and brush again with butter. Put a chicken breast at narrow end, spread the breast with duxelles and fold to make a rectangular package. Butter a jellyroll pan and place chicken on it. Brush tops with butter. (May be prepared in advance up to this point and wrapped in plastic wrap and refrigerated.) Bake at 400° for 25 to 30 minutes until puffed and browned. Serve with sauce.

Sauce:
½ cup white wine
Pan juices
2 cups chicken stock
2 or 3 shallots, chopped
2 sprigs chopped parsley
1 carrot, peeled and sliced
1 bay leaf
Thyme
Salt and freshly ground pepper
1 tablespoon arrowroot or
   cornstarch
1 tablespoon butter or margarine
   (optional)

Add wine to cognac and juices in pan in which chicken was sauteed; cook to reduce slightly, scrapping up brown bits. Add stock, shallots, parsley, carrot, bay leaf and thyme to taste and simmer for 30 minutes; strain the stock. If time allows, place in freezer or refrigerate overnight so that fat rises to the top and can be removed. Heat, season with salt and pepper. Make a paste with arrowroot and a hot sauce or water and add to the sauce; stir until thickened. Just before serving, beat in butter if desired.

Chicken Or Shrimp Fettucini

Serves 4 to 6
Quick and easy-always a favorite

1 (8-ounce) package fettucini
  pasta
4 chicken breasts, skinned, boned
  and cut into bite-size pieces or
2 pounds shrimp, peeled,
  deveined and cut into
  bite-size pieces
3 tablespoons butter or margarine
2 whole cloves garlic
6 scallions, finely chopped

1 tablespoon all-purpose flour
1 tablespoon lemon juice
1 cup heavy cream
½ cup freshly shredded Gruyere
  or Swiss cheese
¼ cup grated Parmesan cheese
Salt and pepper to taste
3 tablespoons finely chopped
  fresh parsley

Cook pasta according to package directions. Saute chicken or shrimp in hot butter for 3 minutes. Stir in garlic and onions; saute over moderate heat for 3 minutes. Discard garlic cloves. Stir in flour; add lemon juice and cream. Stir until hot then add cheeses and seasonings. Stir until cheese is melted. Drain noodles and toss with chicken mixture. Serve with a lovely green salad.

Baked Chicken Luncheon

Serves 6 to 8

4 whole chicken breasts, halved,
  boned and skinned
¼ teaspoon salt
⅛ teaspoon pepper
1 (16-ounce) can sauerkraut,
  drained and squeezed

4 (4x6-inch) slices Swiss cheese
1¼ cups bottled Thousand Island
  salad dressing
1 tablespoon chopped fresh
  parsley

Place chicken in buttered baking pan; sprinkle with salt and pepper. Spoon sauerkraut over chicken and top with Swiss cheese. Pour salad dressing evenly over cheese. Cover with foil and bake at 325° for 1¼ hours or until chicken is tender. Sprinkle with parsley.

Chicken Or Turkey Tetrazzini

Serves 6 to 8
A good way to use turkey leftovers

1 pound spaghetti, cooked
and drained
½ cup plus ⅓ cup butter or
margarine, divided
½ cup all-purpose flour
1 teaspoon salt
¼ teaspoon pepper

2½ cups chicken broth
½ cup milk
¼ cup sherry
1 (4-ounce) can mushrooms,
drained or ½ pound fresh
mushrooms
3 cups cooked chicken or turkey

Place cooked and drained spaghetti in a 3-quart casserole. In a large saucepan melt ½ cup butter; add flour, salt and pepper. Stir until smooth. Add broth, stirring until thickened; add milk and sherry. In another saucepan melt remaining ⅓ cup butter; add mushrooms and chicken or turkey. Heat thoroughly and add to white sauce in other pan, then pour over spaghetti. Liberally sprinkle casserole with grated Parmesan cheese and bake at 400° for 20 to 25 minutes until brown. Serve with tossed salad and garlic bread.

Veronika's Walnut Chicken

Serves 4

¼ cup soy sauce
1 tablespoon dry sherry
½ teaspoon ground ginger
1 pound boneless chicken
breasts, cut into 1-inch pieces

5 tablespoons vegetable oil,
divided
⅓ cup sliced green onions
1 clove garlic, halved
1 cup coarsely chopped walnuts

Combine soy sauce, sherry and ginger in a medium bowl; add chicken pieces and let stand 15 minutes. Meanwhile heat wok or large skillet; add 3 tablespoons oil and heat until smoking. Add green onions, garlic and walnuts. Cook 3 minutes, tossing mixture with slotted spoon; discard garlic halves and remove walnut-onion mixture to a small bowl. Add remaining oil to wok; heat and add chicken pieces and soy mixture. Stir-fry until chicken is done and soy mixture begins to coat the chicken, about 5 minutes. Add walnut-onion mixture and toss together. Serve with hot, cooked rice if desired.

Erin's Favorite Chicken Divan

Serves 6
Everyone loves this–my daughter's request every birthday

¼ cup butter or margarine
¼ cup all-purpose flour
1½ cups chicken broth
2 teaspoons sherry
⅛ teaspoon nutmeg
½ cup heavy cream, whipped

1 cup grated Parmesan cheese,
  divided
2 (10-ounce) packages frozen
  broccoli spears or 1 bunch fresh
  broccoli
6 to 8 large boned chicken breasts

In a medium saucepan melt butter over low heat. Add flour to make a roux. Add chicken broth and bring to a boil, stirring constantly. Remove from heat; stir in wine and nutmeg. Gently fold in whipped cream and ½ cup Parmesan cheese. Place broccoli in an ungreased 11x7-inch baking dish. Top with chicken; pour sauce over all. Sprinkle with remaining ½ cup Parmesan. Bake, uncovered, at 350° about 90 minutes until bubbly and nicely browned. Serve with wild rice.

Note: If fresh broccoli is used, cook ½ normal time before topping with chicken and sauce.

Chicken Marsala With Muenster Cheese

Serves 4
Serve over spatzle

4 chicken breasts, boned and
  skinned
2 eggs, beaten
Seasoned breadcrumbs
¼ cup butter or margarine

¼ cup vegetable oil
¼ cup Marsala wine
1 (4-ounce) can mushrooms,
  drained
Muenster cheese slices

Soak chicken in eggs for 1 hour. Roll in breadcrumbs and brown in a mixture of butter and oil in frying pan. Remove to a baking pan. Add wine and mushrooms; pour over chicken. Top each chicken breasts with a slice of Muenster cheese. Bake at 350° for 20 minutes.

Polynesian Chicken

Serves 6
May be made hours in advance and reheated-makes a colorful buffet

½ pound bacon
5 onions, quartered
1 green pepper, cut up
¾ cup celery, cut into strips
1 (29-ounce) can peach halves,
    drained and syrup reserved

1¼ tablespoons cornstarch
1 tablespoon soy sauce
2 tablespoon vinegar
6 chicken breasts, halved
2 or 3 medium tomatoes,
    quartered

Cook bacon, onions, green pepper and celery in large skillet; set aside. Drain peaches, reserving liquid, and set aside. Combine peach syrup, cornstarch, soy sauce and vinegar. Cook over medium heat until thickened and transparent. Cook (fry) chicken breasts in serving casserole on buffet server. When done, cover with cooked vegetables and top with peaches and tomatoes. Pour syrup over all. Serve with hot, cooked rice. Reheat to serve.

Oriental Chicken Breasts

Serves 4
Very lo-cal and delicious

2 pound chicken breasts, cut into
    2-inch pieces
2 tablespoons vegetable or
    olive oil
1 bunch broccoli, cut into
    1-inch pieces
1 rib celery, cut into 1-inch pieces
1 large carrot, cut into matchstick
    pieces

4 scallions, chopped
1 large green pepper, chopped
1 large red sweet pepper, chopped
1 (1-pound) package frozen
    Chinese pea pods
1 tablespoon low-salt soy sauce

Brown chicken lightly in oil in non-stick pan; set aside. In same pan saute all vegetables until tender crisp, adding the pea pods last. Return chicken to pan and sprinkle soy sauce on chicken. Gently fold together all ingredients and simmer for about 5 minutes. Serve with hot, cooked rice.

Gov's Favorite Chicken

Serves few to many

2 to 8 chicken breasts, split
1 (16-ounce) jar apricot preserves
1 (1 ⅜) package onion soup mix

1 (8-ounce) bottle Italian salad
 dressing

Place breasts in large flat casserole dish. Spoon preserves over chicken. Sprinkle soup mix over chicken and top with Italian dressing. Cover with foil and bake at 350° for about 45 minutes; remove foil last 15 minutes to crisp up chicken.

Note: I've cooked chicken for ½ hour (earlier in the day) and later threw it on the grill to reheat and crisp it up.

Nikki O'Neill
Governor's Mansion
Hartford, CT

Nanny's Chicken Delight

Serves 6
Everyone's favorite served over rice

1 large onion, sliced
1 green pepper, sliced
1 (8-ounce) can mushrooms,
 drained
3 tablespoons butter or margarine
3 tablespoons molasses
2 tablespoons Worcestershire
 sauce

¼ teaspoon paprika
1 cup catsup
⅔ cup water
4 pounds chicken, cut into pieces
1 cup all-purpose flour seasoned
 with salt and pepper
Vegetable oil

Saute onion, pepper and mushrooms in butter. Add next 5 ingredients, mix thoroughly and bring to a boil. Wash chicken parts, dry and roll in seasoned flour; brown in hot oil. Place chicken in 2-quart casserole. Cover with sauce. Bake at 325° for 45 minutes in oven or cook in electric skillet.

Crescent Chicken Squares

Serves 4
Quick-prepare ahead

1 (3-ounce) package cream cheese
3 tablespoons butter or
    margarine, melted and divided
2 cups chicken, cooked and cubed
¼ teaspoon salt
⅛ teaspoon pepper
2 tablespoons milk
1 tablespoon chives
1 (8-ounce) package crescent rolls
Breadcrumbs

In medium bowl blend cream cheese and 1 tablespoon melted butter until smooth. Add next 5 ingredients and mix well. Separate rolls into 4 squares. Firmly press perforation to seal. Spoon ½ cup chicken mixture into center of each square. Pull 4 corners to top and twist to seal. Brush with remaining butter and dip in crumbs. Place on ungreased baking sheet and bake at 350° for 20 to 25 minutes.

Mushroom Stuffed Chicken Breasts

Serves 6
Great for company or Sunday dinner

3 boned chicken breasts
6 ounces mushrooms, sliced
1 clove garlic, crushed
1 or 2 tablespoons butter or
    margarine
Salt and pepper to taste
1 tablespoon all-purpose flour
½ packet chicken bouillon
½ cup water
1 cup breadcrumbs

Cut breasts in half and pound thin enough to be able to roll; set aside. Saute mushrooms and garlic in butter in small skillet until mushrooms are tender. Season to taste with salt and pepper. Put flour and bouillon into mushrooms; cook to thicken. Add water to make a thick sauce (just to hold mushrooms together). Pour breadcrumbs onto plate; place chicken breasts on crumbs. Place small amount (1½ tablespoons) mushrooms on 1 end of chicken breast; roll up. Place, seam side down, in buttered baking dish. Bake at 350° for 45 to 60 minutes.

Chicken Fondue

Serves 4 to 6
Serving suggestions: spinach salad and light dessert

4 whole boned chicken breasts
1 cup vegetable oil
2 tablespoons plus 1 teaspoon
   lemon juice, divided
1½ teaspoons salt, divided
2 tablespoons paprika

3 tablespoons butter or margarine
4 tablespoons all-purpose flour
1½ cups chicken broth
½ pound fresh mushrooms
2 eggs yolks
¼ cup heavy cream

Cut chicken into bite-size pieces. Combine oil, 2 tablespoons lemon juice, 1 teaspoon salt and paprika and marinate chicken in mixture, uncovered, for 1 hour. In heavy sauce pan melt butter; add flour. Stir until lumps are gone and mixture is thick. Remove from heat. Add broth, remaining ½ teaspoon salt, remaining 1 teaspoon lemon juice, egg yolks and cream. Saute sliced mushrooms and add to sauce. Return to medium heat, stirring constantly until thickened. Cover and set aside while cooking chicken in fondue pot. Fill fondue pot with a little over ½ full with oil. Add ½ cup butter (no substitutes) and a few grains of dried minced garlic; heat. Cook chicken for 5 minutes before dipping into the sauce.

England Flounder Stuffed With Crab

Serves 4

4 large flounder filets
Salt and pepper to taste
1 (6-ounce) package frozen
   crabmeat, thawed, drained
   and shredded

1 (10¾-ounce) can condensed
   cream of mushroom soup
1 cup frozen peas

Sprinkle flounder with salt and pepper and top with crabmeat. Roll up jellyroll style and place in greased 1½-quart oblong baking dish. Mix soup and peas; pour over fish rolls. Cover and bake at 350° for 30 to 40 minutes or until fish flakes.

Flounder Florentine

Serves 4 to 6
Great make-ahead company dinner

1 pound fresh spinach	Dash of salt, pepper and nutmeg
2 tablespoons butter or margarine	1 tablespoon lemon juice
2 tablespoons water	Lemon slices
1 to 1½ pounds flounder fillets	Chopped parsley

Wash spinach, chop and place in saucepan with butter and water. Steam gently over low heat until spinach is just wilted, about 2 minutes. Place drained spinach in greased, shallow oven-proof dish. Arrange fish fillets on top, sprinkle with salt, pepper and nutmeg; pour over lemon juice. Cover with greased aluminum foil and bake at 350° for 20 to 30 minutes or until fish is tender. Remove fish from oven and spoon over hot Mornay Sauce, garnish with lemon slices and chopped parsley.

Mornay Sauce:

2 tablespoons butter or margarine	¼ cup shredded firm Cheddar cheese
2 tablespoons all-purpose flour	Dash of salt, pepper, nutmeg
1 cup milk	
¼ cup grated Parmesan cheese	

Melt butter in saucepan. Add flour and cook 1 minute. Remove from heat; gradually add milk. Return to heat and bring to a boil.

In 1978, the longest East Coast charity run ever made was by Adam West from Farmington, at age twenty. West ran from Caribou, Maine to Marathon, Florida, a distance of 2,500 miles

Red Snapper With Matchstick Vegetables

Serves 6

2 tablespoons butter or margarine
1½ pounds fresh red snapper
¼ teaspoon salt
Freshly ground white pepper
2 shallots, finely minced
12 sprigs lemon thyme
2 cups mixed vegetables (carrots,
  yellow squash, zucchini, red
  peppers), cut into matchstick
  pieces

3 ounces snow peas, cut into
  diagonal pieces
3 ounces white wine
1 lemon, sliced into 6 portions

Cut butter into thin shavings and divide it among 6 (9x12-inch) pieces of parchment paper. Cut the fish into six 4-ounce servings and place on top of butter, skin side down. Season with salt and pepper. Sprinkle minced shallots and lemon thyme over fish. Surround the fish with the matchstick vegetables and snow peas. Pour 1 tablespoon wine over each fish and top with a lemon slice. Completely enclose the fish in the parchment paper by loosely rolling the paper. Fold the ends and use a 6-inch string to tie them together like a handle. Make sure the paper has not torn. Bake at 400° for 15 to 20 minutes. Transfer from the baking dish to a warmed platter. Cut the packets open just before serving.

In 1840, the first bolt shop in America was founded in Southington.

Scrod Dijon

Serves 4

¼ cup chopped green pepper
¼ cup minced onion
1 tablespoon Dijon mustard
2 teaspoons Worcestershire sauce
¼ teaspoon hot pepper sauce
Salt and pepper to taste
Thyme and garlic powder to taste

3½ tablespoons lemon juice
½ cup butter or margarine
2 cups bread or cracker crumbs
1½ to 2 pounds scrod fillets
2 tablespoons grated Parmesan
cheese

Combine green pepper, onion, mustard, Worcestershire, pepper sauce seasonings and lemon juice. Melt butter; stir in crumbs and add to vegetable mixture, blending well. Cut scrod into 4 serving-size pieces, season with salt and pepper and dot with additional butter. Place on foil-lined rack with surface about 4 inches below heat source and broil 5 minutes. Remove from broiler. Turn scrod, top with mixture and return to broiler for 5 to 7 minutes or until fish flakes easily with fork. Sprinkle with Parmesan and broil 1 minute longer.

Sole Aubergine

Serves 6

2 tablespoons olive oil
3 cups chopped eggplant or
squash
3 tablespoons chopped shallots
3 cloves garlic, minced
⅓ cup chopped green pepper

1½ teaspoons basil
½ teaspoon thyme
¼ teaspoon pepper
3 cups chopped tomato
6 filets of sole (1 per person)
6 thin slices Swiss cheese

Heat olive oil in a large skillet. Saute eggplant, shallots, garlic, pepper and spices until eggplant is brown and tender. Stir in tomato. Arrange fish in a baking dish. Place a slice of cheese on each filet. Spoon eggplant mixture evenly over all. Bake at 450° for 5 to 10 minutes or until fish flakes and cheese is melted.

Poached Salmon With Caper Sauce

Serves 2 to 4
Simple and elegant

1 pound salmon filet	Pinch of dill seed
1 small onion, sliced	1 to 2 carrots, sliced
2 teaspoons dill weed	Salt to taste
5 peppercorns	

Place salmon in deep, wide skillet (or use a fish poacher) with all above ingredients. Bring to a boil, then simmer 10 to 15 minutes, turning as needed. Drain and reserve onions and carrots. Reserve 1 cup stock for sauce.

Caper Sauce:

2 tablespoons butter or margarine	1½ teaspoons dill weed
2 tablespoons all-purpose flour	2 tablespoons small capers
1 cup fish stock	2 tablespoons chopped onion
¼ cup white cooking wine	

Melt butter in saucepan and brown flour. Add liquid slowly, using a wire whisk to blend. Add seasoning, capers and onion. Cook until thickened. Serve over poached salmon.

Spicy Fish Fillet

Serves 6
Easy, tasty dish liked even by people who are not fish lovers

½ cup dry breadcrumbs	½ cup butter or margarine, melted
2 pounds fish fillets (sole or cod are suggested)	1 teaspoon salt
1 tablespoon cider vinegar	1 teaspoon prepared mustard
1 tablespoon Worcestershire sauce	⅛ teaspoon pepper
1 tablespoon lemon juice	Paprika

Cover bottom of a greased 12x9x2-inch baking dish with breadcrumbs. Lay fillets on crumbs. Mix remaining ingredients except paprika. Pour over fish fillets; sprinkle with paprika. Bake at 450° for 10 minutes per inch thickness of fish. Fish is done when it flakes with a fork.

Snapper Pontchartrain

Serves 2

8 to 10 ounces fresh filet of red or yellow tail snapper
Lightly salted butter or margarine
2 ounces fresh mushrooms, including stems, sliced
2 ounces fresh crabmeat (white lump or King crab)

½ fresh tomato, finely diced
2 slices Bermuda or Spanish onion, finely diced
Freshly ground pepper

Rinse fish in cold water, drain and pat dry. Rub both sides with butter and place skin side up on greased, shallow pan. Bake at 350° for 15 minutes. (Fish will not cook completely.) While fish is baking, melt 1 tablespoon butter in an iron skillet over medium low heat. Do not overheat the butter so that it remains yellow. When butter is hot, add sliced mushrooms and toss frequently. Add butter to keep liquid ratio. When mushrooms are heated through, add crabmeat. Add diced tomato and heat through adding butter again if necessary. Add onion and toss with other ingredients in pan until hot. Raise heat and cook until onion is translucent. Season with pepper. Remove saute from pan with a spoon, retaining pan juices. Add fish to the skillet and saute for about 30 seconds. Flip over and saute 30 seconds more. Reduce heat and cook just long enough to assure that the fish is cooked through. Use a fork to test the center of fish for doneness. Transfer fish to a hot platter and top with sauteed vegetables and serve.

In 1899, the first private bird sanctuary in the U.S. was established in Fairfield.

Tuna Vinaigrette

Serves 4 to 6
Serve with thinly sliced French bread

4 cups sliced pared carrots
½ cup water
1 teaspoon salt
¼ teaspoon sugar
¼ teaspoon pepper
¼ teaspoon dry mustard
½ teaspoon dried leaf basil
5 tablespoons white wine vinegar

½ cup vegetable oil
1 tablespoon lemon juice
1 clove garlic, minced
¼ cup chopped parsley
2 tablespoons chopped onion
2 (6½-ounce) cans tuna, drained
2 zucchini, sliced

Place carrots in medium saucepan. Add water, cover and cook over medium heat until tender crisp. Drain and set aside. In large bowl combine seasonings; stir in liquids, garlic, parsley and onion. Add tuna, cooked carrots and zucchini. Toss together, cover and chill several hours.

Scalloped Fish

Serves 4
Easy company supper

5 tablespoons butter or
  margarine, divided
2 tablespoons finely chopped
  scallions
1 cup toasted croutons
2 tablespoons all-purpose flour

1 to 1½ cups light cream
1 to 1½ cups cooked fish (scallops
  are very good)
2 tablespoons dry sherry
Salt and freshly ground pepper to
  taste

Melt 3 tablespoons butter in saucepan. Saute scallions; stir in croutons, toss, then set aside. Melt remaining butter in skillet. Stir in flour and cook 2 minutes, stirring until smooth. Slowly add cream, cooking and stirring until smooth. Add fish, sherry and seasonings. Spread ½ fish mixture in greased baking dish and cover with ½ crouton mixture. Repeat layers twice. Bake at 350° for 30 minutes.

Crab Casserole

Serves 4 to 6

1 pound crabmeat
¼ cup butter or margarine
¼ cup all-purpose flour
⅛ teaspoon pepper
1 teaspoon salt
1½ teaspoons paprika
3½ cups milk
1½ cups shell macaroni,
   uncooked

2 (8-ounce) jars artichoke hearts
   or 1 (12-ounce) package frozen
   artichoke hearts, cooked as
   directed
½ cup sherry
1 cup shredded Cheddar cheese

Flake crabmeat and set aside. Melt butter in a saucepan and remove from heat. Stir in flour and seasonings to make a smooth mixture. Add milk gradually, stirring constantly. Bring to a boil and reduce heat. Simmer 5 minutes; remove from heat. Cook macaroni according to package directions. Drain macaroni and artichokes. Combine crabmeat, sherry, macaroni and artichoke hearts with the sauce. Mix well and put in casserole dish. May refrigerate for 24 hours at this point. Sprinkle with cheese and bake at 350° for 20 minutes until bubbly or longer if refrigerated.

Lobster Fra Diavolo

Serves 2

3 cloves garlic, chopped
½ cup olive oil
1 (16-ounce) can tomatoes,
   crushed
1 teaspoon oregano
1 tablespoon chopped parsley
½ teaspoon salt

⅛ teaspoon red pepper
¼ teaspoon pepper
½ cup sherry or white wine
2 medium-sized live lobsters
   cooked
Little neck clams

Brown garlic in oil; add tomatoes. Add oregano and chopped parsley. Add seasonings. Cook 2 or 3 minutes. Add sherry and simmer 15 minutes. Add chopped lobster pieces. Cover and simmer 20 minutes. Clams may be added the last 5 minutes if desired.

Mussels Steamed In Ouzo Tomato Broth

Serves 10 to 12
An easy to prepare dinner for a crowd

2 Spanish onions, finely diced
4 cloves garlic, minced
2 green peppers, finely diced
⅓ cup chopped parsley
⅓ cup finely chopped celery
¼ cup olive oil
1 (8-ounce) can tomato sauce
7 cups canned tomatoes with
 liquid
½ tablespoon fresh oregano,
 minced
½ tablespoon fresh basil, minced
⅛ teaspoon cayenne pepper
1 cup dry red wine

1 lemon, sliced
2 tablespoons sugar
12 ounces tomato paste
½ tablespoon fresh rosemary,
 minced
½ tablespoon fresh thyme,
 minced
8 whole peppercorns
2 bay leaves
2 cups clam broth
⅓ cup ouzo
1 cup sweet butter or margarine
12 to 16 mussels per person

Saute first 5 ingredients in olive oil until onions turn golden in color, 5 to 7 minutes. Add remaining ingredients, except mussels, to sauteed vegetables. Bring to a low boil, reduce heat and simmer 1 hour, stirring occasionally. Remove lemons. Add mussels to the pot; cover and steam until mussels open. Serve over fresh pasta.

Note: The ouzo may be omitted with great results. To clean mussels, rinse in cold water and pull the "beard" off. For a more elegant variation, substitute scallops or shrimp for the mussels.

In 1910, the first steel golf club shafts were made in Bristol.

Mussels Posillipo

Serves 4
Easy to prepare but looks like it took all day!

48 mussels
½ cup olive oil
1 tablespoon minced garlic
2 dried hot peppers
½ cup dry white wine
3 cups canned tomatoes with
  juice

Freshly ground pepper to taste
1 tablespoon oregano
¼ cup finely chopped fresh
  parsley

Wash mussels well are remove beards. Heat oil in large, heavy skillet. Add garlic and hot peppers. Cook briefly and add wine. Cook to reduce liquid by ½. Add tomatoes with paste. Add pepper and oregano. Cover and bring to a boil. Simmer 15 minutes. Add mussels and cover tightly until mussels open, about 5 to 10 minutes. Sprinkle with parsley and serve.

Risotto Giorgio

Serves 6

2 cups raw rice
2 zucchini, chopped
1 large onion, chopped
1 tablespoon olive oil
1 clove garlic, minced
1 tablespoon basil, fresh
  if possible

2 ripe tomatoes, cubed
½ cup pignolas or walnuts
1 pound shrimp, cleaned and
  cooked
½ cup grated Parmesan cheese
1 tablespoon chopped parsley

Cook rice in 4¼ cups water for 20 minutes (rice should be "wet"). Saute zucchini and onion in oil. Add garlic and basil. Put mixture into food processor and process into puree. Stir in tomatoes and nuts; reheat. Mix thoroughly with rice and shrimp. Add Parmesan and parsley and mix.

Shrimp In Hot Garlic Sauce

Serves 4 to 6
Ruth Podgwaite's recipe

1 pound fresh shrimp
1 egg white
1 teaspoon Chinese wine or dry
  sherry
1 teaspoon salt
2 teaspoons cornstarch
2 cups vegetable oil
3 fresh red chilies, finely
  chopped
1 inch knob fresh ginger,
  finely chopped

1 brown onion, finely
  chopped
2 spring onions (scallions), finely
  chopped
3 cloves garlic, finely minced
5 ounces fish stock
1 tablespoon black bean paste
1 teaspoon sugar
Freshly ground pepper
1 teaspoon sesame oil

Shell, wash, and devein shrimp; cut into halves. Beat egg white, then add wine, salt and cornstarch. Pour mixture over shrimp and let marinate for ½ hour. Heat vegetable oil in pan and deep fry shrimp until pink. Remove from pan and pour off all but about 3 tablespoons oil. Add chilies, ginger, onions and garlic to oil in pan and stir for 5 minutes. Add stock, bean paste, sugar and pepper and bring to a boil. Replace shrimp and simmer for 2 minutes more. If desired, thicken with a little cornstarch mixed with cold water. Arrange in a serving dish and sprinkle with sesame oil.

Grilled Shrimp

Serves 4 to 6
Elegant and easy company dinner

⅓ cup soy sauce
⅓ cup lime or lemon juice
⅓ cup vegetable oil
Onion powder to taste

Pepper to taste
2 pounds jumbo shrimp, cleaned
  and deveined

Mix together soy sauce, juice, oil and seasonings. Marinate shrimp in this mixture for 2 to 3 hours. Place shrimp on skewers and grill 8 to 10 minutes, turning often and basting at each turn. Serve over hot rice with a green salad.

Rita's Stuffed Jumbo Shrimp

Serves 3 to 4

1 to 2 pounds jumbo shrimp
(9 to 10 count), shelled
and deveined
1 or 2 (7-ounce) can(s) tiny shrimp
1 (7½-ounce) can crabmeat,
drained

¾ (12-ounce) package round,
butter-flavored crackers
½ cup butter or margarine,
melted

Split shrimp almost through from the back after shelling and deveining. Rinse under cold water, pat dry with paper toweling and set in buttered baking dish. In large bowl mix remaining ingredients thoroughly. Do not use any water. Generously stuff shrimp, pressing extra stuffing over all. Bake at 375° for 30 minutes or until nicely browned.

Wine and Cheese Shrimp Strata

Serves 8
Great as a company dish or delete the shrimp for an everyday family meal

1 loaf French bread, cubed
⅓ pound shredded Swiss cheese
¼ pound shredded Monterey
Jack cheese
1 pound shrimp, cooked
1 bunch broccoli, steamed or 1
(10-ounce) package broccoli,
thawed
¼ cup white wine

⅛ teaspoon pepper
Dash of cayenne pepper
8 eggs
1¼ cups milk
2 scallions, minced
1¼ teaspoons prepared mustard
¾ cup sour cream
⅔ cup grated Parmesan cheese

Spread bread cubes in bottom of a 13x9x2-inch pan. Sprinkle with Swiss and Jack cheeses, then add shrimp and broccoli. Beat together remaining ingredients and pour over pan's contents. Cover and refrigerate for several hours or overnight. Bake, covered, at 350° about 1 hour or until set. Uncover and spread sour cream and Parmesan on top. Bake about 10 minutes longer or broil until Parmesan turns golden. Leftovers freeze and reheat well.

Glazed Scallops and Mushrooms/Coquilles Saint-Jacques

Serves 4

4 scallions, white parts, thinly
  sliced
5 tablespoons butter or
  margarine, divided
1 cup medium dry white wine
½ cup water
½ teaspoon salt
⅛ teaspoon white pepper
1 pound scallops
½ pound fresh mushrooms,
  sliced

2 tablespoons all-purpose flour
2 egg yolks
1 cup heavy cream
1 teaspoon strained lemon juice
2 tablespoons grated Parmesan
  cheese
2 tablespoons fine wine white
  breadcrumbs

In a saucepan, gently saute the scallions in 1 tablespoon butter. Add the wine, water, salt and pepper and cook at simmer for 10 minutes. If sea scallops are used, halve or quarter them; use bay scallops whole. Add scallops and mushrooms to wine broth and cook for 5 minutes or just until the scallops are tender. Do not overcook. Drain scallops and mushrooms, reserving cooking liquid and put them in 6 buttered scallop shells or individual heat proof dishes. If cooking liquid is in excess of 1 cup, reduce it in the saucepan over high heat to that quantity. In another saucepan, heat 2 tablespoons butter. Blend in flour and cook gently, without browning, for 2 minutes. Add reserved cooking liquid gradually, stirring constantly to produce a smooth sauce; remove from heat. In a mixing bowl, thoroughly combine egg yolks and cream, and stir the mixture vigorously, a little at a time, into the sauce. Add the lemon juice. Pour sauce equally over the scallops and mushrooms and sprinkle each serving with 2 teaspoons of the cheese and breadcrumbs combined. Dot each with 1 teaspoon of remaining butter, cut into small bits and brown lightly under a hot broiler. Serve at once.

In 1866, the first steam automobile was one manufactured by
H.A. House in Bridgeport.

Seafood Newburg

Serves 10 to 12

6 tablespoons unsalted butter
  or margarine
1 clove garlic, minced
½ cup all-purpose flour
1 teaspoon sugar
1 teaspoon paprika
¼ teaspoon curry powder
1 tablespoon Worchestershire
  sauce
3½ cups milk or light cream,
  scalded
½ cup dry sherry

1 chicken bouillon cube,
  crumbled
1 pound medium to large shrimp,
  cooked, peeled and deveined
¾ pound fresh lobster meat from
  the tail (frozen may be used)
1 pound fresh backfin crabmeat,
  picked over
2 tablespoons chopped fresh
  parsley
Salt and freshly ground pepper
to taste

In a large saucepan, melt butter over moderate heat. Add garlic and saute until soft. Add flour and cook, whisking for about 5 minutes. Stir in sugar, paprika, curry powder and Worcestershire. Gradually whisk in milk, sherry and bouillon cube; cook until thick. Add shrimp, lobster and crab-meat. Stir in parsley and season with salt and pepper. Serve on toast or with rice pilaf.

Note: The roux may be made ahead of time. Use double boiler to heat before adding seafood.

In 1829, the first coffee mill was patented by James Carring-ton of Wallingford

Seafood In A Wok

Serves 2 to 3
Quick and easy

⅓ cup teriyaki sauce
⅓ cup white wine or sherry
Dash of ground ginger
½ pound shrimp, cleaned
   and deveined
¼ pound bay scallops
2 tablespoons peanut oil
¼ pound snow peas, sliced
   on the diagonal

½ green pepper, chopped
6 to 8 scallions, sliced
6 to 8 mushrooms, sliced
2 teaspoons arrow root or
   cornstarch
Cashew nuts

Mix together teriyaki sauce, wine and ginger. Marinate seafood in sauce for 1 to 2 hours. Saute seafood in peanut oil in wok; set aside. Saute vegetables in remaining oil until tender crisp; return seafood to wok. Add marinade with arrow root or cornstarch. Heat until thickened. Add cashews. Serve over hot rice or chow mein noodles.

Elephant Stew

Serves 3800
Good for a laugh

1 medium size elephant
2 rabbits (optional)

Salt and pepper

Cut the elephant into bite-size pieces. This should take about 2 months. Add enough brown gravy to cover. Cook over kerosene fire for about 4 weeks at 465°. This will serve 3800 people. If more are expected, 2 rabbits may be added, but do this only if necessary as some people do not like to find a hare in their stew.

Company Casseroles

Easy Beef Burgundy

Serves 4
Hearty winter supper

1½ pounds lean stew beef,
   trimmed of fat and cut into
   1½-inch cubes
1 large onion, chopped
½ pound or more fresh
   mushrooms, sliced

1 (10¾-ounce) can condensed
   cream of mushroom soup
1 (10¾-ounce) can condensed
   golden cream of mushroom
   soup
1 cup hearty burgundy wine

In a large, covered casserole, mix beef, onion, mushrooms, soups and wine. Mix together and cover. Bake at 350° for about 1 hour or until beef appears done and mixture is bubbly. If mixture appears watery, add 1 tablespoon flour or cornstarch for thicker gravy. Serve hot over rice or noodles.

In 1841, the first course in normal school instruction was given at a university in Middletown.

Corned Beef Von Reuben

Serves 6 to 8
A different casserole for taking to a pot luck meal

6 ounces croutons
1 (12-ounce) can corned beef,
   sliced
1 (16-ounce) can sauerkraut,
   drained and squeezed

2 cups shredded Swiss cheese
3 eggs
2 cups milk

In a 12x8x2-inch baking dish layer croutons, corned beef, sauerkraut and cheese. Beat eggs; add milk and pour over top. Bake at 325° for 35 minutes.

One Dish Casserole

Serves 6
Good for a complete meal, may be prepared ahead

1 (8-ounce) package egg noodles
1 tablespoon butter or margarine
1 pound ground beef
½ cup chopped onion
1 (10¾-ounce) can condensed
  cream of mushroom soup
8 ounces plain yogurt
1 cup shredded Cheddar cheese,
  divided

1 (2½-ounce) jar sliced
  mushrooms, drained (optional)
½ teaspoon salt
⅛ teaspoon pepper
1 (10-ounce) package frozen
  whole green beans, thawed
1 tablespoon chopped pimiento
  (optional)

Cook noodles according to package directions, drain and toss noodles with butter. Put noodles into a well-greased 2-quart baking dish and set aside. Brown ground beef with onion in a large skillet; drain. Combine soup, yogurt, ½ cup cheese, mushrooms, salt and pepper. Stir into meat mixture. Spoon meat mixture down center of noodles. Arrange green beans around meat. Bake at 325° about 25 minutes until hot and bubbly. Remove from oven and sprinkle with remaining ½ cup cheese and pimiento. Return to oven just until cheese begins to melt, about 3 minutes. Serve hot!

Heavenly Hamburger

Serves 8
Casual company supper

1½ pounds lean ground beef
2 tablespoons butter or margarine
1 teaspoon salt
1 teaspoon sugar
Dash of garlic salt
2 (8-ounce) cans tomato sauce

1 (8-ounce) package egg noodles
1 cup sour cream
1 (3-ounce) package cream cheese
6 green onions, chopped
1 cup shredded sharp Cheddar
  cheese

Brown meat in butter; add salt, sugar and garlic salt. Mix in tomato sauce. Cook noodles and drain. Mix sour cream, cream cheese and onions. Layer noodles, meat mixture and cream cheese mixture in greased casserole; top with shredded cheese. Bake, covered, at 350° for 30 minutes. May add 1 (8-ounce) can water chestnuts if desired.

Dad's Dish

Serves 10 to 12
Great prepared ahead meal

1 small onion, chopped
1 small green pepper, chopped
Corn oil
12 small meatballs
6 Italian sausage
1 (9-ounce) can tomatoes
1 (4-ounce) can mushrooms,
    drained

16 ounces ziti
16 ounces Italian tomato sauce or
    your own Italian sauce
2 to 3 cups shredded mozzarella,
    Cheddar or grated Parmesan
    cheese

Saute onion and pepper in oil; remove from pan and brown meatballs and sausage. Pour off oil. Return onions, peppers and meat to pan and add tomatoes and mushrooms. Cook ziti. In a 14x11-inch pan pour ½ the sauce, add ziti, meat, onion and peppers and remaining sauce. Sprinkle with cheese. Bake at 350° for ½ hour. May be made ahead and baked when needed.

Cheese Pasta in a Pot

Serves 10 to 12
Good super bowl dish, winter party, large crowd

2 pounds ground beef chuck
2 medium onions, chopped
1 clove garlic, crushed
1 (28-ounce) jar spaghetti sauce
1 (8-ounce) can mushrooms
    (optional)

1 (16-ounce) package small shell
    macaroni
2 cups sour cream
8 ounces sliced provolone cheese
8 ounces sliced mozzarella cheese

Cook ground beef; drain excess fat. Add onions, garlic, spaghetti sauce and mushrooms; mix well. Simmer. Cook shells, drain and rinse with cold water. Pour half the shells into a large, deep casserole or 2 smaller casseroles. Spread with ½ the sauce. Spread ½ sour cream over sauce. Top with slices of provolone. Repeat layers ending with mozzarella. Bake covered at 350° for 35 to 40 minutes. Uncover and continue baking until mozzarella melts and browns slightly.

Eggplant and Meat Casserole

Serves 4
Great

1 pound ground beef	Salt and pepper to taste
½ cup butter or margarine, divided	½ cup breadcrumbs
	2 egg whites
3 onions, finely chopped	7 or 8 small eggplant
¼ cup water	White sauce
1 tablespoon tomato paste	1 cup shredded cheese
1 tablespoon chopped parsley	

Saute meat in 1 teaspoon butter for 5 minutes. Add onions, water, tomato paste, parsley, salt and pepper. Cook 25 minutes, stirring occasionally. Add crumbs and beaten egg whites; mix well. Slice eggplant lengthwise and brown in remaining butter. Place a layer of eggplant in a buttered pan, then a layer of meat until all ingredients are used ending with eggplant. Top with white sauce and sprinkle with cheese. Bake at 350° for ½ hour until brown.

White sauce:

3 cups milk	7 tablespoons all-purpose flour
6 tablespoons butter or margarine	Dash of salt and nutmeg

Bring milk to a boil; melt butter then stir in flour, salt and nutmeg. Slowly pour in milk and stir until smooth sauce is obtained. Pour over moussaka.

Corned Beef Casserole

Serves 6

1 (8-ounce) package medium
   egg noodles
1 (12-ounce) can corned beef,
   chilled
1 cup shredded Cheddar cheese

1 (10¾-ounce) can condensed
   cream of mushroom soup
1 cup milk
¼ cup finely chopped onion
¾ cup buttered breadcrumbs

Cook noodles according to package directions; drain. Cut chilled corned beef into small cubes. Combine with remaining ingredients, except breadcrumbs. Turn into 2-quart casserole; top with buttered breadcrumbs. Bake at 350° for 30 minutes.

Canadian Casserole

Serves 15 to 18
Excellent for pot luck suppers and family gatherings

3 slices bacon
1 onion, chopped
6 ribs celery, chopped
3 pounds ground beef
1 (10¾-ounce) can condensed
   cream of celery soup
1 (10¾-ounce) can condensed
   cream of mushroom soup

1 (10¾-ounce) can tomato soup
1 (10¾-ounce) can condensed
   cream of chicken soup
1 (1-pound) package egg noodles,
   cooked
Potato chips and slivered
   almonds for topping

Fry bacon until crisp and add onion and celery. Cook until soft, add meat and brown. Mix all ingredients together, except topping. Top with crushed potato chips and slivered almonds. Bake at 325° for 1½ hours.

Ham and Artichoke Casserole

Serves 6
Great for brunch or company luncheon

¼ cup butter or margarine
4 tablespoons all-purpose flour
2 cups warm milk
Dash of seasoned salt
Dash of cayenne pepper
¼ teaspoon nutmeg
Paprika
Pinch of pepper

⅓ cup shredded Swiss cheese
⅓ cup grated Parmesan cheese
4 tablespoons sherry
2 (1-pound) cans artichoke hearts, drained
12 thin slices ham
Topping

Melt butter; blend in flour until smooth. Remove from heat and stir in warm milk. When smooth, return to medium heat; stir until thick. Add seasonings and cheese. Stir over low heat until melted. Remove from heat; add sherry. Cut hearts in half if large. Wrap 2 halves in 1 slice ham. Arrange in buttered casserole with sides touching. Pour sauce over and sprinkle with topping. Bake at 350° for 25 minutes.

Topping:
⅔ cup buttered breadcrumbs
⅓ cup shredded Swiss cheese

⅓ cup grated Parmesan cheese

Combine all ingredients; sprinkle over casserole.

In 1840, the first American wooden Gothic house was built in Fairfield for Jonathan Sturgis by the architect J.C. Wells.

Lamb Chop Casserole

Serves 6
Nice, company dish—can be made ahead

1 pound small white onions
  (about 18)
12 loin lamb chops, ¾-inch thick
Onion salt
3 large baking apples

½ lemon
1 pound cooked or canned whole
  young carrots
1 (10-ounce) jar currant jelly

The day before or early in day, cook onions in boiling, salted water until almost tender. Sprinkle chops with onion salt and brown on both sides. Halve, core and rub surface of apples with lemon half. Around sides of a large shallow casserole, stand 10 chops; lay 2 more on bottom. Place carrots against chops, apples against carrots and onions in center. Melt some of jelly and spoon over casserole. Cover and refrigerate. When ready to serve, bake at 350° for 30 minutes or until apples are tender and glazed. Brush once or twice during baking with rest of jelly, melted.

Baked Veal Scallopini

Serves 4 to 6
Easy, do-ahead veal dish

¼ cup chopped onions
¼ cup vegetable oil (more as
  needed)
1½ pounds boned veal steak
  or veal stew meat, cut into
  bite-size pieces
¼ cup all purpose flour

½ teaspoon salt
⅛ teaspoon pepper
1 (4-ounce) can mushrooms,
  drained
1 cup tomato or vegetable juice
½ teaspoon sugar
1 cup dry white wine

Saute onions in heated oil. Remove to casserole. Roll veal in flour with salt and pepper; brown. Add to casserole. Brown mushrooms slightly; add to casserole. Combine juice, sugar and wine and pour over other ingredients in casserole. Bake, covered, at 350° for 45 minutes; uncover and bake 30 minutes longer.

Veal Casserole

Serves 8
May be made the day before serving

2 tablespoons butter or margarine
8 green peppers, cut into chunks
4 medium onions, cut into
  chunks
4 pounds veal, cut into 1-inch
  pieces

4 to 8 cloves garlic, chopped
12 ounces white wine, divided
2 to 3 cups water or soup stock
2 or 3 bouillon cubes

Melt butter in an electric skillet or heavy frying pan. Add green peppers and onions and stir until softened. Push to the side of pan and add veal; cook to seal in juice but do not brown, about 10 minutes. Mix green peppers and onions with veal in pan and add garlic. Pour 8 ounces wine into pan and stir. Cook about 5 minutes. Add 1 cup hot water with bouillon added. Stir and cook about 30 minutes over very low heat. If liquid is needed, add another ½ to 1 cup bouillon. Keep moist but not puddled. Cook a total of 1½ hours. Add remaining 4 ounces wine 5 minutes before removing from pan. Pour mixture into a buttered casserole dish and bake at 325° for about 30 minutes.

Extremely Easy Weeney Casserole

Serves 4 or more
Serve with a Waldorf salad and corn muffins for a cozy fall dinner

2 (16-ounce) cans baked beans
  in molasses sauce
1 (8-ounce) can regular (tomato
  based) baked beans
⅓ cup chopped onions
⅛ teaspoon dry mustard

1 tablespoon maple syrup
8 frankfurters
3 or 4 slices bacon, crumbled
Cheddar cheese cubes (optional)
½ cup grated Parmesan cheese

In an ungreased 11x7-inch casserole combine baked beans, onions, mustard and syrup. Cut frankfurters into 1-inch pieces and put in with beans. Stir to coat the pieces with the bean liquid. Stir in about 1 tablespoon crumbled bacon and some cheese chunks, if desired. Sprinkle evenly with Parmesan and more bacon. Bake at 350° about 10 minutes until bubbly.

Helen's Chicken

Serves 4
Even better the 2nd day

4 whole chicken breasts
Paprika
Salt and pepper to taste
½ cup butter or margarine, divided
1 (15-ounce) can artichoke hearts, drained

½ pound fresh mushrooms, sliced
Pinch of tarragon
3 tablespoons all-purpose flour
⅓ cup sherry
1½ cups chicken bouillon

Split breasts and cover with paprika, salt and pepper. Saute in half the butter until golden. Place in large casserole with artichokes. Put mushrooms and remaining butter in same skillet; season with tarragon and saute 5 minutes. Sprinkle flour in gently and add sherry and bouillon. Simmer for 5 minutes, stirring to prevent lumps. Pour over chicken. Cover casserole and bake at 375° for 45 minutes.

Chicken and Broccoli Casserole

Serves 4

2 (10¾-ounce) cans condensed cream of mushroom or cream of chicken soup
½ cup butter or margarine
½ cup mayonnaise
1 cup milk
1 teaspoon lemon juice

½ cup all-purpose flour
2 (10-ounce) packages frozen broccoli
4 chicken breasts, boned and cooked
Buttered breadcrumbs

In saucepan combine soup, butter, mayonnaise, milk, juice and flour; stir and heat. Cook broccoli according to package directions and drain. Place broccoli on bottom of a large casserole, top with chicken breasts and cover with sauce. Top with buttered breadcrumbs. Bake at 350° for 45 minutes until bubbly.

Chicken Macaroni Casserole

Serves 6 to 8

1 (10¾-ounce) can condensed cream of chicken soup, undiluted
1 cup mayonnaise
1 (4-ounce) can mushrooms, drained and chopped
⅓ cup chopped onions
⅓ cup chopped green pepper
½ cup chopped celery
2 cups cooked chicken, cubed
1¼ cups macaroni twists, cooked and drained
¾ cup shredded Cheddar cheese
Cracker or breadcrumbs

Mix together soup and mayonnaise; add chopped vegetables. Fold in chicken and macaroni. Pour into a casserole; top with cheese and sprinkle with crumbs. Bake at 350° for 30 minutes until heated through.

Wild Rice Chicken Casserole

Serves 8
May be made ahead, frozen, thawed and baked. Easy-tossed salad and hot bread–yum!

1 (6-ounce) package wild rice mix
1 (10¾-ounce) can condensed cream of chicken soup
4 cups cooked chicken, cubed
1 cup chopped celery
¼ cup chopped onions
1 (5-ounce) can water chestnuts, sliced
1 (4-ounce) can mushrooms, drained
3 tablespoons soy sauce
1 cup chicken broth
Topping

Cook rice according to package directions. Blend in soup and next 6 ingredients; mix gently. Add broth and mix. Spread in a 13x9x2-inch dish. Sprinkle with topping; bake at 350° for 1 hour.

Topping:
1½ cups seasoned stuffing mix
½ cup butter or margarine, melted

Toss together and sprinkle on top of casserole.

Grandma's Casserole

Serves 8
Easy company supper

1 cup chopped onion
1 green pepper, chopped
1 pound ground turkey
1 teaspoon salt
¼ teaspoon pepper
1 tablespoon sugar
1 tablespoon oregano

1 (28-ounce) can crushed tomatoes
1 (15-ounce) can tomato sauce
2 cups water
1 (8-ounce) package noodles,
    uncooked
1 cup shredded Cheddar cheese

Saute onion, green pepper and ground turkey in large skillet. Add seasonings. Stir in tomatoes, sauce and water. Bring to a boil. Reduce heat and simmer 15 minutes. Layer meat and tomato mixture with uncooked noodles in a 13x9x2-inch baking pan. Top with cheese. Cover and bake at 350° for 45 minutes.

Golden Cheddar Turkey Bake

Serves 6

3 cups cooked diced turkey or
    chicken
1½ cups sliced celery
1 cup cubed sharp Cheddar
    cheese
¾ cup mayonnaise

¼ cup toasted slivered almonds
¼ cup chopped onion
1 tablespoon lemon juice
1 teaspoon salt
½ cup corn flakes, crushed
2 tablespoons butter or margarine

Combine all ingredients except last two and mix lightly. Spoon mixture into buttered 10x6-inch baking dish. Toss together corn flake crumbs and butter and sprinkle over casserole. Bake at 325° for 40 minutes.

Creamy Turkey-Mushroom Casserole

Serves 6 to 8
Exceptional hot dish for any occasion, especially special ones

6 slices bacon
¾ cup chopped onion
½ cup chopped celery
1¼ cup chopped green pepper
1 (4-ounce) can mushrooms,
  drained and cut-up
1 (10¾-ounce) can condensed
  cream of celery soup
1 cup sour cream

3 cups cut-up cooked turkey
¼ teaspoon salt
⅛ teaspoon pepper
2 cups biscuit baking mix
½ cup milk
2 eggs
½ cup shredded Cheddar or
  American cheese

Fry bacon in 10-inch skillet until crisp; remove and crumble. Cook and stir vegetables in bacon fat until tender. Stir in soup, sour cream, turkey, salt, pepper and bacon. Heat until bubbly. Spread in casserole. Mix remaining ingredients just until moistened. Spread over turkey mixture. Bake, uncovered, at 350° for 30 to 35 minutes until golden brown. Enjoy!

Clam Casserole

Serves 4
Reheats well; half the recipe serves 1 or 2

2 eggs
2 (6½-ounce) cans minced clams
8 milk crackers, crushed

3 tablespoons butter or margarine
1¼ cups milk
Pepper

Beat eggs slightly; add clams and juice. Add cracker crumbs, butter and a little pepper. Turn into a 1-quart casserole. Set casserole in a shallow pan of water. Bake at 375° for 50 minutes or until brown.

Wild Crab Casserole

Serves 8 to 10
Easy company dinner

1 cup butter or margarine,
   divided
1½ cups chopped celery
1 cup chopped onion
1 cup chopped fresh mushrooms
1 teaspoon dried thyme, crushed
Salt and pepper to taste
1 cup wild rice, cooked or ½ cup
   wild rice and ½ cup brown
   rice, cooked

3 shallots, chopped
2 cloves garlic, minced
½ cup all-purpose flour
4 cups light cream
2 egg yolks, beaten
1 cup grated Parmesan cheese
1½ pounds crabmeat

In a large skillet heat ¼ cup butter and cook celery, onion, mushrooms, thyme, salt and pepper until tender. Stir together vegetable mixture and cooked rice. Place in a 13x9x2-inch baking dish; set aside. In a large saucepan cook shallots and garlic in remaining butter until tender. Stir in flour; add cream. Cook and stir until mixture is thickened and bubbly. Stir about 1 cup cream mixture into egg yolks; return to saucepan. Cook and stir until mixture comes to a boil. Remove from heat; stir in half the cheese. Place crabmeat on rice mixture. Pour sauce over crab. Sprinkle with remaining cheese. Bake at 425° for 13 to 15 minutes or until cheese is lightly browned and sauce bubbles.

In 1819, the first industrial or manual training school was established by Josiah Holbrook in Derby.

Crab Lasagna

Serves 6 to 8
Good dish to make 1 day ahead. I serve it with Caesar salad

1 large egg, beaten
2 (8-ounce) packages cream
  cheese
1 large onion, diced
1 (10¾-ounce) can condensed
  cream of mushroom soup
2 cups cottage cheese

¼ cup olive oil
1 clove garlic, crushed
1 pound crabmeat
1 (8-ounce) package lasagna
  noodles, cooked
1 pound grated fresh Parmesan
  cheese

Beat egg and cream cheese together. Add next 6 ingredients; mix well until creamy. It will appear lumpy. In a glass 11x9-inch casserole dish coated with non-stick vegetable spray, layer crab/cheese mixture, about ⅓ of the Parmesan cheese and about 3 noodles. Repeat layers twice ending with crab mixture and Parmesan. Bake at 350° for 1½ hours or until top is browned.

Casserole of Halibut with Almonds

Serves 4
Easy company supper

½ cup butter or margarine
3 tablespoons slivered almonds
2 teaspoons dry mustard
1 tablespoon tarragon vinegar

1 tablespoon water
3 tablespoons sliced green onions
4 small or 2 large halibut steaks

Heat butter in skillet; saute almonds until just beginning to color. Add mustard, vinegar, water and onions. Stir for a few minutes until onions just start to soften. Arrange fish in a shallow buttered casserole. Pour sauce over fish. Cover with foil and bake at 350° for 25 to 30 minutes until fish flakes.

Note: May use fillet of sole or cod but cooking time will be about 15 minutes.

Jane's Company Lobster

Serves 10 to 12
Make enough copies of this recipe for your guests–it will be asked for

1 pound macaroni, broken
   in 2½-inch pieces
1 small onion, minced
¼ cup butter or margarine
3 tablespoons all-purpose flour
½ teaspoon dry mustard
1½ teaspoons salt
⅛ teaspoon pepper
3 cups milk
4 cups shredded sharp American
   cheese, divided

½ cup sherry
6 cups cooked or canned lobster
   meat (rock lobster tails are nice)
¼ cup lemon juice, fresh, frozen
   or canned
1 teaspoon mace
1 cup crushed round buttery
   crackers

Cook macaroni according to package directions; drain and set aside. In double boiler combine onion, butter, flour, mustard, salt and pepper until smooth; stir in milk. Cook, stirring often, until smooth. Add 3 cups cheese; stir until melted. Add sherry. In a 13x9x2-inch baking dish or 3-quart large shallow casserole place macaroni. Arrange lobster meat on top; sprinkle with lemon juice and mace. Pour sauce over all. Sprinkle cracker crumbs around edge of dish. Sprinkle remaining 1 cup cheese over crackers. Bake at 400° for 35 minutes until mixture is hot and bubbly and crackers are browned. For foursome: Halve all ingredients. Bake in 12x8x2-inch greased baking dish for 20 minutes or until hot and bubbly.

In 1966, the first Ecumenical Easter Sunrise Service was held on April 10 at Constitution Plaza in Hartford.

Lobster Casserole

Serves 4 to 6
Melts in your mouth

2 cups lobster meat
½ cup plus ⅓ cup butter or
    margarine, divided
⅓ cup all-purpose flour
2 teaspoons salt
¼ teaspoon pepper

1½ teaspoons paprika
3½ cups milk
⅓ cup sherry
1 (8-ounce) package elbow
    macaroni or shell macaroni
½ cup grated Parmesan cheese

Cut lobster meat into small pieces; saute in ¼ cup butter. Melt ⅓ cup butter in large saucepan. Blend in flour, salt, pepper and paprika. Add milk gradually, stirring constantly; cook until thickened. Add lobster and sherry. Cook macaroni in boiling salted water until tender. Drain. Add macaroni to lobster mixture. Turn into lightly greased 2-quart casserole. Sprinkle top with Parmesan. Pour remaining ¼ cup melted butter over top of casserole. Bake at 350° for 20 to 30 minutes until sauce is bubbly and cheese is melted and delicately browned.

Shrimp Curry for a Crowd

Serves 10 to 12

½ cup butter or margarine
1½ cups chopped onion
1½ cups chopped celery
2 pounds cleaned raw shrimp
    (about 3 pounds in shell)
1 (1-pound) can applesauce

4 (10¾-ounce) cans condensed
    cream of celery soup
1 (6-ounce) can broiled sliced
    mushrooms, undrained
2 tablespoons curry powder
¼ teaspoon salt

Melt butter in a 12-inch skillet; add onion and celery. Cook until almost tender. Add remaining ingredients; stir. Simmer, uncovered, stirring frequently, about 15 minutes.

Seafood Casserole

Yields 3 quarts

1 pound scallops	Salt and pepper to taste
Water	1½ pounds cleaned, cooked
1½ cups butter or margarine	shrimp
1½ cups all-purpose flour	½ pound lobster meat, cooked
Milk	½ pound crabmeat, cooked
½ cup sherry	Buttered bread cubes

Put scallops in pan with water just to cover; cook only until they turn white; remove scallops from pan and set aside. Use about ½ the liquid to start cream sauce. Melt butter with liquid and stir in flour until bubbly. Gradually add milk, stirring constantly, until desired thin consistency is reached. Stir in sherry, salt and pepper. Add all seafood, pour into 3-quart casserole and top with bread cubes.

In 1784, the first law school in America, the Litchfield Law School, was founded by Judge Tapping Reeve in Litchfield.

Asparagus Casserole

Serves 6 to 8

3 (14½-ounce) cans cut up green asparagus, drained and liquid reserved	⅛ teaspoon pepper
	2 eggs, beaten
	2 cups breadcrumbs, divided
¼ cup water	1 cup milk
¼ teaspoon salt	1 cup diced American cheese

Mix asparagus and reserved liquid and water. Add salt, pepper, eggs, half the breadcrumbs and milk. Fold in cheese; top with remaining breadcrumbs. Bake at 350° about 40 minutes until custard is set and firm and very hot.

Ethnic Cooking

Huevos Rancheros

Serves 3

2 tablespoons minced onion
2 tablespoons bacon fat
1 (4-ounce) can green chilies, chopped
1 (1-pound) can peeled tomatoes

¼ pound Cheddar cheese, cubed
6 eggs
¼ teaspoon salt

In 10-inch skillet saute onion in fat until golden. Add chilies and tomatoes and simmer until almost dry. Add cheese cubes and stir. When almost melted, drop in whole eggs, 1 at a time and cook until eggs are desired consistency.

Avgolemono Soupa (Egg and Lemon)

Serves 6
A Greek favorite

6 cups chicken stock
⅓ cup short grain rice
Salt to taste

3 eggs, separated
Juice of 1 large lemon
White pepper

Bring stock to a boil; add rice and salt to taste. Stir until stock returns to a slow boil, cover and simmer for 20 minutes. In a bowl beat egg whites until stiff. Add yolks and beat until creamy. Slowly blend in lemon juice. Whisking constantly, add ¼ of boiling soup to egg mixture. Remove soup from heat, gradually add egg mixture, stirring vigorously. Salt and pepper to taste and serve immediately.

Note: Reheating soup is not recommended. Stock may be prepared ahead.

Linguine Genovese

Serves 4

½ cup olive oil
1 cup plus 2 tablespoons butter or margarine, divided
1½ pounds onions, chopped
3 carrots, chopped
2 or 3 ribs celery, chopped
2 tablespoons chopped parsley
Salt and pepper to taste

2 pounds veal shank, cut into pieces
1 cup white wine
2 Italian plum tomatoes
1 pound linguine
2 tablespoons grated Parmesan cheese

Very slowly heat olive oil and 1 cup butter. Add vegetables, parsley, salt, pepper and veal. Cover and stew gently for 45 minutes. Add wine and after 15 minutes mash tomatoes into sauce. Cook another ½ hour or until veal is tender (total cooking time 1½ hours). Boil linguine until just done and drain. Return to pot; add about 2 tablespoons of sauce, 2 tablespoons butter and Parmesan. Mix well and heat briefly. Serve and cover with remainder of sauce.

Applesauce Matzoh Kugel

Serves 12
Unusual and may be used all throughout the year–recipe for all seasons

6 regular size matzohs (plain)
Water
6 eggs
½ teaspoon salt
¾ cup sugar

2½ teaspoons vanilla extract
1 cup butter or margarine, melted
1 (35-ounce) jar applesauce
1 cup golden raisins

Soak matzohs in cold water; set aside. Beat eggs; add salt, sugar and continue to beat until creamy. Add vanilla while beating. Blend in melted butter. Stir in applesauce and raisins. Squeeze water from matzohs and fold into mixture. Pour into greased large lasagna pan and bake at 375° for 1 hour. Watch during last 15 minutes.

Note: Recipe may be halved and baked in an 11x7-inch pan. Also, if unsweetened applesauce is used, increase sugar to 1 cup for full recipe.

Pierogi

Serves 4 to 6
A favorite dish of Poland

Dough:

2 cups all-purpose flour	½ teaspoon salt
1 large egg	⅓ to ½ cup water

Mix flour, egg and salt. Stir in water until a stiff dough forms. Divide dough in half; roll paper-thin. Cut circles in dough with biscuit cutter. Place a teaspoon of filling on half the circle. Moisten, fold over and seal edges. Drop into boiling, salted water; cook for 3 to 5 minutes. Using a slotted spoon lift out of water. Serve with sour cream and/or sauteed onions. Pierogis freeze well after they are cooked. Freeze in single layer; re-boil when ready to serve.

Filling:

1 cup mashed potatoes	½ teaspoon salt
½ cup shredded Cheddar cheese	¼ teaspoon pepper
1 egg, beaten	

Combine all ingredients.

Breakfast Burritos

Serves 6
Delicious for a company brunch

6 (10-inch) flour tortillas	2 cups chopped tomatoes
18 eggs, scrambled	2 cups shredded Cheddar cheese
12 slices crisply cooked bacon	1 cup picante sauce

Heat tortillas in frying pan or microwave until soft. At serving time, spoon eggs onto tortillas and top each with 2 slices bacon. Guests may choose their own additional toppings and spoon them on; roll up tortillas.

Hungarian Goulash

Serves 4
Wonderful on a winter day

1 pound beef, cut into cubes
2 medium onions, minced
¼ teaspoon dry mustard
1¼ teaspoons paprika
2 tablespoons firmly packed
  brown sugar
1¼ teaspoons salt
3 tablespoons Worcestershire
  sauce

¾ teaspoon cider vinegar
6 tablespoons catsup
Dash of cinnamon (optional)
1½ cups water, divided
3 tablespoons all-purpose flour
1 (8-ounce) package egg noodles

Brown meat in Dutch oven; add onions, mustard, paprika, brown sugar and salt. Combine Worcestershire, vinegar, and catsup and add to meat. Add 1 cup water, stir, cover and cook over low heat 2½ hours or until meat is tender. Blend flour with remaining ½ cup water and add to meat mixture. Stir until thickened. Cook noodles according to package directions. Serve meat mixture over hot noodles.

Hungarian Short Ribs

Serves 6 to 8

4 pounds beef short ribs
2 tablespoons vegetable oil
2 medium onions, sliced
1 (15-ounce) can tomato sauce
2 cups water, divided
¼ cup firmly packed brown sugar

¼ cup vinegar
1 teaspoon salt
1 teaspoon dry mustard
1 teaspoon Worcestershire sauce
4½ cups cooked medium noodles

In Dutch oven brown meat in hot oil; add onions. Blend tomato sauce, 1 cup water, sugar, vinegar, salt, mustard and Worcestershire; pour over meat. Cover and simmer for 2 to 2½ hours or until meat is tender. Skim off fat. Stir in noodles and remaining 1 cup water. Cover and cook, stirring occasionally, for 15 to 20 minutes.

Stuffed Beef Rolls (Farsu Margru)

Serves 10

Farsu Margru means "false lean" in Italian. Simply delicious with pasta!

1 pound top round steak, cut 1-inch thick (about 1½ pounds)
½ pound ground beef or veal
1 egg
1 cup fresh breadcrumbs
2 tablespoons chopped parsley
1 tablespoon grated onion
1¼ teaspoon salt, divided
1 (4-ounce) package sliced salami
1 (8-ounce) package mozzarella cheese, cut into ¼-inch strips
2 hard cooked eggs, cut lengthwise into 4 wedges
½ cup frozen peas
2 tablespoons vegetable oil
2 medium carrots, sliced
1 medium onion, sliced
1 (16-ounce) can tomatoes
½ cup dry wine
½ teaspoon basil

Two hours before cooking, butterfly steak. Holding knife parallel to work surface and starting from the long side of the steak, cut steak horizontally almost but not all the way through; spread steak open to form 1 large piece. With meat mallet or dull edge of French knife, pound steak to about ¼-inch thickness. In a medium bowl, mix ground beef, egg, bread-crumbs, parsley, grated onion and ½ teaspoon salt. Spread ground meat mixture over steak. Place salami slices along center in a lengthwise row over the ground beef mixture, overlapping slices, if necessary. Place cheese strips along 1 side of salami; place egg wedges along other side of salami. Sprinkle peas over entire steak. Starting at long side, roll steak jelly roll fashion. With string, tie crosswise in several places. Place oil in an 8-quart Dutch oven; heat until sizzling. Add beef roll and brown on all sides. Reduce heat to medium; add carrots and onions. Cook until vegetables are lightly browned and tender, stirring occasionally. Stir in tomatoes with their liquid, wine, basil and ¾ teaspoon salt. Stir to break up tomatoes and heat over high heat until boiling. To serve, arrange beef roll in deep platter; discard strings and spoon sauce onto roll.

In 1859, William Delius of Waterbury made the first ferro-types or tintypes in this country.

Spudini

Serves 6
A wonderful and unusual Italian main course

1 medium onion, diced
Butter or margarine
6 very thin (the thinner the better)
   sirloin breakfast steaks
Olive oil

Italian breadcrumbs
1 large very ripe tomato, diced
1 pound shredded Cheddar
   cheese

Brown onion in butter; set aside. Dip steaks in olive oil and coat with breadcrumbs. Fill with onions, tomatoes and cheese. Roll up and broil 2 to 3 minutes on each side until browned.

In 1847, the first Christian Mission was founded in Foochow, China, by Stephen Johnson of Griswold, Connecticut.

Bubble and Squeak Hash (Irish)

Serves 4
As the hash fries in skillet, it bubbles and squeaks–hence its unique name

3 tablespoons butter or margarine
1 small onion, diced
2 cups shredded cooked cabbage

2 cups mashed potatoes
2 cups diced cooked roast beef

Melt butter over low heat; add onion and saute until tender. Combine cabbage, potatoes and beef. Add to skillet pressing with fork to form large cake. Cook over moderate heat until well browned. Loosen cake with spatula; slide onto plate. Flip back into skillet, uncooked side down. Cook until well browned. Cut into wedges to serve. Irish people make this as a Monday night supper with rye bread.

Stifatho (Braised Beef and Onions)

Serves 6
Winter favorite

2 pounds stew beef, cut into
  2-inch cubes
3 tablespoons butter or margarine
  or vegetable oil
1 medium onion, finely chopped
2 cloves garlic, crushed
1 cup tomato puree
½ cup red wine

2 tablespoons wine vinegar
1 bay leaf
1 (3-inch) cinnamon stick
4 whole cloves
1 teaspoon sugar
Salt and pepper to taste
1½ pounds small onions

In large stock pot brown beef on all sides in oil; set aside. Add onion and garlic to pan, adding more butter if necessary. Fry until onion is soft. Add tomato puree, wine and vinegar; stir to lift pan juices. Return meat to pot. Add bay leaf, spices, sugar and season to taste with salt and pepper. Cover and cook over low heat for 1 hour. Meanwhile, remove the tops and roots from small onions and cross cut ends. Cover with boiling water for about 2 minutes and drain. Slip off skins and add onions to meat. Continue to cook, covered, for 1 to 1½ hours until meat and onions are tender and sauce has thickened. Serve stifatho over rice or buttered noodles.

Korean Meatballs

Serves 4 to 6

1 egg
2 tablespoons milk
1 teaspoon sugar
2 tablespoons soy sauce
½ teaspoon salt
¼ teaspoon MSG

¼ teaspoon hot pepper sauce
½ cup breadcrumbs
1 clove garlic, pureed
¼ cup chopped onions
1 pound ground beef

Combine all ingredients and mix well. Shape into small meatballs and broil for 1 minute. Turn and broil until done to your liking. Serve warm in Grab Bag Dip. Freeze well if you want to make ahead.

Pork Chops in Wine

Serves 4
A specialty of Modena, Italy, and simply delicious

3 tablespoons olive or vegetable
   oil
½ pound small fresh mushrooms
1 medium onion, sliced
1 clove garlic, crushed
4 pork loin blade, rib, or sirloin
   chops, ¾-inch thick

¾ cup cooking or dry white wine
¾ cup water
½ teaspoon salt
½ teaspoon basil
⅛ teaspoon pepper
2 medium tomatoes, chopped
1 tablespoon chopped parsley

About 1½ hours before serving in a 12-inch skillet over medium heat in hot oil, cook mushrooms, onions and garlic until tender, stirring occasionally. With slotted spoon remove mushroom mixture to small bowl. In drippings remaining in skillet (add oil if necessary) over medium heat, cook pork chops until browned on both sides. Add wine, water, seasonings; bring to a boil, stirring to loosen brown bits from bottom of skillet. Reduce heat to low; cover and simmer 45 minutes. Return mushroom mixture to skillet and add tomatoes. Cover and cook until vegetables and meat are fork tender, about 15 minutes. Skim off fat from liquid in skillet; sprinkle with parsley and serve.

Hoppelpoppel (German for Hodgepodge)

Serves 2 to 4
Can be eaten any time of day. In Germany it is regarded as a snack

5 tablespoons butter or margarine
1 large onion, chopped
3½ cups cooked diced potatoes
1 cup diced cooked pork or
   beef roast

4 eggs, beaten
1 tablespoon chopped parsley
Salt and pepper to taste

Melt butter in a large skillet over low heat. Add onions and saute for about 1 minute, stirring constantly. Add potatoes and saute for about 3 minutes. Add pork and stir for 2 minutes. Add eggs, parsley, salt and pepper, stirring constantly. Continue cooking until eggs are set.

Norwegian Brown Hash

Serves 6
For brunch or lunch, can't be beat

4 cups diced cooked pork
4 cups diced cooked potatoes
½ cup butter or margarine

1½ cups chopped onions
1 cup beef broth or bouillon
Salt and pepper to taste

Brown pork and potatoes in melted butter in large skillet, stirring occasionally. Add onion; mix lightly. Stir in beef broth. Salt and pepper to taste. Cover and bring to a boil; reduce heat and simmer 45 minutes, stirring occasionally, until all the broth is absorbed.

In 1835, the first music school in this country was founded at Salem, Ct. under the name of "Music Vale Seminary."

Cantonese Spareribs

Serves 4
Great on a cold night with rice pilaf and red wine

4 pounds country-style pork ribs,
    cut in half
¾ cup soy sauce
¾ cup catsup
3 tablespoons firmly packed
    brown sugar

2 teaspoons ground ginger or
    gingerroot
2 teaspoons garlic powder
2 ounces cream sherry or bourbon
1 teaspoon salt

Mix ingredients together in large bowl and marinate in sauce overnight or for 10 to 12 hours. Place ribs on rack in roasting pan and bake at 325° for 1 hour. Baste frequently with sauce while baking. Leftover sauce may be heated and served over meat.

Spanish Chicken

Serves 4 to 6

2 pounds boneless chicken
  breasts
Salt and pepper to taste
All-purpose flour
⅓ cup olive oil
1 red onion, chopped

1 cup chicken broth
1 cup orange juice
¾ cup firmly packed brown sugar
½ cup golden raisins
Dash of cinnamon and cloves
Toasted almonds (optional)

Sprinkle chicken pieces with salt and pepper; roll in flour. Heat olive oil in skillet. Add chicken, a few pieces at a time, and brown on all sides. Place browned chicken in a shallow baking pan. Add onions to pan drippings; saute for 5 minutes. Add broth, juice, brown sugar, raisins and spices. Bring to a boil; pour over chicken. Bake, uncovered, at 350° for 45 minutes or until tender. Place chicken on a serving platter. Pour sauce over chicken; sprinkle with almonds if desired. Serve with rice.

Clams in Sherry Wine (Almejas Al Faro)

Serves 3 to 4
Excellent clam appetizer

2 tablespoons olive oil
¼ pound onion, finely chopped
½ cup (about 2 ounces) cubed
  cured ham, cut ⅛-inch thick

2 tablespoons semi-sweet
  (oloroso) Spanish sherry
1 dozen very small clams

Heat oil in a skillet; saute onion for 1 minute, cover and cook very slowly until onion is tender but not colored, about 15 minutes. Stir in ham, then add sherry and clams. Turn the heat to medium, cover and cook, removing clams as they open. Return clams to sauce making sure the clam meat is covered by the sauce.

Chicken Stemperato

Serves 8 to 10
Great picnic dish! Make a day ahead

2 (3¼ to 4-pound) chickens, cut
   into pieces (cut large breasts
   in half)
1 pound green Italian olives
½ cup capers, well-rinsed
1 cup chopped celery, ½ to 1-inch
   pieces

½ cup red wine vinegar
Mint leaves (from 4 or 5 stalks–
   optional)
Garlic powder
Salt
Pepper
1 tablespoon olive oil

Wash and trim all fat and excess skin from chicken, pat dry and set aside. Remove pits from olives by hitting the olives with a kitchen mallet or saucepan to smash the olive, then remove pit. Place olive pieces, capers and celery in a baking pan. Pour half the vinegar over them and sprinkle with most of the mint leaves. Place chicken in single layer in pan; sprinkle with garlic powder, salt and pepper. Pour remainder of vinegar over them and sprinkle with rest of mint leaves. Sprinkle with olive oil (use more if chicken is skinned). You may need 2 pans. Bake at 375° about 20 to 30 minutes until meat sizzles and turns golden. Lower temperature to 325°, turn chicken over and cook about 30 to 45 minutes longer until chicken is cooked thoroughly. Ideally eaten cool or at room temperature. The vinegary taste goes away as the meat cools. Serve with Italian bread and Mangia! Use lots of napkins.

Carol's Italian-Style Eggs

Serves 3 to 6
Good on a cold Lenten day with a tossed salad

2 tablespoons butter or margarine
1 tablespoon Worcestershire sauce
3 to 5 tablespoons catsup
1 tablespoon prepared mustard

1 teaspoon paprika
1 teaspoon salt
6 eggs

Mix well all ingredients except eggs in a heavy skillet. Bring to a boil. Break and drop in eggs; cook slowly until set. Serve on buttered toast, spooning sauce over eggs.

Bill's Fried Rice with Shrimp (Har Chow Fon)

Serves 6

1½ cups raw rice
2½ cups water
¼ cup peanut oil
3 eggs
1 teaspoon salt
½ teaspoon pepper
1 pound shrimp, shelled, cleaned
    and coarsely chopped

3 onions, chopped
¼ pound fresh mushrooms,
    sliced
3 tablespoons soy sauce
1 teaspoon sugar

Cook rice in water according to package directions. Heat oil in large skillet or wok. Break eggs into pan and mix. Fry until firm, then turn over and fry 1 minute. Remove pan from heat and cut eggs into very fine shreds while still in pan. Return pan to heat and add salt, pepper, shrimp, onions and mushrooms. Cook over low heat for 5 minutes, stirring frequently. Add rice, soy sauce and sugar. Cook over medium heat for 5 minutes, stirring almost constantly.

Tomato Raita

Serves many
Compliments Indian fare

1 tablespoon vegetable oil
1 teaspoon mustard seeds
¼ teaspoon cumin
¼ teaspoon coriander
½ teaspoon crushed red pepper

2 cups plain yogurt
2 ripe tomatoes, chopped
2 tablespoons chopped jalapeno
    or canned hot red peppers

Heat oil in a small skillet; add mustard seeds, cumin, coriander and crushed red pepper. Heat until seeds begin to jump and snap. Pour into yogurt; add tomatoes and hot peppers stirring until mixed. Refrigerate. Serve this spicy dip with quartered pita bread and chutney with other Indian dishes.

Baklava

Serves 30

3 to 4 cups finely chopped nuts
½ cup sugar
¼ teaspoon ground cloves
2 teaspoons cinnamon

20 sheets phyllo pastry
2 cups sweet butter or margarine,
    melted
Syrup

Mix nuts, sugar and spice together in a bowl. Place 1 pastry sheet in a well-buttered 13x9x2-inch baking pan and brush with butter. Repeat for 5 sheets. Sprinkle evenly with nuts; brush top with butter. With a sharp knife, cut diagonal line the length of pan to make diamond shaped pieces. Bake at 350° for 1 hour or until golden brown. Remove from oven and pour the hot syrup over the hot baklava.

Syrup:
1 cup honey
2 cups water
2 cups sugar
1 cinnamon stick or ½ teaspoon
    cinnamon

1 teaspoon grated lemon or
    orange rind

In a saucepan combine all ingredients; bring to a boil and simmer for 15 minutes.

Mazurka

Yields 200 cookies
Christmas favorite

2 egg yolks
1 cup sugar
1 teaspoon vanilla extract
1 egg white
½ cup all-purpose flour

1 cup chopped figs
1 cup chopped apricots
1 cup chopped almonds
1 cup chopped pecans (or other
    nuts)

Mix together egg yolks and sugar until frothy. Add vanilla and egg white; mix well. Mix in flour then all remaining ingredients. Spread in 2 greased and floured 11x9-inch cookie pans. Bake at 350° for 20 minutes. Cut into 1-inch squares while still warm.

Greek Pear Cookies

Yields 50 cookies

1 cup vegetable oil	Juice and grated rind of 1 orange
1 cup sugar	4 cups all-purpose flour
2 eggs	Whole cloves
2½ teaspoons baking powder	

Beat oil and sugar until thick and cream-like. Add eggs. Mix baking powder with orange juice and add to sugar and egg mixture. Add 2 cups flour, orange rind then remaining flour; mix well. When shaping the dough, take a piece the size of a walnut and shape like a pear; stick clove on end. Bake at 350° for 20 to 25 minutes.

Syrup:

2 cups water	¼ cup confectioners' sugar
1 cup sugar	1 tablespoon cinnamon

In large frying pan bring water and sugar to a boil. Reduce heat to low; dip cookies in mixture and turn over. Remove and place in pan with space between; allow to sit for a few minutes. Put confectioners' sugar and cinnamon in strainer and sprinkle over cookies.

Pastry Custard (Frangi Pane) France

Serves 3 to 4
May be used as dessert or to fill creme puffs

⅓ cup sugar	3 eggs
¼ cup all-purpose flour	1 teaspoon vanilla extract
2 cups milk, scalded	

Combine sugar, flour and eggs in top of a double boiler or heavy saucepan; add hot milk gradually, stirring often. Cook until custard begins to thicken; remove from heat and add vanilla.

Note: For variation add 1 ounce chocolate to milk, heat and beat well. Fold in ½ cup whipped cream into chilled custard.

Zavonicky Cookies

Yields 6 to 8 dozen
Grammie's "olde country" cookies

4 cups cake flour
½ teaspoon soda
½ teaspoon ginger

2 whole eggs plus 6 egg yolks
1 (16-ounce) package
   confectioners' sugar

Sift flour, soda and ginger together. Beat all eggs until lemon in color; add sugar. Add dry ingredients to eggs; knead 35 minutes or in food processor with mixing blade until machine begins to labor. Put on floured board and roll out ⅓-inch thick. Cut into 1x3-inch strips. Let sit overnight on board. Place on greased cookie sheets, upside down and 1 inch apart. Bake at 325° for 15 to 20 minutes.

Kringler

Serves 16

2 cups all-purpose flour, divided
1 cup butter or margarine,
   divided
1 cup plus 1 tablespoon water,
   divided

3 eggs, beaten
½ teaspoon almond extract

Combine 1 cup flour, ½ cup butter and 1 tablespoon water as for pastry and divide in half. Pat each half on a cookie sheet in a long strip 3 inches wide. Put 1 cup water in saucepan with ½ cup butter; bring to a boil. Remove from heat and add 1 cup flour. Stir until smooth. Stir in eggs, a little at a time and beat after each addition. Add extract; spread over first mixture. Bake at 375° for 40 minutes. Do not underbake. Frost when done.

Frosting:
1 cup sifted confectioners' sugar
1 tablespoon butter or margarine

About 1 tablespoon light cream
½ teaspoon almond extract

Combine and mix well.

The Inn Thing

Bull's Bridge "Cold-Beater"

Serves 6 to 8
Great on a cold day!

Batter:

2 eggs, separated
1 cup confectioners' sugar

¼ teaspoon vanilla

Beat egg whites with ½ cup sugar until stiff peaks form; set aside. In a separate bowl, beat egg yolks and remaining sugar until mixture is thick and lemon colored. Add vanilla to yolk mixture. Fold egg yolks into whites with spatula.

¾ ounce rum
¾ ounce brandy
1 heaping teaspoon Batter

Boiling water
Nutmeg

Place first 3 ingredients in heat-proof mug. Fill with boiling water; stir to keep frothy. Top with nutmeg.

Bull's Bridge Inn
Rt 7
Kent, CT

Chicken Curry Salad

Serves 4 to 6

1 whole chicken, cooked,
  deboned and cut into
  bite-sized pieces
½ cup plain yogurt
¼ cup mayonnaise

¼ cup diced green pepper
¼ cup diced green onion
¼ cup diced celery
1 tablespoon curry powder
Salt and pepper to taste

Combine ingredients in order listed; mix until well blended. Chill before serving.

Norwich Inn
Norwich, CT

Curry House Dressing

Serves 8

1 cup 75/25 blended oil
   (soy/olive)
4 whole eggs
1 tablespoon paprika
2 tablespoons curry powder

1 tablespoon dried mustard
Scant teaspoon salt
Full ½ tablespoon black pepper
1 tablespoon onion finely diced

Measure oil and eggs in blender container. Blend on high until mixture is emulsified. Add remaining ingredients; blend until well mixed. Place in jar with lid and chill before using.

Cobbs Mill Inn
Weston, CT

Raspberry Vinaigrette Salad Dressing

Yields about 1 quart dressing

1 egg
⅔ cup raspberry vinegar
1 tablespoon whole grain mustard
1 quart olive oil
2 tablespoons plus
   2 teaspoons sherry

⅔ cup heavy cream
1 tablespoon thyme
1 tablespoon tarragon
1 tablespoon basil
Salt and pepper to taste

Combine 1 egg, ⅓ cup raspberry vinegar and 1 tablespoon whole grain mustard in mixing bowl; whisk until evenly distributed. Slowly, whip in olive oil. Add ⅓ cup raspberry vinegar; blend thoroughly. Add sherry; blend thoroughly. Add cream; blending thoroughly. Add remaining seasonings. Mix until thoroughly incorporated. Store in large container with tight fitting lid. Shake or whisk well to incorporate ingredients before serving.

Note: To make House Dressing: Mix same as above but substitute red wine vinegar for the raspberry vinegar. Add more mustard to taste and dill can also be substituted for other herbs, if desired.

Old Lyme Inn
85 Lyme St
Old Lyme, CT

Butterscotch Biscuits

Yields 12 biscuits
Very good on a cold winter day!

½ cup melted butter or margarine
1¼ cups brown sugar, firmly
  packed
2½ cups sifted all-purpose flour
3¾ teaspoons baking powder

1 teaspoon salt
¼ cup sugar
5 tablespoons shortening
½ cup milk
1 egg, beaten

Combine butter and brown sugar in small saucepan. Cook over low heat, stirring constantly, until sugar and butter are melted; set aside to cool. Sift flour, baking powder, salt and sugar into mixing bowl. Add shortening; cut into mixture with pastry blender until mixture resembles coarse cornmeal. Combine milk and egg; mix. Add to flour mixture, a little at a time; mix after each addition. If dough is still too dry, add a little more milk. Roll dough into a 13x10x¼-inch rectangle. Spread with melted butter and brown sugar mixture. Sprinkle with cinnamon if desired. Roll up like a jelly roll, starting on the long side of the rectangle. Cut roll into ¾-inch slices. Place slices, cut side down, in buttered muffin tins. Bake at 425° for 15 to 20 minutes. Serve hot or cold.

Note: These freeze well. It is a good idea to put a pan below the muffin pan when baking as these will sometimes run over a little while baking.

Old Babcock Tavern
Tolland, CT

In 1817, the first hospital established as an eye infirmary was set up by Elisha North in New London.

Pumpkin Nut Bread

Yields 2 loaves
My mom's bread delights our guests

3 cups sugar
1 cup vegetable oil
4 eggs
1 (16-ounce) can pumpkin
⅓ cup water
3½ cups all-purpose flour
½ teaspoon baking powder

2 teaspoons baking soda
2 teaspoons salt
1 teaspoon cinnamon
1 teaspoon cloves
1 teaspoon allspice
1 cup raisins
½ cup chopped walnuts

Combine sugar, oil, eggs, pumpkin and water in a large mixing bowl; mix until well blended. Combine flour, baking powder, soda, salt spices, raisins and nuts in a separate bowl; mix well. Stir in pumpkin mixture and mix until well blended. Pour batter into 2 greased 9x5x3-inch loaf pans. Bake at 325° for 1 hour or until bread tests done.

Jared Cone House
Bolton, CT

Mainstay French Toast

Serves 6 to 8
Great for Sunday Brunch

1 cup brown sugar, firmly packed
½ cup butter
2 tablespoons light corn syrup
2 tart apples, peeled and sliced

5 eggs
1½ cups milk
1 teaspoon vanilla
1 loaf French bread

Combine sugar, butter and corn syrup in saucepan. Cook over medium heat until mixture becomes "syrupy". Pour mixture into a 13x9x2-inch baking dish. Spread apple slices over this. Slice bread into ¾-inch slices and place on top of apple slices. Whisk remaining ingredients together and pour over bread slices. Cover and refrigerate overnight. Bake, uncovered, at 350 for 40 minutes. Serve with spicy apple syrup.

Mainstay Inn
Cape May, NJ

Pumpkin Soup

Serves 4 to 6

2 tablespoons olive oil
1 tablespoon butter or margarine
3 large cloves garlic, minced
1 cup chopped onion
¼ cup fresh parsley
¼ teaspoon freshly chopped thyme
2 pounds smooth textured pumpkin, cut into 1-inch cubes

4 cups chicken stock (homemade if possible)
2 shakes angostura bitters
Salt and pepper to taste
½ cup heavy cream
Homemade croutons

Combine olive oil and butter in a large saucepan; heat over medium-high heat. Add garlic and onion; saute for 3 to 5 minutes or until soft. Add parsley, thyme, pumpkin and 2 cups chicken stock. Bring mixture to a boil, reduce heat and simmer until pumpkin is softened. Add angostura, mix and allow to cool enough to puree in blender or put through food mill. Return puree to pan. Add remaining chicken broth and salt and pepper to taste. Heat through; stir in cream just before serving. Garnish with chopped fresh parsley and homemade croutons.

Bull's Bridge Inn
Rt 7
Kent, CT

In 1831, William Redfield of Cromwell first discovered the laws of cyclonic storms.

Granola Cereal: Old Lyme Inn Style

Serves 24 to 30

12 cups quick cooking oats
4 cups wheat germ
2 cups coconut
4 cups chopped nuts

4 cups raisins
2 cups vegetable oil
2 cups honey
8 teaspoons vanilla

Measure dry ingredients into a large container; mix well. Combine oil, honey and vanilla; mix until well blended. Pour liquid mixture over dry ingredients and mix until dry ingredients are coated with liquids. Pour onto flat baking sheets. Bake at 275° for 1 hour, stirring mixture at 15 minute intervals. Cool and store in air-tight containers.

Old Lyme Inn
85 Lyme St
Old Lyme, CT

Chicken Breast Williamsburg

Serves 8

8 double center cut boneless
   chicken breasts
4 Granny Smith apples, skinned,
   cored, ½-inch cubes
6 tablespoons coarsely chopped
   walnuts

4 tablespoons maple syrup
2 tablespoons honey
½ cup dark raisins
1 teaspoon cinnamon

Flatten breasts to ½-inch thickness. Combine remaining ingredients and heat, slowly, to boiling in a heavy saucepan. Stuff each breast by rolling around an equal mound of stuffing. Bake at 375° for 45 minutes to 1 hour or until browned. Serve with Brown Raisin Sauce.

Note: Brown Raisin Sauce can be made by reducing chicken stock married with raisins and a brown demi-glaze.

Cobbs Mill Inn
Weston, CT

Cornish Hens with Basil and Walnut Pesto Sauce

Serves 4
This has been requested many times by our guests!

2 cornish hens
½ cup chicken stock
2 tablespoons Basil and Walnut
  Pesto

¼ cup heavy cream
Whole walnuts and basil leaves,
  if desired as garnish

Split and quarter cornish hens. Saute in ¼ cup butter until cooked; cook legs additional time as needed. Remove to serving platter. Drain grease from saute pan, add chicken stock and continue to cook until stock is reduced by half. Add cream and continue to cook until mixture is reduced in half or until desired "sauce" consistency is attained. Swirl in pesto. Adjust seasonings to taste. Pour over hens on platter and serve. Garnish with basil leaves and walnut pieces, if desired.

Basil and Walnut Pesto:
1 bunch fresh basil
  (approximately 1 ounce,
  cleaned)
½ cup grated Parmesan cheese

1 clove garlic
Salt and black pepper to taste
¼ cup shelled walnuts

Add ingredients to blender container or food processor. Puree until a smooth paste is formed.

Old Lyme Inn
85 Lyme St
Old Lyme, CT

Grilled Salmon with Spinach Cream

Serves 4

4 (8-ounce) salmon filets
½ cup olive oil
¼ cup lemon juice
1 (8-ounce) package fresh
   spinach, thoroughly washed
1 tablespoon butter

2 cloves shallots, minced
2 ounces white wine
1 cup cream
¼ teaspoon nutmeg
Salt and pepper to taste

Marinate salmon filets in a mixture of olive oil and lemon juice for 30 minutes. Place spinach in a saucepan, add about ½-inch boiling water, cover and cook for about 10 minutes or until done. Do not over cook. Remove from heat; drain thoroughly. Melt butter in a heavy saucepan over medium-high heat. Add shallots and saute for about 3 minutes. Stir in wine, reduce heat and simmer until volume is reduced to ⅓ the original amount. Add cream, simmer until reduced about half its original volume, stirring mixture constantly. Chop spinach and add to the cream. Season with nutmeg, salt and pepper. Place salmon on broiler rack. Broil for 4 to 6 minutes on a side, depending on the thickness. Be careful not to over-cook. Serve by spooning the spinach mixture on a warmed plate and topping with salmon. Garnish with lemon slices and additional chopped fresh spinach.

Longleaf Plantation, Inc.
Lumberton, MI

In 1937, the first permanent license plates were issued in Connecticut.

Salmon and Sole Crepe

Serves 4

2 tablespoons minced shallots
1 tablespoon butter
¼ cup white wine
¼ cup fish stock
½ cup heavy cream

1 teaspoon tarragon
Salt and pepper to taste
½ pound each: salmon and sole
1 (10-ounce) bag fresh spinach
Spinach leaves for garnish

Saute ½ shallots in butter until tender; coat with flour. Add white wine and fish stock. Simmer until mixture is reduced to ½ its original volume. Add cream, cooking until slightly reduced. Saute remaining shallots. Add fish, spinach and cream sauce. Simmer until fish is cooked. Mixture should not be runny. Fill crepes, roll and coat with remaining sauce. Garnish with fresh spinach leaves.

Old Lyme Inn
85 Lyme St
Old Lyme, CT

Sauteed Swordfish Au Poivre

Serves 1
One of our most popular specials

1 (12-ounce) swordfish steak
All-purpose flour
3 tablespoons vegetable oil
2 ounces brandy
¼ teaspoon Dijon mustard

¼ cup heavy cream
Salt
1 tablespoon cracked black
  peppercorns or to taste

Slice swordfish in half lengthwise, making 2 (½-inch) steaks. Flour steaks and shake off excess. Heat oil and saute swordfish over medium heat until fully cooked on both sides. Pour off oil, add brandy and saute until sauce is reduced. Add mustard and cream. Increase heat to high and cook until sauce becomes a semi-thick consistency. Salt and pepper to taste and serve on heated platter

Captain Daniel Packer Inne
32 Water Street
Mystic, CT

Hunter's Platter with Red Cabbage

Serves 1

Broccoli	**Dry mustard**
Cauliflower,	**Green peppercorns**
Carrot mousse	**1 (6-ounce) fillet of venison**
Shredded red cabbage	**1 rabbit thigh, wrapped in bacon**
Balsamic vinegar	**1 (5-ounce) Napa Valley quail**

Marinate first 4 ingredients in a mixture of balsamic vinegar with dry mustard and green peppercorns added to taste. Grill meats for approximately 10 minutes or until the desired doneness is reached. Serve on a large platter with marinated vegetables.

Note: For added touch, heat cabbage in a non-stick frying pan before serving.

Cobbs Mill Inn
Weston, CT

In 1843, the first typewriter that successfully typed was patented by Charles Thurber of Norwich.

Sweet Potatoes, As Served at The King's Arms Tavern, Williamsburg, Virginia

Serves 4 to 6 servings
Looks and tastes like a souffle. Good with ham!

2½ to 3 pounds sweet potatoes,
    cooked, drained and mashed
¾ cup sugar
1 teaspoon salt

½ teaspoon nutmeg
¼ teaspoon cinnamon
½ cup butter, melted
2 cups milk

Combine ingredients in mixing bowl. Mix until well blended. Pour into a 11x8x2-inch glass baking dish. Cover and allow to sit before baking. May be refrigerated overnight. Bake, covered, at 350° for approximately 50 minutes.

Note: A souffle dish can be used to prepare this recipe.

King's Arms Tavern
Williamsburg, VA

Apple Glazed Carrots

Serves 8 to 10
A great dish with quail

¼ cup butter
3 medium to large apples, peeled,
    cored and coarsely chopped
6 to 8 medium-sized carrots,
    sliced or julienne cut

Salt
Dash of nutmeg
3 tablespoons honey

Melt butter in heavy saucepan over low heat. Add apples, cover tightly and cook over medium heat until soft. Add carrots, cover and cook until carrots are crisp soft. Stir in nutmeg and honey just before serving. Continue to cook until mixture boils.

Longleaf Plantation Inn
Lumberton, MI

Mushrooms Aux Champignons

Serves 4

½ pound fresh mushrooms
3 tablespoons butter, divided
1 shallot, chopped or 1 teaspoon
  chopped onion
3 tablespoons all-purpose flour
1¼ cups hot milk

1 teaspoon salt
Cayenne to taste
Grated nutmeg to taste
4 eggs, separated
1 egg white

Clean mushrooms; caps and stems. Chop until very fine. Place 1 table-spoon butter in saucepan, add shallot and saute over medium-high heat until shallot is soft but not brown. Add chopped mushrooms and slowly cook until all moisture is evaporated; set aside. In another saucepan, melt 2 tablespoons butter. Gradually, stir in flour and cook until mixture begins to turn golden. Add milk and cook, stirring constantly with a wire whisk or slotted spoon, for 5 minutes or until sauce is reduced to a scant 1 cup. Season with salt, cayenne and nutmeg. Add the mushrooms and bring to a boil. Remove from heat. Beat egg yolks lightly; add a small amount of hot sauce to yolks. Stir until yolks are slightly heated and return to remaining sauce; stir. Cool slightly. Beat 5 egg whites with electric mixer until stiff but not dry. Fold into sauce mixture. Fill a buttered souffle dish ¾ full and bake at 375° for about 30 minutes or until souffle is well puffed and delicately browned on top.

Dilworthtown Inn
Old Wilmington Pike
West Chester, PA

In 1783, the perfection of the self-winding clock was accomplished in Litchfield.

Mustard Sauce with Dill

Yields about 2½ cups

1 teaspoon wine vinegar
½ cup sugar
1 cup sweet mustard

1 cup vegetable oil (Do not use
  olive oil)
½ cup finely chopped dill

Combine vinegar, sugar and mustard. Whisk until blended. While constantly stirring, pour in oil. Stir in dill.

Note: Golden spicy brown mustard works well for the sweet mustard in this recipe. This works extremely well if prepared in blender.

Dilworthtown Inn
Old Wilmington Pike
West Chester, PA

Toll House Inn Butterscotch Sauce

Serves 10 to 12
Real butterscotch for those special desserts

1¼ cups sugar
¾ cup light corn syrup
1 cup light cream

1 tablespoon butter or margarine
½ teaspoon salt
Milk if needed

Combine ingredients in heavy saucepan. Cook over medium-high heat until mixture reaches the soft ball stage on a candy thermometer (234°). Watch and stir occasionally as it cooks. Remove from heat. Dilute with milk if too thick. Serve hot or cold over ice cream or cake. This will keep for a long period of time if refrigerated. To reheat, place over hot water and thin with milk or cream if too thick.

Note: I have used ½ cup light corn syrup and 4 tablespoons honey in place of the regular recipe amount.

Toll House Inn
West Cornwall, CT

Gravlaks

Serves 2

1 tablespoon sugar
1 tablespoon coarse salt
1 to 2 teaspoons crushed black
  peppercorns
1 good size bunch of dill,
  coarsely chopped, stems and all

½ teaspoon monosodium
  glutamate
1 pound fresh midsection salmon,
  deboned

Mix sugar, salt and pepper in small mixing bowl. Using a glass, enamel or plastic square dish (not metal) just big enough to hold salmon, sprinkle some spice mixture in the bottom of the dish along with small portion of dill. Rub salmon well with spice mixture on all sides. Place 1 piece of salmon in dish, skin side down. Sprinkle with large portion of dill/MSG mixture. Place remaining piece of salmon on top of first piece fitting thick part against thin part of lower piece. Sprinkle remaining spices and dill on top. Cover with foil and place flat dish and heavy object on top. Refrigerate for 48 hours turning occasionally. Drain liquids.

Dilworthtown Inn
Old Wilmington Pike
West Chester, PA

In 1870, Maria Sanford, a native of Old Saybrook, was the first woman professor appointed in the United States.

Baked Apples

Serves 4
Our guests love these on wintery mornings!

4 large, firm cooking apples	**¼ cup chopped walnuts**
¼ cup light brown sugar	**4 teaspoons butter**
1½ teaspoons cinnamon	**1 to 2 cups cranberry-raspberry**
¼ cup raisins	**juice**

Wash and core apples without poking through bottoms. Remove peel from top ¼-inch apples. Combine next 4 ingredients in mixing bowl; set aside. Place apples in glass baking dish. Spoon sugar mixture to fill apples. Dribble cranberry-raspberry juice into apples and pour remainder into bottom of baking dish until ¼-inch deep. Top each apple with 1 teaspoon butter. Cover and bake at 350° for 30 minutes or until apples are soft but not split. To test, insert narrow knive into white of apple. Apple is done if knife pushes easily into pulp. Serve at once with sauce from bottom of pan spooned over apples.

Note: Cider or cran-apple juice can be substituted for cranberry-raspberry juice. Extra sauce can be made by heating additional sugar mixture, butter and juice in a saucepan.

The Tolland Inn
Tolland, CT

In 1829, the first double reflecting tin baker was invented by
Isaac Dobson of Farmington.

Vegetables

Asparagus Casserole

Serves 6 to 8
Easy vegetable dish

3 cups asparagus, cut into 1-inch
   pieces and cooked
1 teaspoon salt
3 eggs, beaten
1 cup grated medium-sharp
   Cheddar cheese

1¼ cups cracker crumbs
1 cup milk
2 tablespoons butter or
   margarine melted

Combine ingredients in order listed in large mixing bowl. Pour into a
buttered 2½-quart casserole dish. Bake, uncovered, at 350° for 35 to 40
minutes.

Baked Broccoli Continental

Serves 8
Prepare ahead vegetable

2 pounds fresh broccoli, cleaned,
   crisp cooked and drained
½ cup sliced ripe olives
¼ cup pimiento strips

½ cup grated cheese
¼ cup fine breadcrumbs
¼ cup melted butter or margarine
1 tablespoon lemon juice

Arrange broccoli, olives and pimiento in a buttered 2-quart shallow baking dish. Combine cheese and breadcrumbs; sprinkle over broccoli mixture. Combine butter and lemon juice. Pour over the top of the casserole.
Bake, uncovered, at 350° for 30 minutes or until hot.

Note: A combination of broccoli, cauliflower and carrots is also tasty and colorful.

Carrot and Cranberry Casserole

Serves 4 to 6
Unusual sweet-sour flavor

1 apple, peeled and grated
1 cup whole cranberries
4 cups grated carrots
4 tablespoons brown sugar,
    packed

½ teaspoon salt
½ cup cider or apple juice
2 tablespoons butter

Combine ingredients in order listed; mix well. Pour into a buttered 2-quart casserole. Dot the top with butter. Bake, uncovered, at 350° for 40 minutes, stirring once during baking.

In 1858, the first air-tight fruit jars with a spring-fastened glass top was patented by W.W. Lyman of Meriden.

Carrot-Apple Casserole

Serves 6

1 (16-ounce) bag carrots, sliced
    and par-boiled
1 (21-ounce) can apple pie filling

½ teaspoon nutmeg
½ teaspoon cinnamon

Mix carrots and pie filling until well blended. Pour into a buttered 2-quart casserole. Sprinkle with cinnamon and nutmeg. Bake at 325° for 1 hour.

Wined Onions

Serves 6

3½ to 4 pounds onions, sliced
½ cup butter
1 tablespoon sugar

½ cup red wine
1 teaspoon vinegar
½ teaspoon salt

Saute onions in skillet over a medium-high heat in butter-sugar mixture for 3 to 5 minutes or until tender. Add wine, vinegar and salt. Reduce heat and simmer for 3 to 4 hours.

Swiss Chard Casserole

Serves 6

2 pounds Swiss chard
4 tablespoons butter or
   margarine, divided
2 tablespoons all-purpose flour
½ cup milk

½ pound shredded sharp
   Cheddar cheese
½ to ¾ cup flavored breadcrumbs
Thinly sliced sharp Cheddar
   Cheese

Wash Swiss chard and cut stalks from leaves. Cut stalks into 1-inch pieces and cut leaves into 1-inch pieces. Place stalks in boiling water and boil, covered, for 5 minutes. Add leaves and continue to boil, covered, for an additional 5 minutes. Drain well. (This will make approximately 5 cups cooked chard.) Melt 2 tablespoons margarine in saucepan over low heat; blend in flour, stirring constantly. Slowly, add milk, stirring constantly, so it does not lump. Add cheese. Continue to cook, stirring constantly, until cheese melts. Grease a 2-quart casserole dish. Place chard in casserole and stir in sauce. Melt remaining 2 tablespoons margarine in skillet and stir in breadcrumbs until evenly coated. Spread on top of casserole. Bake at 350° for about 25 minutes or until bubbly and browned.

Note: Breadcrumbs can be flavored with garlic powder and oregano according to your own individual tastes.

Cauliflower-Broccoli Medley

Serves 6 to 8

1 head cauliflower
1 bunch fresh broccoli
2 small onions, sliced and
  separated into rings
½ cup mayonnaise
⅓ cup vegetable oil

⅓ cup vinegar
¼ cup sugar
½ teaspoon salt
¼ teaspoon pepper
2 slices bacon, cooked and
  crumbled

Wash cauliflower, removing green leaves. Separate into flowerets, slicing the large ones into bite-sized pieces. Trim leaves from broccoli. Remove tough ends of lower stalks and wash thoroughly. Cut into bite-sized pieces. Combine vegetables in a large mixing bowl. Combine remaining ingredients in small mixing bowl, except for bacon. Mix and pour over vegetables. Toss gently until vegetables are coated with dressing. Chill several hours or overnight before serving. Garnish with bacon just before serving.

Stir-Fried Green Beans

Serves 4 to 6
Serve as a side dish

1 pound fresh green beans
⅔ cup water
1 vegetable bouillon cube

2 tablespoons sesame oil
5 cloves garlic, chopped
½ teaspoon salt

Wash beans thoroughly. Snap off and discard the tips of the beans. Break into 2-inch pieces. Place water in a small saucepan over a low heat. Add bouillon cube; stir until dissolved. Set aside. Heat oil in wok over high heat. Drop in garlic and stir until slightly browned. Add salt and beans; stir for 1 minute. Add water and bouillon, cover and cook for about 4 minutes. Uncover, stir the beans and cook until most of the liquid has disappeared. Beans will still be crunchy. Store beans in a covered container in the refrigerator until thoroughly chilled. Serve cold.

Nooney's Mushroom Florentine

Serves 6 to 8
My grandmother made this dish to accompany our family's annual
Easter Dinner together.

1 pound fresh mushrooms	¼ cup chopped onion
2 (10-ounce) packages frozen	¼ cup melted butter
spinach, thawed and drained	1 cup grated Cheddar cheese
1 teaspoon salt	Garlic salt to taste

Gently, wipe mushrooms clean with a paper towel. Carefully, remove the
stems from the mushrooms. Saute mushrooms in a skillet with a small
amount of butter, browning the cap sides first; set aside. Combine the
spinach, salt, onion and melted butter in mixing bowl. Place in a buttered
11x8x2-inch baking dish. Sprinkle ½ cheese mixture over the spinach.
Arrange the mushrooms over the cheese. Season with garlic salt to taste.
Cover with remaining cheese. Bake at 350° for 30 minutes.

Mushrooms Parmesan

Serves 4 to 6
Don't peel or scrub the mushrooms; just rinse. The experts tell us you
lose flavor if you wash them too well.

1½ pounds whole fresh	½ cup Italian-style breadcrumbs
mushrooms	2 tablespoons parsley flakes
¼ cup olive or vegetable oil,	¼ cup Parmesan cheese
divided	1 teaspoon garlic salt

Toss mushrooms with ½ the oil in a 1½-quart casserole. Combine dry
ingredients and sprinkle over mushrooms. Pour the remaining oil over
the entire casserole. Bake at 350° for 25 minutes.

Potato Logs

Serves 8 to 10

2 eggs, separated
½ cup chopped onion
½ teaspoon celery seed
6 servings leftover mashed
potatoes or prepared instant
potatoes

¼ cup all-purpose flour
½ cup milk
1½ cups breadcrumbs
Oil for frying

Combine egg yolks, onion and celery seed to mashed potatoes. Mix until thoroughly blended. Shape approximately 2 tablespoons of this mixture into small logs or balls. Roll into flour. Repeat this process until all mixture is used. Combine egg whites and milk. Dip floured potato logs into mixture. Roll in breadcrumbs. Deep fry logs in oil heated to 375° degrees for 2 to 3 minutes or until golden brown.

Potatoes Au-Gratin Kaleel

Serves 10 to 12 servings
The best scalloped potatoes you'll ever make!

6 to 8 cloves garlic
1½ teaspoons salt
1 tablespoon butter
6 small shallots, finely minced
5 to 6 large potatoes, peeled and
thinly sliced

¾ teaspoon pepper
¾ pound freshly grated Parmesan
cheese, divided
2 cups heavy cream, divided
½ pound Swiss cheese, grated

Chop garlic, add salt and pulverize using a mortar and pestle until no garlic is visible. Generously grease a 2-quart casserole with 1 tablespoon butter. Sprinkle ⅓ shallots and ⅓ of garlic-salt mixture into the bottom of the casserole. Add a layer of potato slices ½ to ¾-inch thick. Sprinkle with ½ teaspoon pepper, ⅓ of Parmesan cheese and cover with ⅓ cup cream. Sprinkle with shallot and garlic-salt mixture. Continue 2 more layers in same order until pan is nearly full. Add remaining Parmesan cheese, gently mixing throughout casserole. Top with grated Swiss cheese. Cover with foil and bake at 350° for 45 minutes or until potatoes are tender.

Make Ahead Potato Casserole

Serves 10 to 12

2 (24-ounce) packages shredded
  frozen hash browns
2 cups half and half
⅔ cup pasteurized processed
  cheese spread

½ cup margarine
1 teaspoon salt
¼ cup grated Cheddar cheese

Thaw potatoes overnight in the refrigerator. Crumble the thawed potatoes in a buttered 13x9x2-inch baking dish. Combine half and half,
cheese, butter and salt in a small saucepan. Cook over a medium heat,
stirring constantly, until cheese melts. Pour over potatoes. Mix potatoes
with a fork to completely separate. Sprinkle Cheddar cheese over top.
Bake, uncovered, at 350° for 1 hour or until set and lightly browned.

Delmontico Potatoes

Serves 8
Always a crowd pleaser!

¼ cup butter
3 tablespoons all-purpose flour
2 teaspoons salt (less, if desired)
¼ teaspoon pepper
½ teaspoon garlic salt or garlic
  powder

1½ cups hot milk
½ cup grated sharp cheese
4 hard cooked eggs, sliced or cut
  into large pieces
4 cups cold cooked potatoes,
  sliced into ¼-inch pieces

Melt butter in 10-inch skillet over medium-high heat. Stir in flour and
seasonings. Slowly, stir in milk and cook for 5 minutes, stirring constantly, or until mixture thickens. Blend in cheese. When cheese melts,
add potatoes, stir until coated with sauce and pour into a buttered
2½-quart casserole. Bake at 400° for 20 minutes. Brown under broiler
before serving.

Snow Pea Delight   Very Good

Serves 4
Easy for entertaining

2 cups snow peas
6 slices bacon, cut into
    1-inch pieces
1 diced scallion, including top
1 tomato, peeled, seeded and
    diced

½ cup water chestnuts, sliced
Salt and pepper to taste
Soy Sauce

Boil snow peas in water for 1 minute. Drain and blanch in cold water. Saute bacon in skillet until crisp, remove and drain. Pour off ½ of drippings. Saute scallion, tomato and water chestnuts in remaining drippings for 2 minutes. Add bacon, salt and pepper and snow peas. Toss and serve with soy sauce.

Feta-Spinach Kugel

Serves 8
A great dish on a buffet meal!

1 (12-ounce) package fettucini
1 medium-sized onion, chopped
3 tablespoons vegetable oil
1 (10-ounce) package frozen
    chopped spinach, thawed
    and drained
3 large eggs

1 (8-ounce) package feta cheese,
    crumbled
1 cup sour cream
2 tablespoons melted butter
½ teaspoon nutmeg
Pepper to taste

Prepare noodles according to package directions; drain. Saute onion in oil until brown and crispy, stirring constantly. Combine onions and remaining ingredients except for noodles in a large mixing bowl. Add noodles and mix until well blended. Pour mixture into a greased 13x9x2-inch baking dish. Bake at 350° for 30 to 45 minutes.

Butternut Squash

Serves 4 to 6

1 butternut squash, cleaned
   and halved
1 tablespoon chopped nuts

1 tablespoon honey
1 tablespoon brown sugar,
   packed

Place squash halves on baking sheet cut side down; add small amount of water to the bottom of the pan. Bake at 350° for 30 minutes. Turn and add nuts, honey and brown sugar mixture to the inside of the squash. Cook an additional 10 minutes or until squash is tender.

Country Squire Squash

Serves 6
Good hot or cold

8 slices bacon
¼ cup finely chopped onion
1 cup vegetable cocktail juice
2 cups mashed, cooked acorn or
   butternut squash

3 large eggs, slightly beaten
1 cup shredded Swiss cheese
Dash of pepper
Ground nutmeg

Place bacon in a 10-inch skillet. Cook over medium heat until crisp. Remove bacon and drain. Pour off drippings except for 2 tablespoons. Saute onions in reserved bacon drippings for 3 to 5 minutes or until tender. Stir in remaining ingredients including all but 2 tablespoons of crumbled bacon and nutmeg. Pour mixture into a well greased 9-inch pie plate. Bake at 350° for 1 hour or until knife inserted in the center of the mixture comes out clean. Garnish with reserved bacon and nutmeg; serve warm or cold.

Note: This can be made ahead and frozen. Reheat at 350° until warmed.

Squash Onion Egg Pie

Serves 4

1 (9-inch) unbaked pastry shell
1 medium-sized onion, chopped
3 tablespoons margarine
1 cup sliced apples
5 eggs

½ cup heavy cream
½ teaspoon nutmeg
1 cup cooked acorn or winter
   squash

Prepare pastry shell and line pie plate; set aside. Saute onions in margarine over medium-high heat until golden; add apples. In small mixing bowl, whip egg and cream until well blended and foamy. Add nutmeg; mix. Pour egg mixture into pie shell. Top with squash and sauteed onions and apples. Bake, uncovered, at 350° for 20 to 30 minutes or until mixture is firm.

Squash Medley

Serves 5 to 6

2 slices bacon, diced
1 medium-sized onion, chopped
3 medium-sized yellow squash,
   sliced
1 medium-sized zucchini, sliced
2 medium-sized tomatoes, sliced
   into eighths

1 teaspoon salt
Dash of pepper
½ teaspoon basil
½ teaspoon sugar

Fry bacon in a 10-inch skillet over medium heat until almost crisp. Add remaining ingredients. Reduce heat to low, cover and cook for 15 minutes. Serve hot.

Autumn Butternut Casserole

Serves 8
A perfect, nutritious accompaniment for pork

3 cups mashed, cooked
   butternut squash
¼ cup plus 3½ tablespoons
   butter, divided
½ cup plus 1 tablespoon brown
   sugar, packed
¼ teaspoon salt

Dash of white pepper
6 cups unpared sliced Jonathan
   apples
¼ cup sugar
1½ cups cornflakes, coarsely
   crushed
½ cup chopped pecans

Season squash with ¼ cup butter, 1 tablespoon brown sugar, ¼ teaspoon salt and pepper. Heat 1½ tablespoons butter in a skillet; add sliced apples, sprinkle with ¼ cup sugar, cover and simmer over low heat until barely tender or about 5 minutes. Spread in a buttered 3-quart casserole. Spoon squash evenly over apples. Mix cornflakes with pecans, ½ cup brown sugar and remaining melted butter. Sprinkle over squash. Bake at 350° for 15 minutes or until heated through.

Verdant Summer Fry

Serves 6

3 medium-sized zucchini,
   thinly sliced
1 tablespoon salt
1 cup green onions, chopped
1 large green pepper,
   thinly sliced

¼ cup vegetable oil
¼ cup fresh sweet basil, chopped
½ cup sour cream or plain yogurt
1 teaspoon Dijon mustard
Chopped chives

Place sliced zucchini in a colander. Mix with salt and set aside for 30 minutes. Squeeze out accumulated moisture. Saute onions and peppers in oil in a 10-inch skillet over a medium-high heat for 5 minutes or until onions are limp. Add zucchini and basil. Reduce heat and cook for 5 to 8 minutes, stirring occasionally. Blend in sour cream and mustard; cook until heated through. Garnish with chives before serving.

My Sweet Potato Praline

Serves 6 to 8

3 cups cooked mashed yams
2 eggs, beaten
⅓ cup sugar
⅓ cup butter, melted

⅓ cup cream
1 teaspoon vanilla
½ teaspoon allspice
½ teaspoon nutmeg

Combine ingredients in order listed; mix until well blended. Spread in a buttered 2½-quart baking dish. Top with topping mix. Bake at 350° for 60 minutes or until bubbly. Garnish with pecans.

Topping:
1 cup brown sugar, packed
⅓ cup all-purpose flour
⅓ cup butter, cut into small
  pieces

Pecans for garnish

Measure ingredients into a small mixing bowl. Mix until well blended.

Crowd-Pleasing Vegetable Bake

Serves 10 to 12
Delicious, great with turkey, chicken or beef!

1 (20-ounce) package frozen
  cauliflower
1 (10-ounce) package cut broccoli
1 (17-ounce) can cream-style corn
1 (17-ounce) can whole kernel
  corn, drained

2 cups shredded Swiss cheese
1 (10¾-ounce) can cream of
  celery soup
1 (4-ounce) can sliced mushrooms
1½ cups soft rye breadcrumbs
2 tablespoons melted butter

Cook cauliflower and broccoli according to package directions. Combine next 4 ingredients; mix until blended. Fold in cooked vegetables and mushrooms. Pour into a buttered 13x9x2-inch baking dish. Toss breadcrumbs with butter until evenly coated. Sprinkle over the top of the casserole. Bake, uncovered, at 375° for 30 to 35 minutes. Remove from oven and allow to stand 10 minutes before serving.

Tomatoes Filled with Rice

Serves 6 to 8
Good way to use summer tomatoes

½ pound fresh mushrooms,
   sliced
1 to 2 bunches scallions, sliced
2 tablespoons butter

6 to 8 fresh tomatoes, tops and
   pulp removed
1 (10-ounce) package long grain
   and wild rice

Saute mushrooms and scallions in butter in skillet over medium-high heat for 3 to 5 minutes or until tender; set aside. Sprinkle tomatoes with seasoned salt; drain upside down on paper towels. Cook rice according to package directions. Add mushrooms and onions to rice, mix well and set aside to cool. Fill tomatoes with rice mixture. Place in shallow casserole dish. Bake at 325° for 20 to 30 minutes.

Note: Tomatoes may be prepared ahead. This dish is lovely with charcoaled steak.

In 1908, the first use of a confectionery machine to manufacture lollipops was in New Haven by Bradley & Smith Co.

Desserts

Apple Cake

Serves 16 plus
A family favorite–good for breakfast, snack, dessert

5 apples, peeled and sliced
1¾ cups plus 3 tablespoons
   sugar, divided
1 tablespoon cinnamon
2¾ cups all-purpose flour

¼ cup unprocessed bran
2 teaspoons baking powder
4 eggs
¼ cup orange juice
1 cup vegetable oil

Combine apples, 3 tablespoons sugar and cinnamon and set aside. Mix together flour, remaining sugar, bran and baking powder. Combine eggs, orange juice and oil. Mix together liquid and dry ingredients. Put 1 inch batter into a large greased and floured tube pan. Next put a layer of apples (don't push down) then remaining batter and smooth out. Put last half of apples on top. Bake at 350° for 1½ hours. Cool slightly before turning over to remove from tube pan.

Wooden Spoon Apple Cake

Serves 16 to 20

¾ cup vegetable oil
1 cup sugar
2 eggs
2 cups all-purpose flour
1 tablespoon cinnamon
1 teaspoon baking soda

Pinch of salt
2 teaspoons vanilla extract
½ cup chocolate chips
½ cup chopped walnuts
3 cups firm cooking apples,
   peeled, cored and chopped

Mix together oil, sugar and eggs. Sift in flour, cinnamon, soda and salt; blend thoroughly. Add vanilla, chocolate and nuts; fold in apples. Batter is very thick! Spoon into greased and floured tube pan. Bake at 350° for 1 hour.

Banana Split Cake Supreme

Serves 8 to 12
Simple but delicious

2 cups graham cracker crumbs
1 cup butter or margarine, melted
  and divided
2 cups confectioners' sugar
1 (8-ounce) package cream cheese
5 bananas, split lengthwise

1 (22-ounce) can crushed
  pineapple, drained
1 (13½-ounce) container frozen
  non-dairy whipped topping,
  thawed
¼ cup chopped nuts

Combine graham cracker crumbs with ½ cup butter; cover bottom of a 13x9x2-inch pan. Cream confectioners' sugar with cream cheese and remaining melted butter. Spread over crust. Place bananas over cream cheese mixture. Spoon pineapple over bananas; spread with whipped topping. Sprinkle with nuts. Refrigerate for 2 hours.

Cream Cheese Cherry Nut Cake

Yields 1 (10-inch) tube or bundt pan
Wonderful for Christmas holidays–nice gift too

1 (8-ounce) package cream cheese
1 cup butter or margarine
1½ cups sugar
1½ teaspoons vanilla
4 eggs
2¼ cups all-purpose flour,
  divided

1½ teaspoons baking powder
¾ cup well-drained maraschino
  cherries, halved
½ cup chopped nuts

Blend first 4 ingredients. Add eggs, 1 at a time, and mix well after each. Gradually add 2 cups flour mixed with baking power. Mix remaining ¼ cup flour with cherries and nuts. Add to batter and blend. Pour into greased and floured 10-inch tube or bundt pan. Bake at 325° for 1 hour 20 minutes.

Caramel Nougat in Milk Chocolate Cake

Serves 16 to 20

1 cup butter or margarine,
   divided
3 large or 6 small caramel nougat
   in milk chocolate candy bars
2 cups sugar
4 eggs

2½ cups sifted all-purpose flour
½ teaspoon baking soda
1¼ cups buttermilk
1 teaspoon vanilla
1 cup chopped nuts

Melt ½ cup butter and candy over low heat. Cream remaining ½ cup butter and sugar until fluffy. Add eggs, 1 at a time, and beat well. Add flour and soda alternately with buttermilk; stir well. Add melted candy and mix well. Stir in vanilla and nuts. Bake in a greased and floured 10-inch bundt pan at 350° for 1 hour 20 minutes. Cool a few minutes before removing from pan.

Chocolate-Covered Toffee Candy Bar Cake

Serves 10 to 12
Rich and good

2 cups brown sugar, firmly
   packed
2 cups sifted all-purpose flour
½ cup butter or margarine
1 egg, beaten
1 cup milk

1 teaspoon salt
1 teaspoon baking soda
1 teaspoon vanilla extract
6 chocolate-covered toffee candy
   bars, frozen
½ cup chopped pecans

Stir sugar into flour; mix well. Cut in butter with pastry blender until mixture is like cornmeal. Measure 1 cup mixture; set aside. Add egg, milk, salt, soda and vanilla to remaining mixture; beat well. Pour into greased and floured 13x9x2-inch pan. Remove broken bars from wrappers (break with hammer). Blend broken bars with pecans and reserved crumb mixture. Spread topping over batter. Bake at 350° for 35 minutes.

Black Magic Cake

Serves 10 to 12–Yields 1 cake
My favorite chocolate cake, the family loves it

1¾ cups all-purpose flour
1¾ to 2 cups sugar
¾ cup cocoa
1 teaspoon salt
1 teaspoon baking powder
2 teaspoons baking soda
2 eggs

1 cup strong coffee or 2 teaspoons
  instant coffee plus 1 cup
  boiling water
1 cup buttermilk or sour milk
½ cup vegetable oil
1 teaspoon vanilla extract

Combine flour, sugar, cocoa, salt, baking powder and soda in a large mixing bowl. Add eggs, coffee, milk, oil and vanilla. Beat at medium speed of mixer for 2 minutes (batter will be thin). Pour batter into a greased and floured 13x9x2-inch pan or 2 (9-inch) layer cake pans. Bake at 350° for 35 to 40 minutes for oblong pan or 30 to 35 minutes for layer pans. Frost with your favorite frosting.

Prize Fudge Cake

Yields 2-layer cake

¼ cup shortening
2 cups sugar, divided
2 eggs, separated
4 (1-ounce) squares chocolate,
  melted
2 cups cake flour

1 tablespoon baking powder
½ teaspoon salt
1½ cups milk
1 teaspoon vanilla
1 cup chopped nuts

Cream shortening, gradually adding 1½ cups sugar. Add well-beaten egg yolks and blend thoroughly. Blend in melted chocolate. Sift flour before measuring, then sift flour, baking powder and salt together and add to creamed mixture alternately with milk. Beat just enough to make batter smooth, 5 to 10 seconds. Blend in vanilla and nuts. Beat egg whites until stiff enough to hold a point, then gradually beat in remaining ½ cup sugar. Fold this meringue into batter. Pour into well-greased and floured 9-inch layer cake pans or 10-inch tube pan and bake at 350° for 40 to 45 minutes for layer pans, 50 to 60 minutes for tube pan. Frost with your favorite chocolate frosting.

Amaretto Cheese Cake

Serves 16 to 20

1½ cups graham cracker crumbs
1 cup plus 2 tablespoons sugar,
  divided
1 teaspoon ground cinnamon
¼ cup plus 2 tablespoons butter
  or margarine, melted
3 (8-ounce) packages cream
  cheese, softened

4 eggs
⅓ cup plus 1 tablespoon
  Amaretto liqueur, divided
1 (8-ounce) carton sour cream
¼ cup toasted sliced almonds
1 (1.2-ounce) chocolate candy bar,
  grated

Combine crumbs, 2 tablespoons sugar, cinnamon and butter. Mix well and press mixture firmly into bottom and ½ inch up sides of a 9-inch springform pan. Beat cream cheese until light and fluffy. Gradually add 1 cup sugar; mix well. Add eggs, 1 at a time, beating well after each. Stir in ⅓ cup Amaretto. Pour into pan and bake at 375° for 45 to 50 minutes or until set. Mix sour cream, 1 tablespoon plus 1 teaspoon sugar and remaining Amaretto; stir well. Spoon over cheese cake and bake 500° for 5 minutes. Let cool to room temperature. Refrigerate 24 to 48 hours for best flavor. Top with almonds and candy.

Ladyfinger Cake

Serves 8 to 10
So easy–so good

2 or 3 (4-ounce) packages
  ladyfingers
2 cups heavy cream
1 teaspoon vanilla

1 (8-ounce) package cream cheese
½ cup sugar
1 (21-ounce) can cherry pie filling

Tightly line the sides and bottom of a 9-inch springform pan with ladyfingers; set aside. In large bowl whip cream with vanilla until stiff. In another bowl beat cheese with sugar until creamy. Gently, but thoroughly, fold in cheese mixture with whipped cream. Spread half the cheese mixture over ladyfingers. Place another layer of ladyfingers and then rest of cheese. Cover and chill 24 hours. Spoon fruit over top; chill several more hours.

No Bake Lemon Cheese Cake

Yields 20 squares
Great for parties, showers, meetings

Crust:

2 cups all-purpose flour
1 cup butter or margarine,
    softened

2 tablespoons confectioners'
    sugar

Mix ingredients together and pat into a 13x9x2-inch glass baking dish. Bake at 375° for 10 to 15 minutes; cool.

Filling #1:

2 (8-ounce) packages cream
    cheese
2 cups confectioners' sugar

1 (9-ounce) container frozen non-
    dairy whipped topping,
    thawed

Beat cream cheese and sugar until smooth. Fold in whipped topping and spread over crust.

Filling #2:

2 (3¾-ounce) packages lemon flavor pudding mix

Cooking filling according to package directions; pour over whipped topping.

In 1780, Zadoc Benedict of Danbury established the first hat manufactory in this country.

White Chocolate Cheese Cake

Serves 16 to 20

2 (8-ounce) packages cream
   cheese
¾ cup sugar
3 eggs

1 (8-ounce) carton sour cream
1 pound white chocolate
3 tablespoons light cream
Graham cracker crust

In blender or mixer bowl blend together cream cheese, sugar and eggs. Add sour cream; mix well. In double boiler melt chocolate until soft; stir in cream. Mix with spoon until well blended. Add to cream cheese mixture, mixing well. Pour into graham cracker crust. Bake at 350° for 25 minutes; turn heat off in oven and let cake sit in oven 1 hour.

Crust:
1 sleeve of graham crackers
¼ cup sugar

¼ cup butter or margarine

Finely roll graham crackers. Pour crumbs into a bowl. Add sugar and softened butter; blend well. Pour crumbs into a 9-inch springform pan; press firmly. Bake at 350° for 8 to 10 minutes; cool.

Note: For delicious plain cheese cake, omit the chocolate.

In 1818, the first "knock-down" furniture was produced by Lambert H. Hitchcock of Riverton.

Free Wheeling Coffee Cake

Serves 12 to 15
Easy–but fantastic

4 cups fresh fruit
1 cup water
2 tablespoons lemon juice
2 cups sugar, divided
⅓ cup cornstarch
3 cups all-purpose flour
1 tablespoon baking power
1 teaspoon salt

1 teaspoon cinnamon
¼ teaspoon mace
1 cup butter or margarine
2 eggs, slightly beaten
1 cup milk
1 teaspoon vanilla extract
Strusel topping

In large bowl combine fruit, water, lemon juice, 1 cup sugar and corn-starch. Microwave on High until thick and boiling, about 5 minutes, stir-ring occasionally. Set aside to cool. Mix flour remaining, 1 cup sugar, baking power, salt, cinnamon and mace. Cut in butter. Combine eggs, milk and vanilla and add to dry ingredients just until blended. Spread ½ the batter into a greased 13x9x2-inch pan. Spread with fruit mixture, then add rest of batter. Sprinkle with strusel topping. Bake at 350° for 50 min-utes until done in center

Strusel topping:
½ cup sugar
¼ cup butter

½ cup chopped nuts
½ cup all-purpose flour

Mix together ingredients and sprinkle over cake batter.

In 1826, David C. Collins of Canton organized the first com-pany to manufacture axes with ground edges.

Sour Cream Cake and Apple Filling

Serves 12 to 15

1 teaspoon baking soda	1 teaspoon baking powder
1 cup sour cream	1 teaspoon vanilla
½ cup butter or margarine	3 cooking apples, peeled and
1 cup sugar	thinly sliced
2 eggs	Topping
2 cups all-purpose flour	

Add soda to sour cream; set aside. Cream butter, sugar and eggs until fluffy. Sift flour and baking power; add alternately to creamed mixture with sour cream; add vanilla. Spread half mixture in greased and floured 13x9x2-inch pan. Sprinkle with half the topping. Place sliced apples on top and spread with remaining batter. Sprinkle with remaining topping. Bake at 350° for 35 minutes.

Topping:

1 cup chopped nuts	1 teaspoon cinnamon
½ cup sugar	

Walnut Cake

Serves 10
Rich and delicious. This recipe has been handed down several generations

1 cup butter or margarine	1 teaspoon baking powder
2 cups sugar	1 cup sour cream
6 eggs	1 teaspoon vanilla
2 cups all-purpose flour	1 cup chopped nuts
1 scant teaspoon baking soda	

Cream butter and sugar; add eggs, 1 at a time. In a separate bowl mix flour, soda and baking powder together. Add flour mixture to butter mixture alternately with sour cream; add vanilla and nuts. Fill tube pan less than ¾ full. Bake at 325° for 1 hour or until done. Frost with your favorite chocolate frosting.

Pineapple Announcement Cake

Serves 12 to 14
A great "special occasion" cake

6 eggs, separated
½ teaspoon salt
½ teaspoon cream of tartar
1 cup sugar, divided
Water
1 tablespoon lemon juice
1 teaspoon vanilla extract
1 cup sifted cake flour

2 (3⅛-ounce) packages vanilla
 flavor pudding and pie filling
 (not instant)
1 (30-ounce) can crushed
 pineapple, undrained
⅓ cup light rum
Golden whipped cream

Separate eggs; beat whites until foamy. Add salt and cream of tartar; continue beating until stiff. Gradually beat in ½ cup sugar, 1 tablespoon at a time. Continue beating to stiff meringue. With same beater, beat yolks. Gradually beat in remaining ½ cup sugar until thick and light yellow. Add 3 tablespoons water, lemon juice and vanilla, beating until very light. Fold in flour. Pour egg yolk mixture over beaten egg whites, folding together until no streaks of yolk remain. Turn into 2 ungreased 9-inch layer cake pans. Bake at 350° for 15 to 18 minutes until cake springs back when touched lightly in center and is browned on top. Invert pans, resting rim on custard cups; cool completely. Meanwhile, combine ¼ cup water and pudding mix, stirring until smooth. Add undrained pineapple. Cook, stirring constantly, over moderate heat until mixture boils and becomes clear. Remove from heat and cool. Blend in rum. Split each layer to make 2 layers. Spread each of 4 layers with thin coating of golden whipped cream. Place 1 layer on serving plate. Spread ¼ of pineapple filling over cream; cover with second layer. Repeat until cake is reassembled. Use remaining cream to frost sides of cake and pipe ruffle around top.

Golden Whipped Cream:
2 cups heavy cream
¼ cup confectioners' sugar

1 teaspoon vanilla
⅛ teaspoon yellow food coloring

Whip cream with sugar, vanilla and food coloring until stiff.

Waldorf Red Cake

Yields 2 (8-inch) layers or 1 (13x9-inch) cake

2½ cups all-purpose flour
1 teaspoon baking soda
¼ teaspoon salt
2 teaspoons cocoa
1 cup butter or margarine
1½ cups sugar

1 cup buttermilk
2 eggs
1 teaspoon vinegar
1 ounce red food coloring
1 teaspoon vanilla

Sift dry ingredients together. Cream butter and sugar together. Add dry ingredients alternately with buttermilk. Add eggs, vinegar and food coloring. Add vanilla. Beat 2 minutes on high speed of mixer. Pour into 2 greased and floured 8-inch round pans or a 13x9x2-inch oblong pan. Bake at 350° for 30 to 40 minutes. Frost with Cream Cheese Frosting when cooled.

Cream Cheese Frosting:
¼ cup butter or margarine,
    softened to room temperature
1 (3-ounce) package cream cheese,
    softened

2 cups confectioners' sugar
1 teaspoon vanilla

Mix all together and beat well until smooth.

In 1836, America's first tacks were made in Derby.

Pecan Praline Cake

Serves 16 or more
A bit of New Orleans

2 cups buttermilk
1 cup butter, melted
4 cups brown sugar, firmly
  packed
4 eggs

4 cups all-purpose flour
2¾ teaspoons baking soda
¼ cup cocoa
2¾ teaspoons vanilla

Heat buttermilk and butter in saucepan; add sugar and eggs and beat well. Pour into a bowl. Combine flour, soda and cocoa; add to liquid mixture and beat well. Add vanilla. Pour into well-greased 13x9x2-inch pan. Bake at 350° for 25 minutes.

Topping:
1 cup butter or margarine, melted
2 cups brown sugar, firmly
  packed

¾ evaporated milk
2 cups chopped pecans

Mix ingredients in order listed. When cake is done, spread topping over cake and return to oven to brown.

Grapefruit Chiffon Loaf Cake

Yields 1 (9x5x4-inch) loaf

1 cup all-purpose flour
¾ cup sugar
1½ teaspoons baking powder
¼ teaspoon salt
3 eggs, separated

¼ cup vegetable oil
1½ teaspoons finely grated
  grapefruit rind
⅓ cup grapefruit juice
¼ teaspoon cream of tartar

Sift together flour, sugar, baking powder and salt; make a well in the middle. Add in order the egg yolks, oil, rind and juice. Beat briefly with electric mixer until smooth. In another bowl beat egg whites with cream of tartar until stiff. Pour the flour mixture in a thin stream over the whites and fold in gently. Pour batter into an ungreased 9x5x4-inch loaf pan and bake at 350° for 35 minutes until top is light brown. Invert to cool.

Mrs. Darling's Cuppies

Yields 2½ to 3 dozen cupcakes
Daughter's favorite

1 cup molasses
1 cup sugar
¾ cup shortening
1 teaspoon baking soda
    dissolved in water
1 teaspoon vinegar
1 teaspoon cinnamon

1 teaspoon nutmeg
½ teaspoon salt
½ teaspoon ground ginger
3 cups all-purpose flour
2 cups raisins
1 cup hot water or brewed coffee

Combine all ingredients well and fill greased or paper-lined muffin tins. Bake at 350° for 15 to 20 minutes.

Frosting:
2 (1-ounce) squares unsweetened
    chocolate
1 cup sugar

1 teaspoon butter or margarine
Milk or light cream

Melt chocolate in double boiler; add sugar and blend in butter. Add enough milk or cream to form a smooth paste. Spread over cooled cupcakes.

Fluffy White Frosting

Yields frosting for 1 (9-inch) cake
Not too sweet, but oh, so tasty

6 tablespoons all-purpose flour
½ cup shortening
½ cup butter or margarine

1 cup sugar
1 tablespoon vanilla
½ cup warm milk

Mix all ingredients with electric mixer at high speed for at least 10 minutes. Beat longer for even fluffier texture.

Blackbottom Cupcakes

Yields 24
Delicious

1½ cups all-purpose flour
1 cup sugar
¼ cup cocoa
1 teaspoon baking soda
½ teaspoon salt

1 teaspoon vinegar
1 cup water
⅓ cup vegetable oil
1 teaspoon vanilla

Mix together first 5 ingredients. Add remaining ingredients and mix well. Pour into baking cups ⅓ full then top with 1 teaspoon topping in center of each cup. Bake at 350° for 30 minutes.

Topping:
1 (8-ounce) package cream cheese
1 egg, unbeaten
⅓ cup sugar

⅛ teaspoon salt
1 (6-ounce) package chocolate
   chips

Combine first 4 ingredients in mixing bowl; beat well then stir in chocolate chips.

Bakers Cream

Yields 1½ to 2 cups

1 cup milk
2 tablespoons all-purpose flour
¾ cup shortening
¼ cup butter or margarine

2 teaspoons vanilla
1 (1-pound) package
   confectioners' sugar

Shake together milk and flour in a small covered container to remove lumps. Pour in small saucepan over medium heat. Cook until thick; remove from heat. Cover with plastic wrap and cool to room temperature (crucial!) When cool, add remaining ingredients. Whip 10 minutes until very creamy and silky smooth. This may also be used for some fillings.

Birthday Frosting

Yields 1 to 2 cups
Was my daughter's favorite, especially on chocolate cake

2 tablespoons water
4½ tablespoons sugar
2⅓ cups sifted confectioners'
  sugar

1 egg
⅔ cup shortening
1 teaspoon vanilla extract

Boil water and sugar together for 1 minute; beat confectioners' sugar and egg together until creamy. Slowly pour syrup, while beating, into sugar mixture. Add shortening and vanilla and beat until creamy.

Boiled Frosting

Yields enough to cover layer cake
Delicious on a yellow cake

1 cup sugar
½ cup water

3 egg whites
½ teaspoon vanilla

Cook sugar and water until it forms a string. Cook without stirring after sugar dissolves. Remove from heat and allow to cool. Meanwhile beat egg whites until stiff. Pour syrup in a thin stream over the stiffly beaten egg whites, beating constantly with electric mixer until thick enough to spread; add vanilla.

Danish Apple Pie

Serves 6 to 8

6 or 7 large apples, sliced
½ cup honey
½ cup butter or margarine
1½ cups all-purpose flour

Pinch of salt
1 teaspoon cinnamon
½ cup sugar

Place apples in a buttered 8-inch square baking dish or 2-quart casserole. Drizzle with honey. Combine remaining ingredients; sprinkle over apples. Bake at 375° for 30 minutes.

Apple Dumplings

Serves 8
Great for dessert

12 small or 8 large apples
1 (10-ounce) package refrigerated
  pastry for 9-inch pies

¼ cup sugar
½ teaspoon cinnamon
Topping

Peel and core apples. Cut pastry into pie shaped wedges. Wrap a pastry wedge around each apple tucking down into core. Mix together sugar and cinnamon and fill apple cavities. Put topping in bottom of a 13x9x2-inch pan and place dumplings in pan. Bake at 425° for 40 to 45 minutes, basting every 15 minutes.

Topping:
⅓ cup sugar
1 cup water

1 tablespoon butter or margarine
⅛ teaspoon cinnamon

Combine in a small saucepan and boil for 3 minutes.

French Apple Pie

Serves 6 to 8

Pastry:

⅔ cup plus 2 tablespoons 1 teaspoon salt
 vegetable shortening   4 or 5 tablespoons cold water
2 cups all-purpose flour

Cut shortening into flour and salt until particles are size of small peas. Sprinkle in water, 1 tablespoon at a time, tossing with fork until all flour is moistened and pastry almost cleans side of bowl (1 or 2 teaspoons water may be added if necessary). Gather pastry into a ball, shape into flattened round on lightly floured cloth-covered board. Roll pastry 2 inches larger than inverted 9-inch pie plate with floured stockinette-covered rolling pin. Fold pastry into quarters, unfold and ease into plate pressing firmly against bottom and side.

Apple Pie Filling:

¾ cup sugar   Dash of salt
¼ cup all-purpose flour   6 cups thinly sliced, pared tart
½ teaspoon ground nutmeg   apples (about 6 medium)
½ teaspoon ground cinnamon

Mix dry ingredients; stir in apples. Turn into prepared pastry shell. Top with crumb topping and bake at 425° for 50 minutes. Cover with aluminum foil during last 10 minutes of baking. Best served warm.

Crumb Topping:

1 cup all-purpose flour   ½ cup brown sugar, firmly
½ cup firm butter or margarine packed

Mix all together until crumbly. Sprinkle over pie filling.

Spicy Banana Rum Pie

Serves 6
Nice holiday pie amidst the fruitcakes and cookies

2 (3⅛-ounce) packages vanilla
flavor pudding and pie filling
(not instant)
¼ teaspoon nutmeg

1 teaspoon cinnamon
1 teaspoon rum extract
2 medium bananas
1 (9-inch) baked pastry shell

Combine pudding mix with spices then prepare according to package directions. Stir flavoring into cooked filling. Cool slightly. Slice bananas into baked and cooled crust. Spoon filling over bananas; chill. Garnish with sliced bananas arranged on top of pie and a dollop of whipped cream or whipped topping.

Blueberry Cream Cheese Pie

Serves 8

1 (8-ounce) package cream
cheese, softened
¾ cup sugar, divided
¼ cup sour cream
½ teaspoon vanilla
1 (9-inch) baked pastry shell,
cooled
2 to 3 cups fresh blueberries,
divided

½ cup water
2 tablespoons cornstarch
1 tablespoon lemon juice
2 to 3 tablespoons sifted
confectioners' sugar
Dash of nutmeg and ground
cinnamon

Blend together cream cheese, ¼ cup sugar, sour cream and vanilla until smooth. Spread evenly in pastry shell; chill until firm. In small saucepan mash 1 cup blueberries. Add water and bring to a boil. Strain; add water to blueberry juice to make 1 cup. Combine remaining sugar and cornstarch; stir in blueberry liquid. Return to suacepan and cook, stirring constantly, until mixture thickens and bubbles. Remove from heat, stir in lemon juice and cool. Place remaining blueberries over cream cheese layer. Spoon glaze evenly over all. Chill well about 3 hours. To serve, combine confectioners' sugar, nutmeg and cinnamon; sift over pie.

Date Pie

Serves 6 to 8
A good "guess what's in it" pie

12 singles saltines, crushed finely
12 dates, finely chopped
½ cup chopped nuts
1 cup sugar
¼ teaspoon baking powder

1 teaspoon almond extract
3 egg whites, stiffly beaten
1 cup heavy cream
1 tablespoon confectioners' sugar

Combine first 6 ingredients; mix and fold into beaten egg whites. Spread mixture into a well-greased 9-inch glass pie plate. Bake at 325° for 30 minutes. Cool pie. Whip cream with confectioners' sugar; spread on cooled pie, then refrigerate.

Egg Nog Pie

Serves 6 to 8

1 envelope unflavored gelatin
3 tablespoons cold water
2 cups egg nog
1 cup heavy cream
¼ cup sugar
¼ teaspoon salt

2 teaspoons vanilla
½ teaspoon almond extract
3 tablespoons whiskey
1 (9-inch) baked pastry shell
Nutmeg

Dissolve gelatin in cold water. Heat egg nog 1 to 2 minutes. Whip cream; add sugar and salt. Stir in flavorings. Stir gelatin into egg nog with whiskey and continue to heat until all is dissolved 1 to 2 minutes. Chill 2 to 4 hours; fold in whipped cream. Pour into pastry shell; sprinkle with nutmeg.

Quick Company Pie

Serves 8
Quick and easy

1 (8-ounce) chocolate almond bar
1 (8-ounce) container frozen
   non-dairy whipped
   topping, thawed

1 (9-inch) prepared graham
   cracker crust

Melt chocolate bar in double boiler until liquid; do not overheat. (May be melted in microwave 2 minutes on High.) Blend together with whipped topping and spoon into crust. Chill in freezer until serving time. Very rich.

Italian Cream Pie

Serves 8 to 10
Great for holidays

Sweet Crust:
2 tablespoons vegetable
   shortening
½ cup sugar
2 teaspoons baking powder

2 eggs
2 cups all-purpose flour
Pinch of salt

Mix all ingredients, 1 at a time; mix well. Cut in half. Roll out each half and place 1 pastry in a 10-inch pie plate. Fill and cover with other pastry. Make slits in top and seal edges. Bake at 350° for 1 hour. Sprinkle cooled pie with powdered sugar.

Italian Cream:
4 eggs
¾ cup sugar
3 tablespoons cornstarch

2 tablespoons all-purpose flour
1 quart whole milk
Lemon rind (about 3 inches)

In mixing bowl combine all but milk and lemon rind and mix well. Gradually add milk and lemon rind. Place in double boiler and cook until thick. When cooked, remove lemon rind. Pour into crust.

Lemon Sponge Pie

Serves 6 to 8

2 cups sugar
6 tablespoons all-purpose flour
4 eggs, separated
2 tablespoons butter or
    margarine, softened

Grated rind and juice of 2 lemons
2 cups milk
1 (9-inch) unbaked pastry shell

Beat sugar, flour, egg yolks and butter with a wooden spoon until creamy. Add grated rind and juice; add milk gradually. Beat egg whites to a froth and fold in. Pour into pastry shell. Bake at 375° for 5 to 10 minutes; reduce heat to 350° and bake 40 to 50 minutes. Pie is done when inserted silver knife comes out clean.

Lemon Cake Pie

Serves 6
Sweet and tangy, excellent dessert for hot summer day

1 cup sugar
¼ cup all-purpose flour
¼ cup butter or margarine,
    melted
⅛ teaspoon salt

2 eggs separated
Juice and grated rind of 2 lemons
1 cup milk
1 (9-inch) unbaked pastry shell

Combine sugar, flour, butter, salt and yolks. Beat until smooth. Beat in lemon juice and grated rind. Add milk, beating slowly. Beat egg whites until stiff, not dry. Fold into egg-lemon mixture. Bake pastry shell at 350° for 5 minutes. Pour filling into shell and bake 40 minutes or until filling is just firm. Serve with dollop of whipped cream.

Peanut Pudding Pie

Serves 10
Sinful

1 cup all-purpose flour
½ cup butter or margarine
1⅓ cups dry roasted peanuts,
   divided
½ cup or more peanut butter
1 (8-ounce) package cream cheese
1 cup confectioners' sugar
1 (8-ounce) container frozen
   non-dairy whipped topping,
   thawed and divided

1 (6⅛-ounce) package chocolate
   flavor instant pudding and
   pie filling
1 (5⅝-ounce) package vanilla
   flavor instant pudding and
   pie filling
2¾ cups milk
Chocolate candy bar

Cream together flour and butter. Add ⅔ cup peanuts. Press into a 10-inch pie plate or 11x8-inch casserole dish. Bake at 350° for 20 minutes; cool. Cream together peanut butter, cream cheese and confectioners' sugar. Fold in 1 cup whipped topping; spread over cooled crust. Prepare pudding with milk; spread over peanut butter filling and top with remaining whipped topping. Sprinkle with remaining peanuts and a shaved chocolate candy bar. Chill 2 to 3 hours.

Cheesy Pecan Pie

Serves 6 to 8
For sweet lovers

1 (8-ounce) package cream
   cheese, softened
1 tablespoon all-purpose flour
2½ teaspoons vanilla, divided
1 (9-inch) unbaked pastry shell
1½ cups brown sugar, firmly
   packed

¼ cup butter or margarine
3 eggs, beaten
1 tablespoon vinegar
1 cup chopped pecans or pecan
   halves

Beat cream cheese, flour and 1 teaspoon vanilla. Spread in pastry shell. In another medium bowl cream sugar and butter. Add eggs and mix until combined. Add remaining ingredients. Slowly and carefully pour over cheese mixture. Bake at 350° for 40 to 50 minutes until knife inserted into center comes out clean.

Peach Melba Pie

Serves 8

1 (10-ounce) package frozen
    raspberries
1 tablespoon fresh lemon juice
2 tablespoons sugar
1 tablespoon cornstarch

1 tablespoon brandy
4 cups sliced fresh peaches
1 (9-inch) baked pastry shell
1 cup heavy cream, whipped

Thaw raspberries and force through a sieve. Place in a saucepan and add lemon juice and sugar. Blend cornstarch with brandy and a little water. When blended, add to raspberries. Cook mixture over medium-high heat, stirring constantly, until thickened. Arrange peaches in single layer in pastry shell. Pour raspberry mixture over peaches and chill until ready to serve. Top with whipped cream before serving.

Frozen Pineapple-Lemon Pie

Serves 8
A fast and easy refreshing summer dessert

1 (20-ounce) can crushed
    pineapple
1 (8-ounce) container frozen
    non-dairy whipped
    topping, thawed

½ cup chopped walnuts
Grated rind of 1 lemon
2 teaspoons lemon juice
1 (9-inch) prepared graham
    cracker crust

Drain pineapple reserving 1 tablespoon juice. In a large mixing bowl combine pineapple, whipped topping, nuts, rind, and juices. Stir together until well blended. Spoon into prepared crust. Cover tightly and freeze until firm or overnight. Let stand at room temperature 10 minutes before serving.

Nantucket Pie

Serves 6 to 8
Freezes well

1⅓ cups whole fresh cranberries,
   rinsed and dried
1 cup sugar, divided
¼ cup chopped walnuts
1 egg, beaten

½ cup all-purpose flour
½ teaspoon almond extract
6 tablespoons butter or
   margarine, melted

Cover bottom of a greased 8-inch pie plate with cranberries, ½ cup sugar
and nuts. In separate bowl combine remaining ingredients. Pour this
thick batter over cranberries and bake at 325° for 45 minutes or until
golden.

Chocolate Chip Cream Cheese Bars

Yields 24 bars

2 (16-ounce) packages refrigerated
   chocolate chip slice and bake
   cookie dough
2 (8-ounce) packages cream
   cheese, softened

2 eggs
1 cup sugar
1 teaspoon vanilla

Slice 1 roll of cookie dough ¼-inch thick and line bottom of a greased
13x9x2-inch pan. Beat cream cheese and remaining ingredients together
until smooth. Spread over cookie crust. Slice second roll of cookie dough
and lay on top of filling. Bake at 350° for 35 to 40 minutes. Freezes well.

By-Cracky Bars

Yields 36 bars

1¾ cups all-purpose flour
½ teaspoon salt
¼ teaspoon baking soda
¾ cup butter or margarine,
  softened
1 cup sugar
⅓ cup milk
2 eggs

1 teaspoon vanilla
1 (1-ounce) envelope pre-melted
  unsweetened chocolate
¾ cup chopped walnuts
15 single graham crackers
1 (6-ounce) package semi-sweet
  chocolate pieces

In large bowl combine all ingredients except chocolate, nuts, crackers and chocolate pieces. Blend well. To half of dough in another bowl, add envelope of chocolate and nuts. Spread in a greased 13x9x2-inch pan. Arrange crackers over dough. Add chocolate pieces to remaining dough. Drop by tablespoon over crackers and spread carefully to cover. Bake at 350° for 25 to 30 minutes. Cool, then cut into bars.

Chocolate Raspberry Bars

Yields 4 dozen bars

2 cups all-purpose flour
1 cup sugar
1 cup butter or margarine
1 large egg, beaten
1 teaspoon almond extract

1 cup seedless red raspberry jam
1 (12-ounce) package semisweet
  chocolate chips
1 cup chopped unblanched
  almonds

Combine flour and sugar; mix well. Cut in butter until mixture resembles coarse crumbs. With fork, stir in beaten egg and almond extract until all ingredients are just moistened. Remove and set aside 1 cup dough. Press remaining dough into bottom of prepared pan. Spread jam evenly over dough to within ½ inch of edge. Combine reserved 1 cup dough, chocolate pieces and almonds; mix well. Sprinkle over jam and press lightly with fork. Bake in a greased 13x9x2-inch pan at 350° for 35 to 40 minutes or until top is golden. Cool pan on rack. While warm, cut into squares; cool in pan.

Apricot Squares

Yields 40

½ cup butter or margarine, softened
½ cup brown sugar, firmly packed

1¼ cups all-purpose flour

Combine ingredients and press into an ungreased 13x9x2-inch pan. Bake at 350° for 10 minutes. Spread with filling and bake 25 minutes or until pick inserted in center comes out clean. Cool and cut into squares. Will keep in airtight container in cool place for 2 weeks or longer time in freezer.

Filling:
2 eggs, beaten
1 cup brown sugar, firmly packed
1 cup chopped apricots
¾ cup flaked coconut
½ cup chopped pecans

3 tablespoons all-purpose flour
½ teaspoon vanilla
½ teaspoon lemon juice
¼ teaspoon salt

Blend all ingredients and spread over baked crust.

Blueberry Squares

Yields 12 to 15 squares

1 cup butter or margarine
2 cups sugar
Pinch of salt
4 eggs

3 cups all-purpose flour
1 teaspoon almond or orange extract
3 cups blueberries

Cream butter and sugar well. Add salt and eggs, 1 at a time, mixing well after each addition. Mix in flour and flavoring. Spread on ungreased cookie sheet. Cover dough with blueberries. Bake at 375° for ½ hour or until brown.

Marble Squares

Yields 15 to 20 squares
Everyone's favorite

1 (8-ounce) package cream cheese, softened
2⅓ cups sugar, divided
3 eggs, divided
½ cup butter or margarine
¾ cup water
1½ (1-ounce) unsweetened chocolate squares

2 cups all-purpose flour
½ cup sour cream
1 teaspoon baking soda
½ teaspoon salt
1 (6-ounce) package chocolate chips

Combine cream cheese and ⅓ cup sugar; mix well until blended. Add 1 egg, mix and set aside. Combine butter, water and chocolate squares in saucepan and melt over medium heat. Remove from heat. Stir in combined flour and remaining sugar; add remaining ingredients except chocolate chips and mix well. Pour into greased and floured 15x10x1-inch jellyroll pan or cake pan. Spoon cream cheese mixture over chocolate batter and cut through for marble effect. Sprinkle chocolate chips over and bake at 375° for 25 to 30 minutes or until knife inserted comes out clean. Best served cold.

Raw Sugar Brownies

Yields 12 to 15
Different texture, delicious

1 cup butter or margarine
2 cups raw sugar
4 eggs

4 ounces unsweetened chocolate
1 cup all-purpose flour
1 cup chopped nuts

Cream butter and sugar. Add remaining ingredients and spread in a 13x9x2-inch pan. Bake at 350° for 18 to 20 minutes.

Potato Chip Cookies

Yields about 4 dozen

1 cup butter or margarine
½ cup sugar
1¾ cups all-purpose flour
½ cup crushed potato chips

½ cup chopped nuts
1 teaspoon vanilla
1 cup chocolate chips (optional)

Cream butter and sugar together. Add flour, potato chips, nuts and vanilla; blend well. Stir in chocolate chips if desired. Bake on ungreased cookie sheet at 350° for 10 to 12 minutes. Dust with confectioners' sugar before serving.

Mondel Bread

Yields 3 dozen
Delicious with tea

1 cup sugar
1 cup vegetable oil
3 eggs
1 teaspoon vanilla extract
1 teaspoon almond extract
1 teaspoon lemon extract

3 to 3½ cups all-purpose flour
2 teaspoons baking powder
¼ teaspoon baking soda
½ teaspoon salt
¾ cup chopped walnuts
Cinnamon-sugar mixture

Mix sugar and oil; stir in eggs, 1 at a time. Mix in the flavorings. Add dry ingredients to creamed mixture and the nuts. Form dough into logs about 1-inch in diameter. Place on an ungreased cookie sheet. Bake at 350° for 25 minutes. Leave the oven on and remove cookies from oven. Slice them diagonally into 1-inch pieces; leave them in place on the sheet. Sprinkle with cinnamon-sugar mixture. Return to oven for 10 minutes. Remove cookies to cool on wire rack. Store in a covered container.

Peanut Delight

Yields 3 to 5 dozen
Yummy

3 cups crispy rice cereal
3 cups crunchy peanut butter

16 ounces dry roasted peanuts
1¼ pounds white chocolate

Combine first 3 ingredients in large bowl. Melt chocolate in microwave or top of double boiler. Pour chocolate over dry ingredients and mix until coated. Quickly spoon onto waxed paper in desired ball size. When hardened, store in airtight container.

Cherry Winks

Yields 60 cookies

2¼ cups all-purpose flour
1 cup sugar
2 teaspoons baking powder
½ teaspoon salt
¾ cup shortening
2 tablespoons milk
1 teaspoon vanilla
2 eggs

1 cup chopped pecans
1 cup chopped dates
⅓ cup chopped maraschino
  cherries
1 cup crushed corn flakes
About 15 maraschino cherries,
  quartered

In large mixer bowl combine dry ingredients, shortening, milk, vanilla and eggs. Blend well at low speed of mixer. Stir in nuts, dates and chopped cherries; mix well. Drop by rounded teaspoon onto ungreased cookie sheet; sprinkle with corn flakes and top with cherry quarter. Bake at 375° for 10 to 12 minutes.

Sour Cream Drop Cookies

Yields 5 dozen

3 eggs, beaten
1½ cups sugar
½ cup butter or margarine
1 cup sour cream
3½ cups sifted all-purpose flour
½ teaspoon baking powder

½ teaspoon baking soda
1 teaspoon grated lemon rind
1 teaspoon grated orange rind
1 teaspoon lemon extract
1 teaspoon orange extract
Cinnamon-sugar mixture

Combine eggs, sugar, butter and sour cream and mix thoroughly. Blend flour, baking powder, soda and grated rinds together. Stir into shortening mixture and add flavorings. Mix well. Drop dough by teaspoonfuls onto greased and floured cookie sheet. Sprinkle with cinnamon-sugar mixture. Bake at 400° for 10 to 12 minutes.

Fresh Strawberry Cookies

Yields 4 to 5 dozen
Fresh fruit in a cookie, wow!

2 cups unbleached flour
1 teaspoon baking soda
½ teaspoon salt
1 cup sugar or ¾ cup honey
½ cup vegetable oil
Water

1 egg, beaten
1 tablespoon lemon grated rind
¼ cup lemon juice
1½ cups minced fresh
    strawberries sprinkled with
    sugar

Combine first 4 ingredients together in a large bowl. Blend oil into flour mixture. Add water until dough is lying flat in bowl. Add remaining ingredients. If stirring is difficult, gradually add drops of water to soften somewhat, but dough should still be fairly stiff. Place rounded teaspoons of dough 2 inches apart on greased cookie sheet. Bake at 350° 10 to 12 minutes or until golden brown. Cool on wire racks.

Kay's Favorite Nut Cookies

Yields 4 dozen
Great crunch, not overly sweet, very satisfying

2 cups unbleached wheat flour
½ cup wheat bran
1 teaspoon baking soda
½ teaspoon salt

1 cup natural sugar
½ cup vegetable oil
Water
1½ cups sliced almonds

Mix first 5 ingredients together thoroughly without sifting. Add oil to flour mixture. Add enough water to dough until it is lying flat in the bowl, though still quite stiff. Fold in almonds. Place teaspoons of dough 2 inches apart on lightly greased cookie sheets. Bake at 350° for 10 to 12 minutes or until golden. Loosen on sheets to dry out.

Chocolate Chip Pudding Cookies

Yields 2 dozen
Delicious

2¼ cups all-purpose flour
1 teaspoon baking soda
1 cup butter or margarine,
    softened
¼ cup sugar
¾ cup light brown sugar, firmly
    packed

1 (3¾-ounce) package vanilla or
    chocolate flavor instant
    pudding mix
1 teaspoon vanilla extract
2 eggs
1 (6-ounce) package chocolate
    chips
1 cup chopped nuts

Mix flour with soda. Combine butter, sugars, pudding mix and vanilla. Beat until smooth. Beat in eggs; gradually add flour mixture, chips and nuts. Batter will be stiff. Bake on greased cookie sheets at 350° for 10 minutes. Cool on racks. Store in cookie jar.

Frosted Italian Cookies

Yields 3 dozen

¼ cup plus 2 tablespoons butter
    or margarine
2 cups sugar
4 eggs
1 tablespoon vanilla or lemon
    extract

6 cups all-purpose flour, divided
4 teaspoons baking powder
1 teaspoon baking soda
¼ teaspoon salt
2 cups sour cream

Cream butter, sugar and eggs with beater. Add flavoring and 4 cups flour, baking powder, soda and salt. Mix well. Add sour cream and beat well with electric mixer. Add remaining 2 cups flour and beat with a wooden spoon. Drop with teaspoon onto ungreased cookie sheet. Bake at 400° for 8 minutes. Frost when cool.

Frosting:
¼ cup milk (scalded)
Confectioners' sugar

Food coloring of your choice

Combine ingredients to desired spreading consistency.

Peanut Blossoms

Yields 4 dozen
Our holiday favorite

1¾ cups all-purpose flour
½ teaspoon salt
½ cup brown sugar, firmly
    packed
½ cup shortening
1 egg

1 teaspoon vanilla
1 teaspoon baking soda
½ cup sugar
½ cup peanut butter
2 tablespoons milk
48 milk chocolate candy kisses

Combine all ingredients, except candy, in large mixing bowl until dough forms. Shape into balls using rounded teaspoonful for each. Roll in sugar and place on ungreased cookie sheets. Bake at 350° for 10 to 12 minutes. Top each cookie immediately with unwrapped candy kiss after removal from oven. Press down firmly so cookie cracks around edge. Cool, then remove to rack.

Chocolate Drop Cookies

Yields 2 dozen

1 cup shortening
½ cup sugar
½ cup brown sugar, firmly
  packed
6 heaping teaspoons cocoa
1 egg, beaten

2 cups all-purpose flour
1 teaspoon salt
½ teaspoon baking soda
½ teaspoon baking powder
1 cup milk
1 teaspoon vanilla

Cream shortening and sugars. Add cocoa and egg. Combine dry ingredients and mix alternately with milk; add vanilla. Drop onto cookie sheet and bake at 350° for 12 to 15 minutes.

Almond Amaretto Parfait

Serves 8

Praline:
½ cup sugar
1 tablespoon water

1 cup sliced natural almonds,
  toasted

Mix sugar and water; cook over medium-low heat until water evaporates and sugar turns golden brown, about 5 minutes. Add almonds and stir until lightly coated. Immediately spread on buttered cookie sheet. Cool, then crush coarsely with rolling pin. Set aside.

Mousse Mixture:
1 (1-ounce) envelope unflavored
  gelatin
½ cup sugar
4 eggs, separated
1½ cups milk

½ cup Amaretto liqueur
Pinch of salt
1½ cups heavy cream

Mix gelatin and sugar in saucepan. Beat egg yolks and milk; add to gelatin mixture. Cook over low heat (do not boil), stirring constantly until gelatin is dissolved, about 5 minutes. Stir in Amaretto. Chill in large bowl, stirring occasionally until mixture mounds slightly when stirred, about 1 hour. Stir in praline. Beat egg whites and salt until stiff. Fold in gelatin mixture. Beat cream until soft peaks form. Fold in egg white mixture. Divide among eight (8-ounce) parfait glasses. Chill at least 3 hours. Decorate with whipped cream and toasted sliced almonds.

Apples Bonne Femme

Serves 6
Very easy and delectable treat

6 good-sized, firm apples
6 rounds toasted white bread,
  well-buttered
12 tablespoons firmly packed
  brown sugar, divided

12 tablespoons butter or
  margarine, divided
12 tablespoons honey, divided
Ground nutmeg
Whipped cream

Core, then peel ⅓ of the way down each apple. Place each apple on a round of toasted bread, well-buttered and sprinkled with 1 tablespoon brown sugar. Place 1 tablespoon brown sugar and 1 tablespoon butter into the center of each apple. Top with 2 tablespoons honey and another tablespoon butter and a pinch of nutmeg. Place apples in a well-buttered oven-proof dish and bake at 350° for 45 minutes to 1 hour, basting every 15 minutes with the pan juices. Add additional butter and sugar if necessary. Apples should be tender but not mushy. Serve warm with whipped cream.

Baked Apples with Nuts and Rum

Serves 6
Good with pork chops or ham

6 baking apples
½ cup chopped English walnuts
6 teaspoons honey

6 teaspoons butter or margarine
½ cup water
6 tablespoons Jamaican dark rum

Peel top ⅔ of each apple, core apple and place in baking dish. Place a few chopped nuts in each cavity along with 1 teaspoon each honey and butter. Pour water into baking dish. Cover with foil and bake at 350° for 35 minutes until apples are tender. Add 1 tablespoon rum to each cavity.

Chocolate Mint Desserts

Yields 24
Nice to have on hand for unexpected company

1 cup butter or margarine,
  softened
2 cups sifted confectioners' sugar
4 squares unsweetened chocolate,
  melted
4 eggs

¾ teaspoon peppermint extract
2 teaspoons vanilla
6 ounces whipped topping
1 cup vanilla wafer crumbs

Beat butter and sugar until light and fluffy. Add melted chocolate and continue beating until thoroughly mixed. Add eggs and beat until fluffy. Beat in flavorings. Add whipped topping and stir until well mixed. Divide half of crumbs evenly among 24 cupcake liners. Add scoop of filling to each and sprinkle with remainder of crumbs. Store in freezer until ready to serve. Additional whipped topping and/or maraschino cherry may be put on top when served.

Fruit Pizza   Easy—Too Sweet

Serves 8
Looks wonderful, takes only a short time to make, yet tastes like summertime

1 (16-ounce) roll refrigerated
  slice-and-bake sugar cookie
  dough
1 (8-ounce) package cream cheese,
  softened
⅓ cup sugar
½ teaspoon vanilla

Fruit of your choice (bananas,
  blueberries, peaches,
  strawberries, etc.)
¾ cup peach, orange, or apricot
  preserves
1 tablespoon water

Cut dough into ⅛-inch slices. Arrange in 14-inch pizza pan. Bake at 375° for 12 minutes. Combine cream cheese, sugar and vanilla. Spread on cooled cookie dough. Arrange fruit over crust. Spoon preserves–water mixture over fruit; chill.

Chocolate Ladyfingers

Serves 8
Our family's favorite dessert

2 (4-ounce) packages ladyfingers	2 eggs, separated
1 (6-ounce) package semi-sweet chocolate chips	1 teaspoon vanilla
	2 cups heavy cream
4 tablespoons sugar, divided	Shaved chocolate or chocolate
2 tablespoons water	shot

Cut ladyfingers apart 2 by 2 and split horizontally for 8 portions. Lay out ⅓ of ladyfingers, cut side up on a serving plate. Melt chocolate chips in top of a double boiler over hot water. Add and mix well 2 tablespoons sugar, water, egg yolks and vanilla. Beat egg whites with 1 tablespoon sugar to meringue consistency. Add to chocolate paste and mix well. Spoon ½ of the chocolate mixture (when smooth) over first layer of ladyfingers. Arrange next layer of ladyfingers on top, cut side up. Spoon rest of chocolate mixture over this layer. Top with last ladyfingers, cut side down. Beat heavy cream until stiff. Sweeten with remaining 1 tablespoon sugar and a dash of vanilla. Top the 8 desserts with the divided whipped cream. Sprinkle with shaved chocolate or chocolate shot. Chill at least 3 hours.

Flan

Serves 1

1 cup sugar	2 cans water
1 teaspoon water	6 eggs, beaten
2 (14-ounce) cans sweetened condensed milk	1 teaspoon vanilla
	Pinch of salt

In an aluminum tube pan on top of range melt sugar with the teaspoon water sprinkled over sugar. Stir until golden brown; set aside to cool. Combine remaining ingredients until well beaten. Put through strainer, then pour into pan with carmel coating. Bake at 350° for 1 to 1½ hours. Check with knife–if comes out clean, flan is done. Cool several hours in refrigerator.

Grapenut Custard

Serves 6 to 8
Wintertime treat

⅓ cup grapenuts (not flakes)
2 cups milk, divided
¼ cup sugar
2 tablespoons maple syrup
½ teaspoon vanilla

¼ teaspoon almond extract
¼ teaspoon salt
¼ teaspoon nutmeg
2 eggs, slightly beaten

Put grapenuts in a greased 1-quart casserole dish. Heat thoroughly, but do not boil, 1 cup milk and pour over the grapenuts. Let stand. Add all other ingredients to beaten eggs and stir well. Pour this mixture over the grapenuts and stir. Place casserole in a larger pan that has been lined with brown paper. Fill the pan with hot water so that water surrounds the casserole. Bake at 325° for 50 minutes or until done. Stir mixture 2 or 3 times during the first half hour.

Brides Pudding

Serves 8 to 10
May be prepared in advance and refrigerated or frozen until served, light German dessert

2 envelopes unflavored gelatin
½ cup cold water
⅓ cup boiling water
6 egg whites, at room temperature
½ teaspoon salt

¾ cup sugar
2 cups heavy cream, whipped
1 teaspoon vanilla
1 (7-ounce) can flaked coconut
1 (12-ounce) package frozen
   strawberries

Soften gelatin in cold water. Pour boiling water into it, stir, then cool. Beat egg whites with salt, gradually beating in sugar until mixture holds stiff peaks. Slowly beat in gelatin at low speed of mixer. Fold in whipped cream and vanilla. Generously butter a 10-inch tube pan or springform pan. Sprinkle generously with coconut. Pour mixture into pan. Chill 4 hours. Unmold, cut into serving wedges and serve with sliced strawberries. Garnish with holly for the holidays!

Note: A double recipe fills a 10-inch tube pan.

Lemon Lush

Serves 10 to 12
Great anytime but especially in summer. Pistachio or chocolate pudding substitutes

First Layer:
¾ cup butter or margarine
1½ cups all-purpose flour

1½ cups chopped nuts

Blend butter and flour well and add nuts. Spread in bottom of a 13x9x2-inch pan. Bake at 350° for 20 minutes; cool and set aside.

Second Layer:
1 cup confectioners' sugar
1 (8-ounce) package cream cheese,
   softened

1 cup whipped topping (use only
   1 cup from 12-ounce container,
   reserve rest)

Mix all well; spread over cooled first layer.

Third Layer:
2 (3¾-ounce) packages lemon
   flavor instant pudding mix

3 cups milk
Chopped nuts

Beat pudding with milk for 2 minutes or until thickened. Pour over second layer and top with remaining whipped topping. Garnish with nuts and refrigerate. May be made a day ahead.

In 1845, the first cutlery factory for the manufacture of pocket cutlery was established in Lakeville.

Heavenly Lemon Cream

Serves 15
Luscious dessert but keep it cool on a hot day

4 cups crushed coconut
   macaroons (crisp type), divided
1½ cups sugar
9 tablespoons lemon juice

3 cups heavy cream, whipped
6 eggs, separated
¼ teaspoon salt

Line bottom of ungreased 13x9x2-inch pan with 2½ cups crumbs; set aside. Dissolve sugar in lemon juice and stir thoroughly. Whip cream and set aside. Beat egg yolks with salt. Add to lemon mixture and beat well until thick and creamy. Fold in whipped cream. Beat egg whites until stiff and fold into mixture. Pour into prepared pan. Top with remaining crumbs. Wrap and freeze. Thaw in refrigerator 2 to 3 hours before serving.

Pineapple Cherry Charlotte

Serves 12
A special dessert

20 ladyfingers
1 tablespoon unflavored gelatin
¼ cup cold water
½ cup boiling water
1 cup sugar
Dash of salt

¾ cup canned pineapple juice
2 tablespoons lemon juice
2 cups heavy cream
7 or 8 pineapple slices
¼ cup chopped maraschino
   cherries, drained

Line bottom and side of a 9-inch springform pan with split ladyfingers. Soften gelatin in cold water; add boiling water, stirring until dissolved. Mix sugar, salt, juices together; stir until sugar is dissolved. Add gelatin and chill mixture until it begins to thicken to a syrupy consistency. Whip cream; fold into gelatin mixture. Pour ½ mixture into prepared pan. Arrange pineapple slices and cherries on first layer of gelatin mixture. Cover with remaining mixture. Refrigerate until firm.

Cranberry Refrigerator Dessert

Serves 12
A little effort, but well worth the time. It's become our Thanksgiving tradition

2 cups (½ pound) fresh or frozen
  cranberries, chopped
1 large banana, diced
1½ cups sugar, divided
2 cups vanilla wafer crumbs

1 cup butter, divided
2 eggs
½ cup chopped walnuts
1 cup heavy cream, whipped

In a bowl mix together cranberries, banana and ½ cup sugar; set aside. In another bowl mix together crumbs and ½ cup melted butter. Press half the mixture into bottom of a 9-inch square pan. In a small bowl cream remaining butter and sugar until light; add eggs and beat until fluffy. Fold in nuts and spread mixture over crumb layer. Top with fruit mixture and remaining crumb mixture. Refrigerate several hours before serving with a dollop of whipped cream on top.

Cranberry Sorbet

Serves 6 to 8
What a hit with a Thanksgiving or Christmas turkey dinner

1 cup water
½ cup sugar

1 (16-ounce) can cranberry sauce
Juice of 1 lemon

In saucepan combine water and sugar. Bring to a boil and let boil for a few minutes, then chill. Mix syrup with cranberry sauce; puree until smooth. Add lemon juice; freeze. When almost frozen, remove and blend in food processor or electric blender until smooth. Freeze again and repeat blending. Freeze once more to improve texture.

Lemon Sherbet

Serves 8
A cool, light dessert

3 eggs, separated
½ cup sugar
2 teaspoons grated lemon rind

¼ cup lemon juice
1 cup heavy cream, whipped
¾ cup graham cracker crumbs

Beat egg yolks until thick and lemon colored. Gradually beat in sugar. Add lemon rind and juice. Fold in cream and stiffly beaten egg whites. Cover bottom of a 13x9x2-inch dish with ½ cup graham cracker crumbs. Pour in sherbet mixture. Top with remaining crumbs. Freeze until firm.

Nut Kuchen

Serves 10 to 12
Great for the holidays

1 cup butter or margarine
2 cups sugar
5 eggs, separated
3 cups all-purpose flour

4 teaspoons baking powder
1 cup milk
10 maraschino cherries, chopped
¾ cup chopped walnuts
Confectioners' sugar

Cream butter and sugar. Add 1 egg yolk at a time, beating after each. Add flour sifted with baking powder alternately with milk. Add cherries and nuts. Add stiffly beaten egg whites. Bake in a greased and floured tube pan at 350° for 1 hour. Remove and sprinkle with confectioners' sugar. May be made 2 or 3 days before serving.

Grandma's Apple Kuchen

Serves 10
Brought from my grandma's home in southern Germany

Pastry for 13x9x2-inch pan
8 to 10 apples, peeled and sliced
2 tablespoons instant tapioca
Cinnamon
Grated rind of 1 lemon
½ teaspoon salt
3 eggs, separated

Pinch of cream of tartar
1 (8-ounce) carton cottage cheese
2 tablespoons all-purpose flour
Pinch of baking soda
1¼ cups sugar
Juice of 1 lemon
1 teaspoon vanilla

Lay pastry in a 13x9x2-inch pan. Sprinkle next 4 ingredients over bottom of pastry and top with apple slices. Bake at 350° for 15 minutes. Whip egg whites with cream of tartar and set aside in a cool place.
Add cottage cheese, flour, soda, sugar, lemon juice and dash of salt to the yolks. Beat at medium speed of mixer for 5 minutes. Add vanilla and fold in whites. Remove pan from oven and spread on topping. Bake 15 minutes longer. Reduce heat to 300° and bake 30 minutes more. Serve with whipped cream.

Tea Time Tarts

Yields 24 tarts

½ (8-ounce) package cream cheese
11 tablespoons butter or
    margarine, divided
1 cup all-purpose flour
Finely ground nuts

1 cup brown sugar, firmly packed
1 egg
1 teaspoon vanilla

Mix cream cheese, ½ cup butter and flour together. Divide into 24 balls and mold into miniature muffin tins. Put ½ teaspoon fine nuts into each well. Mix brown sugar, egg, remaining 3 tablespoons butter and vanilla together. Beat and pour over the nuts. Bake at 350° for 25 to 30 minutes.

English Raspberry Trifle

Serves 8 to 10
So easy and when you hear the compliments, you'll wonder why you hadn't tried it sooner

1 envelope English-style custard
  mix
2 cups milk
3 tablespoons sugar
1 (16-ounce) commercially
  prepared pound cake
1 (18-ounce) jar raspberry
  preserves

1 (12 or 16-ounce) package frozen
  raspberries, thawed, drained
  and juice reserved
1 cup sliced almonds
¾ cup Amaretto liqueur
Whipped cream

Prepare custard according to package directions with the 2 cups milk and sugar; refrigerate promptly. Slice pound cake into ¼-inch slices. Make sandwiches filled with raspberry preserves in equal thickness to the slices. Line a large, clear glass bowl with sandwiches on bottom and up the sides in a single thickness. Cut and fit to cover all areas. If there are sandwiches left, save them for the top. When custard is cool, stir in raspberries (may save a few for garnish) and almonds (save some for garnish). Splash cake slices liberally with raspberry juice and Amaretto. Pour custard into cake-lined bowl. Refrigerate overnight. Just before serving, cover top of trifle with whipped cream and garnish with reserved berries and almonds. Scoop down deeply with a spoon to serve making sure you get cake and custard.

Note: If you have leftover sandwiches, break them up and scatter a few across top, but don't make a solid cover.

In 1775, the first American warship, the "Oliver Cromwell" was built at Essex.

Tipsy Turtle Torte

Serves 16
Very rich–very good

Crust:

1½ cups shortbread cookie
  crumbs
¼ cup brown sugar, firmly
  packed

¼ teaspoon ground nutmeg
¼ cup butter or margarine,
  melted

Lightly butter sides of a 10-inch springform pan; line sides with strips of waxed paper; butter the bottom and paper-lined sides of pan. In small bowl mix crumbs, sugar and nutmeg; stir in melted butter. Pat evenly on bottom of pan; refrigerate.

First Layer:

1 quart butter pecan ice cream
¾ cup Irish cream, divided

1 (12-ounce) jar caramel ice cream
  topping
1 cup coarsely chopped pecans,
  toasted and divided

Spoon slightly softened ice cream into medium bowl and swirl in ½ cup Irish cream. (Do not overmix!) Pack into chilled crust. Pour caramel topping into small bowl and stir in 2 tablespoons Irish cream. Spoon over butter pecan layer; sprinkle with ¾ cup pecans. Freeze 1 hour.

Second Layer:

1 quart chocolate ice cream

1 (12-ounce) jar fudge ice cream
  topping

Spread slightly softened chocolate ice cream on top of frozen first layer. Pour fudge topping into small bowl and stir in remaining 2 tablespoons Irish cream. Spoon over chocolate ice cream. Cover with foil and freeze until firm, about 6 hours or overnight. Remove sides of pan; peel off waxed paper. Place bottom of springform pan on serving plate; garnish top with remaining ¼ cup pecans. Let torte stand 10 minutes before slicing.

Chocolate Pistachio Torte

Serves 12
A child's dream

1 (15-ounce) package chocolate
sandwich cookies, crushed
⅓ cup butter or margarine,
melted
2 (3¾-ounce) packages pistachio
flavor instant pudding mix
1½ cups milk

2 drops green food color
(optional)
1 quart vanilla ice cream,
softened
1 (8-ounce) container frozen non-
dairy whipped topping,
thawed

Mix together cookie crumbs and butter. Pat ⅔ of crumbs into a 13x9x2-inch dish; set aside. Reserve the remaining crumbs for the top. Beat together the pudding, milk and food color until very thick. Add softened ice cream and beat together until well blended. Pour pudding mixture over the crumbs. Spread whipped topping over the pudding mixture and top with remaining crumbs. Refrigerate overnight.

Bavarian Apple Torte

Serves 12 to 15

1 cup butter or margarine
⅔ cup sugar

½ teaspoon vanilla extract
2 cups all-purpose flour

Cream together the butter, sugar and vanilla. Blend in flour. Spread dough on bottom and up sides of a greased 9-inch springform pan.

Filling:
1 (8-ounce) package cream cheese
¼ cup plus ⅓ cup sugar, divided
½ teaspoon vanilla
1 egg

4 cups apples, peeled and sliced
½ teaspoon cinnamon
¼ cup sliced almonds

Combine cream cheese and ¼ cup sugar. Blend well, then add vanilla and egg. Pour into prepared shell. Combine apples with remaining sugar and cinnamon and toss. Spoon apples over cheese filling. Sprinkle with almonds. Bake at 450° for 10 minutes, then reduce heat to 400° and bake 25 minutes longer.

Truffles

Yields 36 truffles
Great for Christmas

1 (12-ounce) package semi-sweet
   chocolate chips
¾ cup sweetened condensed milk
1 teaspoon vanilla

⅛ teaspoon salt
½ cup cocoa or 1 cup chopped,
   flaked coconut

In double boiler over hot, not boiling, water, melt chocolate chips. Stir in condensed milk, vanilla and salt until well mixed. Refrigerate mixture about 45 minutes or until easy to shape. With buttered hands, shape mixture into 1-inch balls. Roll balls in cocoa or coconut.

Fudge Meltaways

Yields 3 to 4 dozen
They melt in your mouth

¾ cup butter or margarine,
   divided
4 (1-ounce) squares unsweetened
   chocolate, divided
¼ cup sugar
2 teaspoons vanilla extract,
   divided

1 egg, beaten
2 cups graham cracker crumbs
1 cup coconut
½ cup chopped walnuts
1 tablespoon milk or cream
2 cups sifted confectioners' sugar

Melt ½ cup butter and 1 square of chocolate in saucepan. Blend in sugar, 1 teaspoon vanilla, egg, crumbs, coconut and nuts. Mix well and press into ungreased 12x8x2-inch or 9-inch square baking dish; refrigerate. Mix remaining ¼ cup butter, milk, confectioners' sugar and remaining 1 teaspoon vanilla. Spread over crumb mixture and chill. Melt remaining chocolate and spread over chilled filling. Cut before firm.

Oven Caramel Corn

Yields 15 cups
Great snack

3¾ quarts (15 cups) popped corn
1 cup brown sugar, firmly packed
½ cup butter or margarine

¼ cup light corn syrup
½ teaspoon salt
½ teaspoon baking soda

Divide popped corn between 2 greased 13x9x2-inch baking pans. In saucepan heat sugar, butter, corn syrup and salt, stirring occasionally until bubbly around edges. Continue cooking over medium heat for 5 minutes. Remove from heat; stir in soda until foamy. Pour into popped corn, stirring until corn is well coated. Bake at 200° for 1 hour, stirring every 15 minutes.

In 1779, the first British prize, the sloop "Hero," was captured by the Wethersfield sloop "Enterprise."

Microwave & Lo-Cal

Crab Canapes

Serves 10 to 12 Yields 20
Shrimp may be substituted

1 (6½-ounce) can crabmeat, rinsed
  and drained
½ cup mayonnaise
¼ cup shredded Cheddar cheese
2 tablespoons chopped green
  onion

1 teaspoon horseradish
1 teaspoon catsup
½ teaspoon Worcestershire sauce
20 Melba toast rounds

In small bowl mix all ingredients except Melba rounds. (Better to prepare several hours ahead so flavors may blend.) Spread evenly on Melba rounds; place on paper towel-lined plate. Microwave on Medium-High for 1½ to 2 minutes until cheese melts. Serve immediately.

Microwave Chicken Stock

Yields 1 quart
Great base for soups, etc.

2 pounds chicken backs, necks,
  wing tips and other scraps
  and bones
1 small onion, chopped
1 medium carrot, sliced

1 cup chopped celery tops
  and leaves
6 peppercorns
1 bay leaf
6 parsley sprigs

Put all ingredients plus 2 quarts water in a 3-quart microwaveproof container; cover with a lid or plastic wrap and microwave on High for 60 minutes. Allow to cool and remove fat. Strain stock and freeze in ice cube trays or small freezer containers. Thaw and use as needed for soups, stews, gravies, etc.

German Potato Supper

Serves 4
May serve without meat or with cooked Kielbasa or Italian sausage

4 medium potatoes, pared
½ teaspoon salt
1¼ cups water, divided
4 slices bacon
½ cup chopped onion
¼ cup sugar
2 tablespoon all-purpose flour
½ teaspoon dill seed

¼ teaspoon dried thyme,
   crumbled
⅛ teaspoon dry mustard
Pinch of pepper
⅓ cup white wine vinegar
¼ cup dry white wine
4 smoked bratwurst or
   knockwurst

Cut potatoes into ¾-inch cubes. Combine with ¾ cup salted water in 2-quart casserole with lid. Microwave, covered, on High until potatoes are fork tender, 9 to 12 minutes; drain potatoes. Microwave bacon on paper towels on High 3 to 4 minutes (a little underdone). Let stand, covered, 5 minutes to complete cooking. Remove bacon; save drippings. Stir onions into 2 tablespoons drippings and microwave on High for 1½ to 2½ minutes until onions are tender. Add sugar, flour, dill seed, thyme, mustard and pepper. Stir until no lumps remain. Stir in vinegar, wine and remaining ½ cup water into onion mixture. Microwave, uncovered, on High until mixture thickens, 4 to 6 minutes. Stir 3 times during cooking. Crumble bacon and add. Gently stir in potatoes. Pierce each sausage in 2 places with fork to prevent bursting. Arrange on top of potato salad. Microwave, uncovered, at High until sausages are hot, 5½ to 7 minutes. Rearrange sausage after about ½ the cooking time.

In 1799, Simeon North, of Berlin, was the first official pistol manufacturer for the United States Government.

Japanese Chicken

Serves 4
Must be prepared the night before

¾ cup soy sauce
½ cup sugar
½ teaspoon ground ginger
½ teaspoon garlic powder

2 tablespoons catsup
2 to 3 pounds broiler/fryer
  chicken pieces

In small mixing bowl combine all ingredients except chicken; mix well.
Place chicken pieces in a 13x9x2-inch pan or large plastic food storage bag.
Pour sauce over chicken; cover or seal tightly. Refrigerate for about 24
hours, turning pieces frequently. In casserole combine chicken and sauce.
Microwave at High for about 15 minutes. Reduce power to Medium-High
and microwave for about 20 minutes longer or until juices run clear and
meat near bone is no longer pink.

Chicken Stroganoff

Serves 6
Easy company supper

1 large onion, chopped
1 tablespoon vegetable oil
1 tablespoon prepared mustard
1 (8-ounce) can tomato sauce
1 (4-ounce) can mushroom stems
  and pieces, drained

3 whole chicken breasts, halved,
  skinned and boned
½ cup sour cream
2 tablespoons minced fresh
  parsley

In 4-cup glass measure, combine onion and oil. Microwave on High for 6
minutes or until onion is transparent. Stir in mustard, tomato sauce,
mushrooms and set aside. Place chicken in shallow 1½-quart microwave-
safe casserole. Spoon tomato sauce over chicken. Cover with plastic
wrap. Cook on High for 14 minutes. Rearrange chicken and cook on High
for 13 to 15 minutes. Use slotted spoon to remove chicken to a warmed
serving platter. Stir sour cream into tomato sauce. Cook at Simmer for 2
to 3 minutes or until hot. Pour over chicken. Sprinkle with parsley and
serve. Serve with noodles or rice if desired. Cooking time 35 to 38
minutes.

Chicken Ranchero

Serves 4 to 6
Great for picnic or any company, easy and quick

¾ cup tomato sauce
1 small onion, finely chopped
2 tablespoons finely chopped
  celery
¼ cup brown sugar, firmly
  packed
¼ cup cider vinegar
1 tablespoon light corn syrup

1 tablespoon Worcestershire sauce
1 teaspoon dry mustard
1 clove garlic, minced
½ teaspoon salt
¼ teaspoon paprika
¼ teaspoon ground cumin
1 (3-pound) broiler/fryer chicken,
  cut into 8 parts

Combine all ingredients except chicken in 4-cup measure or 1-quart casserole; mix well. Microwave, covered, on High for 3 minutes until hot. Stir once while cooking. Microwave, covered, at Medium for 12 to 15 minutes until onion is soft; stir every 3 minutes during cooking. In a 13x9x2-inch pan arrange chicken with thickest portion toward outside; brush with sauce. Cover with waxed paper and microwave on High for 9 minutes. Rotate dish ½ turn halfway through cooking time. Rearrange chicken pieces in dish so less-cooked portions are toward outside. Brush chicken again with sauce. Microwave, covered, at High for 8 to 14 minutes until chicken is cooked through (no pink near bone) and tender. Rotate dish ½ turn after about ½ the cooking time. Brush chicken with any remaining sauce. Serve.

Lemon Chicken

Serves 4
165 calories, 75 mg. cholesterol

1 (½-ounce) envelope natural
  butter flavored mix
2 tablespoons lemon juice
1 teaspoon lemon pepper

2 whole boneless, skinless
  chicken breasts, halved
2 teaspoons parsley flakes
  (optional)

Combine butter mix, lemon juice and lemon pepper. Roll chicken breasts and place in small casserole. Cover with lemon-butter mixture; cover with waxed paper. Microwave on High 3 minutes. Turn dish (if no revolving turntable) then microwave on High another 2 to 4 minutes until chicken is opaque and tender. Sprinkle with parsley flakes if desired and serve.

Chicken Asparagus Rolls

Serves 4
245 calories per serving, 75 mg. cholesterol

¼ teaspoon garlic powder
¼ teaspoon rosemary
2 whole skinless, boneless
chicken breasts, halved and
pounded to flatten
2 (1-ounce) slices mozzarella
cheese, halved

1 (10-ounce) package frozen
asparagus spears, thawed
and drained
¼ teaspoon paprika
2 teaspoons grated Parmesan
cheese

Combine garlic powder and rosemary; sprinkle over chicken. Lay ½ slice cheese on each piece. Top with 4 asparagus spears. Roll up chicken; fasten with toothpicks. Sprinkle paprika on all sides of chicken rolls. Place, seam side down, in a 12x8x2-inch baking dish. Cover with waxed paper; microwave on High 3 minutes. Turn and rearrange chicken rolls. Sprinkle with Parmesan, cover and microwave on High 2 to 4 minutes until chicken is tender.

Microwave Chili

Serves 4

1 pound extra lean ground beef
1 large onion, chopped
1 clove garlic, minced
1 green pepper, chopped
1 tablespoon vegetable oil
1 (28-ounce) can tomatoes,
chopped

1 (15-ounce) can red kidney beans
2 or 3 tablespoons chili powder
2 teaspoons sugar
¼ teaspoon ground cumin

Microwave ground beef in covered bowl 4 or 5 minutes; drain. Place onion, pepper, garlic and oil in 2½ or 3-quart microwave-safe casserole. Cover with waxed paper and cook on High for 2 to 3 minutes. Stir in beef, tomatoes, beans, chili powder, sugar and cumin. Cover and cook 10 to 12 minutes on High, stirring after 5 minutes. May substitute 2 cups catsup for tomatoes and sugar.

Stuffed Shrimp

Serves 2

8 fresh, jumbo shrimp (about ½ pound), shelled
2 tablespoons butter or margarine
1 (6½-ounce) can crabmeat, drained and cartilage removed
2 tablespoons fine dry breadcrumbs
2 tablespoons snipped fresh parsley
2 teaspoons fresh lemon juice
⅛ teaspoon salt
⅛ teaspoon cayenne pepper
Paprika
Lemon wedges

To butterfly and devein shrimp, make a cut down middle of back from tail to thick end, cutting almost all the way through. With point of knife, loosen and remove vein. Arrange shrimp, cut-side up, on bacon/meat rack, tails toward center. Spread cut-side open. Place butter in mixing bowl; melt butter in microwave. Stir in crabmeat, breadcrumbs, parsley, lemon juice, salt and cayenne. Divide stuffing evenly on top of shrimp. Cover with waxed paper. Place rack with shrimp in oven and microwave at Medium for 5 to 7 minutes or until shrimp are opaque. Garnish with paprika and lemon wedges.

Special Fish

Serves 2 to 3

1 pound fresh fish fillets or frozen fillets, thawed
Dash of pepper
1 small sweet onion, thinly sliced
1 large tomato, thinly sliced
1 (4-ounce) can sliced mushrooms, drained
Juice of ½ lemon
⅔ cup shredded Cheddar or Swiss cheese
Paprika (optional)

Arrange fillets in a single layer in a 10x6x2-inch oblong microwave-safe dish. Sprinkle with pepper; layer onion, tomato and mushrooms over fish. Pour lemon juice over all; cover. Microwave at High 4 to 5 minutes or until fish flakes. Turn dish halfway around after 2 minutes. Sprinkle cheese over fish mixture. Cook another 2 minutes or until cheese is melted. Sprinkle lightly with paprika before serving.

Shrimp and Vegetable Mandarin

Serves 3 to 4
Easy company dish

1 (11-ounce) can mandarin
 oranges, drained and liquid
 reserved
2 (¼-ounce) envelopes instant
 chicken broth
1½ tablespoons cornstarch
⅛ teaspoon garlic powder
1 pound medium shrimp, shelled
 and cleaned

1 bunch green onions, thinly
 sliced
1 (6-ounce) package frozen
 Chinese pea pods, thawed
1 (4-ounce) jar sliced mushrooms,
 drained
Slivered almonds

To reserve orange liquid add enough water to equal 1½ cups. In a 2-quart
casserole dish, combine liquid, broth, cornstarch and garlic. Heat 3½ to
4½ minutes on High until mixture is thickened; stir twice. Stir in shrimp,
onions, pea pods and mushrooms. Heat, covered, 2 minutes on High.
Continue cooking on Medium–High an additional 5 to 6 minutes until
shrimp is tender, stirring once. Stir in oranges and almonds and let stand,
covered, for 5 minutes before serving. Serve over rice.

Sukiyaki

Serves 4 to 6

1½ to 2 pounds beef sirloin steak,
 cut into thin strips
½ cup soy sauce
½ cup water
3 tablespoons sugar
1 (5-ounce) can water chestnuts,
 drained and sliced

1 (5-ounce) can bamboo shoots,
 drained
1 (16-ounce) can bean sprouts,
 drained
1 (4-ounce) can mushroom stems
 and pieces
½ cup sliced green onion

Combine steak, soy sauce, water and sugar in 2-quart glass baking dish.
Cover with plastic wrap and marinate 3 to 4 hours at room temperature.
Place remaining ingredients in rows across meat and sauce with mush-
rooms and onion in center rows. Microwave on High for 10 to 12 minutes.
Let stand, covered, for 2 minutes before serving.

Broccoli and Cauliflower Ring

Serves 6 to 8

1 small tomato, cut into 6 wedges
   and seeded
4 cups fresh broccoli flowerets
4 cups fresh cauliflowerets
¼ cup water

¼ cup butter or margarine
1 tablespoon fresh lemon juice
¼ teaspoon salt
⅛ teaspoon pepper

In microwave-safe bundt pan arrange tomato wedges, skin side down, evenly on bottom; set aside. Place broccoli and cauliflower in 3-quart casserole. Sprinkle water over vegetables, cover and microwave at High 9 to 13 minutes or until vegetables are tender-crisp, stirring after half the time; drain. Arrange vegetables over tomatoes in bundt pan pressing to pack firmly; set aside. Place butter in 1-cup measure and microwave on High for 45 to 60 seconds or until melted. Blend in lemon juice, salt and pepper. Pour over vegetables. Place pan or rotating microwave dish. Microwave molded vegetables at High for 3 minutes. Invert onto serving plate.

Cauliflower Au Gratin

Serves 4 to 6

1 medium sized head cauliflower
   (about 1 pound)
2 tablespoons butter or margarine
2 tablespoons all-purpose flour
¼ teaspoon lemon pepper

¼ teaspoon dry mustard
1 cup milk
1 cup shredded sharp Cheddar
   cheese

Remove outer leaves from cauliflower and trim stem close to base. Wash and place cauliflower on a 9-inch pie plate. Cover with plastic wrap and microwave on High 6 to 8 minutes. Let stand, covered, while making cheese sauce. Melt butter 1 minute on High. Blend in flour and seasonings. Stir in milk and microwave on High 2 to 3 minutes or until thickened, stirring every minute. Add cheese and stir to blend. Place cauliflower on serving plate and pour sauce over top. Serve at once.

Note: For quick variation use 1 (8-ounce) jar pasteurized processed cheese spread and heat according to directions on jar.

Zucchini Boats

Serves 4

1 slice bacon
2 medium zucchini, scrubbed
(about 1 pound)
⅓ cup finely chopped Spanish or
yellow onion
1 tablespoon olive oil
1 small clove garlic, minced
½ cup seeded coarsely chopped
fresh tomato
½ cup chopped mushrooms

⅓ cup dry unseasoned
breadcrumbs
1 tablespoon grated Parmesan
cheese
¼ teaspoon dried oregano,
crumbled
½ teaspoon dried basil, crumbled
¼ teaspoon salt
Pinch of cayenne pepper

Place bacon on double thickness of paper toweling; fold toweling over bacon. Microwave at High until slightly underdone, about 45 to 60 seconds. Let stand 5 minutes, covered, to finish cooking. Crumble bacon and set aside. Cut zucchini lengthwise in half. Scoop out centers of zucchini, leaving ¼-inch shells. Chop zucchini pulp coarsely. Combine onion, oil, garlic in medium bowl. Microwave, uncovered, at High until onion is tender, 1½ to 2½ minutes. Add tomato, mushrooms, breadcrumbs, cheese, seasonings, bacon and zucchini pulp; mix well. Spoon mixture into zucchini shells mounding slightly. Arrange evenly spaced in 12x8x2-inch dish. Microwave, uncovered, at High 6 to 8 minutes until shells are tender. If no rotating shelf in microwave, turn dish ½ turn after half cooking time.

In 1767, 22-year-old Seth Dexter began his clothier business in Windsor Locks.

Spinach Surprise

Serves 4
A great side dish and good for you

1 (10-ounce) package frozen
  chopped spinach
2 eggs, beaten
1 teaspoon grated Parmesan
  cheese

2 slices American, Swiss or
  provolone cheese

Cook spinach and drain well. Mix eggs and spinach; fold in Parmesan. Mix well in greased 8-inch pie plate. Microwave on High about 5 minutes or until eggs set. Cut the cheese slices in small squares and cover the spinach. Microwave 1 to 2 minutes longer until cheese melts. Cut into wedges to serve.

Yellow Squash Casserole

Serves 6 to 8
Tasty

1 pound yellow squash, sliced
1 medium onion, chopped
1 medium carrot, grated
1 (10¾-ounce) can condensed
  cream of chicken soup
2 eggs, beaten
1 cup shredded sharp Cheddar
  cheese

¼ cup butter or margarine
¼ teaspoon salt
¼ teaspoon pepper
½ (8-ounce) package seasoned
  breadcrumbs

Microwave squash, onion and carrot of High for 6 to 8 minutes until tender. Drain and add soup, eggs, cheese, butter, salt and pepper. Cover tightly with plastic wrap and cook for 6 to 8 minutes on High. Add crumbs to the top of casserole and cook, uncovered, 1 to 2 additional minutes.

Vegetable Bake

Serves 4 to 6

¼ cup butter or margarine
1½ cups sliced summer squash
1 (10-ounce) package frozen
  broccoli cuts, thawed
1 egg
½ cup shredded Swiss cheese

¼ cup milk
1 teaspoon salt
1 teaspoon dry mustard
3 tablespoons grated Parmesan
  cheese

Place butter in a 1½-quart casserole. Microwave on High until butter melts. Stir in vegetables to coat with butter. Cover and microwave 6 to 8 minutes on High until tender. Beat egg and mix in cheese, milk, salt and mustard. Pour over vegetables. Sprinkle with Parmesan. Microwave 4 minutes on Medium or until cheese melts.

Poached Pears

Serves 4

½ cup water
½ cup cranberry juice cocktail
2 tablespoons honey
1 stick cinnamon, broken into
  small pieces

2 whole cloves
1 thin slice ginger root
4 thin slices orange rind
4 medium pears

In a 2-quart microwave casserole combine water, juice, honey and spices. Add orange rind. Microwave, covered, on High for 4 to 6 minutes or until boiling. Meanwhile, core pears leaving stems intact. Peel pears and add to hot juice mixture. Microwave, covered, on High 4 to 6 minutes or until fruit is tender. Rearrange fruit once during cooking, basting with liquid. Transfer fruit and liquid to individual dessert dishes; garnish with orange rind if desired. Serve warm or chilled.

Chocolate Cherry Cake

Yields 1 bundt cake
Serves 8 to 10

About ½ cup cinnamon-sugar mix
½ cup chopped walnuts
1 (18.5-ounce) package chocolate
  fudge cake mix

2 eggs
2 tablespoons vegetable oil
1 (21-ounce) can cherry pie filling

Grease a 12 to 14-cup non-metallic bundt pan; sprinkle with cinnamon-sugar mix and a layer of chopped walnuts. Mix together remaining ingredients; pour into bundt pan. Microwave at Medium-High for 8 minutes. Turn dish ¼ turn and microwave 10 to 12 minutes more. Let stand 10 minutes; turn onto serving dish. Top with frosting.

Chocolate Pudding Frosting:
¾ cup whole milk
3 tablespoons chocolate chips

1 tablespoon cornstarch
1 tablespoon sugar

In a 2-cup measure combine milk and chocolate chips. Cook on High for 1½ minutes. Stir then add sugar and cornstarch. Cook on High for 30 seconds; stir. Cook on High for 30 seconds. Pour frosting over cake.

Microwave Fudge

Yields 12 to 15 pieces

1 (14-ounce) can evaporated milk
4 cups sugar
1 cup butter or margarine
1 (12-ounce) package chocolate
  chips

1 (7-ounce) jar marshmallow
  creme
1 teaspoon vanilla
1 cup chopped nuts (optional)

In 4-quart microwave bowl mix milk, sugar and butter. Cook on High 20 to 22 minutes (soft ball or 234° on candy thermometer). Stir well every 5 minutes during cooking. Stir in chocolate and marshmallow creme; blend well. Add vanilla and nuts, it used, and mix. Pour into buttered 9-inch square pan for thick pieces or a 12x7x1-inch pan for thinner pieces.

Strawberry Cheese Cake

Serves 8 to 10

3 tablespoons butter or margarine
1 cup graham cracker crumbs
¾ cup plus 2 tablespoons sugar,
  divided
2 (8-ounce) packages cream
  cheese
⅓ cup sour cream
¼ teaspoon salt

4 large eggs
3 tablespoons lemon juice,
  divided
2 teaspoons grated lemon rind
¼ teaspoon vanilla
1 (10-ounce) package frozen
  sweetened strawberries
1 tablespoon cornstarch

Microwave butter in 9-inch round baking dish, uncovered, at High until melted, 30 to 45 seconds. Add crumbs, stirring and tossing with fork until evenly moistened. Stir in 2 tablespoons sugar. Spread crumb mix in even layer in dish; press firmly with fingers. Microwave, uncovered, at High 1½ minutes; rotate dish ½ turn after 1 minute. In large bowl microwave cream cheese at Medium until softened, about 1 minute. Beat until smooth. Beat in remaining ¾ cup sugar, sour cream and salt. Add eggs, 1 at a time, beating well on medium speed of mixer after each addition. Stir in 2 tablespoons lemon juice, rind and vanilla. Microwave cheese mix, uncovered, at High just until very hot, 3 to 5 minutes, stirring every 2 minutes. Pour mix over crumb mixture; spread top smooth. Microwave cheese cake, uncovered, at Medium until filling is almost set in center, 7 to 12 minutes, rotating dish ¼ turn every 3 minutes during cooking. Filling will firm up as cake cools. Cool completely on wire rack. Refrigerate, covered, at least 8 hours or overnight. Microwave strawberries in package on paper plate at High just until soft, 1 to 3 minutes. Berries will be slightly icy. Drain juice from berries into small bowl. Stir in cornstarch until dissolved. Stir in strawberries. Microwave, uncovered, at High until thickened and clear, 2 to 5 minutes; stir mixture after each minute of cooking. Stir in remaining 1 tablespoon lemon juice. Cool completely. Serve with cheese cake or spoon over cake before serving. May top with any canned pie filling if desired.

Cranberry Cooler

Serves 1
Wonderfully refreshing, 42 calories per 12-ounce glass

6 ounces diet cranberry juice

6 ounces diet lemon-lime carbonated soda

Combine juice and soda over ice.

Bean/Carrot Salad

Serves 4

2 cups wax beans
2 cups green beans
2 cups sliced cooked carrots
¼ cup red wine vinegar
¼ cup water
2 tablespoons lemon juice

½ teaspoon dried basil
1 tablespoons plus 1 teaspoon olive oil
Dash of garlic powder
Salt and pepper to taste (optional)

Combine vegetables; add remaining ingredients and mix well. Refrigerate until chilled, about 1 hour, toss again and serve.

Gelatin Cottage Cheese Salad

Serves 8 to 10
For a large group

3 cups cottage cheese
2 (8-ounce) containers frozen non-dairy whipped topping
1 (14-ounce) can mandarin oranges, drained

1 (16-ounce) can crushed pineapple, drained
2 (3-ounce) packages fruit flavor gelatin

Mix cottage cheese and whipped topping; fold in fruit. Sprinkle gelatin over the mixture and blend well. Refrigerate until ready to serve.

Lo-Cal Slaw

Serves 16 Yields 8 cups
Delicious, creamy and garlic-ky

7 cups shredded cabbage
1 cup chopped onion
⅔ cup plain lowfat yogurt
⅔ cup reduced-calorie
  mayonnaise
3 tablespoons white vinegar

1 teaspoon celery seed
1 teaspoon dill weed
½ teaspoon garlic powder or
  2 to 4 cloves, minced
¼ teaspoon pepper

Combine cabbage and onion in large bowl. In separate bowl combine remaining ingredients, mixing well. Pour over cabbage, tossing to mix thoroughly. Cover bowl with plastic wrap and refrigerate for several hours.

Sugar Dusted French Toast Sticks

Serves 6

1 cup egg substitute
½ cup orange juice
½ teaspoon vanilla
¼ teaspoon ground cinnamon
6 (1-ounce) slices firm white
  bread

2 tablespoons reduced-calorie
  margarine
2 teaspoons confectioners' sugar

In shallow bowl, whisk first 4 ingredients until combined; set aside. Cut each slice of bread into four 1x4-inch sticks; press into egg mixture to coat both sides. Melt margarine in a 12-inch non-stick skillet over medium heat. Cook bread about 5 minutes on each side. Dust evenly with sugar.

Note: Each serving provides ½ pro ex, 1 brd. ex, ½ fat ex., 25 cal. opt ex. Reprinted with permission from Weight Watchers Magazine, Copyright 1988.

Beef and Eggplant Casserole

Serves 6
290 calories in each serving

1½ tablespoons olive or vegetable
   oil, divided
1½ pounds lean beef, cut into
   ½-inch cubes
1 eggplant, peeled and thinly
   sliced

2 onions, thinly sliced
4 tomatoes, cubed
2 green peppers, diced
2 teaspoons salt
¾ teaspoon pepper
½ teaspoon oregano

Heat 1 tablespoon oil in a non-stick skillet. Brown the beef over high heat. Grease a casserole with remaining oil. Arrange alternate layers of eggplant, beef, onions, tomatoes and green peppers, seasoning each layer with a mixture of salt, pepper and oregano. Bake, covered, at 350° for 1 hour. Remove the cover and bake 15 minutes longer.

Ginger Beef

Serves 4
185 calories per serving, 80 mg. cholesterol

2 tablespoons water
2 tablespoons light soy sauce
2 tablespoons cornstarch
1 tablespoons minced fresh
   ginger
1 to 2 cloves garlic, finely minced
2 tablespoons sherry or rice wine
1 pound flank steak, thinly sliced

2 medium green peppers, cut into
   thin strips
4 green onions, chopped in 1-inch
   pieces
2 tomatoes, cut into wedges
3 whole canned tomatoes,
   drained

In a 2-quart casserole, blend first 6 ingredients. Add steak, stirring to coat. Add green pepper and onions. Microwave on high for 8 to 10 minutes until meat is tender, stirring 3 times. Stir in tomatoes. Microwave on high for 1 to 2 minutes until tomatoes are heated through. May be served alone or over rice.

Breast of Turkey with Citrus Sauce

Serves 4

2 cups canned unsweetened
   pineapple juice
Dash of cayenne pepper
1 to 1¼ pounds turkey breast
   slices (8 slices about ⅛-inch
   thick)

Vegetable oil
Salt to taste
¼ cup plain lowfat yogurt
1½ tablespoons chopped fresh
   chives

In a medium saucepan combine pineapple juice and cayenne; simmer 15 minutes until reduced to ¾ cup. Meanwhile, brush slices lightly with oil. Season with salt as desired. Broil 1 to 2 minutes per side until slices are opaque. Remove saucepan from heat; whisk in yogurt. Before serving, stir in chives. To serve, arrange 2 slices turkey on each plate; spoon sauce over.

Note: Per serving–246 cal., 31 gm. protein, 5 gm. fat, 18 gm. carbohydrates, 80 mg. cholesterol, 97 mg. sodium.

Pork Chops and Apple Casserole

Serves 6
350 calories in each serving

6 pork chops, ⅓-inch thick
1½ teaspoons salt
¼ teaspoon pepper
6 small white onions
2 cups canned calories-reduced
   applesauce
2 tablespoons seedless raisins

1 tablespoon brown sugar,
   firmly packed
¾ cup beef broth
¼ teaspoon nutmeg
¼ teaspoon thyme
1 bay leaf
2 sprigs parsley

Broil the chops on a broiler rack under a hot broiler for 15 minutes, turning them once. Transfer to a casserole and sprinkle with salt and pepper. Spread the onions, applesauce and raisins over them. Add brown sugar, broth, seasonings and parsley. Cover and bake at 375° for 1¼ hours. Skim the fat; discard bay leaf and parsley. Serve directly from the casserole.

Chicken 'N Noodles Amandine

Serves 2

1 tablespoon butter or margarine, divided
¼ ounce slivered almonds
2 chicken cutlets (¼ pound each)
½ cup sliced mushrooms
½ cup diagonally sliced scallions
½ teaspoon salt

Dash of pepper
½ teaspoon all-purpose flour
½ cup water
2 tablespoons sour cream
½ package chicken broth and seasoning mix
1 cup cooked noodles

In a 8 or 9-inch skillet, heat 1 teaspoon butter until bubbly and hot; stir in almonds and saute, stirring constantly, until golden. Using slotted spoon, remove almonds and set aside. In the same skillet add remaining 2 teaspoons butter until bubbly and hot; add chicken and cook, turning once, until brown on both sides, 2 to 3 minutes. Remove from skillet and set aside. In same skillet combine mushrooms, scallions, salt and pepper and saute until vegetables are tender. Sprinkle flour over the vegetables and stir to combine. Gradually stir in water; add sour cream and broth mix and stir to blend. Reduce heat to low; return chicken to pan and let simmer until chicken is tender, about 5 minutes. Top ½ cup noodles with ½ chicken mixture and ½ almonds to sprinkle on top; repeat for another serving.

Note: 343 calories, 32g. protein, 13 g. fat, 23 g. carbohydrates, 68 mg. calcium, 946 mg. sodium, 97 mg. cholesterol. From Weight Watchers Quick and Easy Cookbook.

Seafood Cocktail Sauce

Yields about 1 cup
Good for shrimp, crabmeat, lobster

1 (8-ounce) bottle low-cal catalina salad dressing
Horseradish to taste

Few drops hot pepper sauce (optional)

Mix salad dressing with horseradish to taste, ½ and ½ or ⅔ to ⅓. Add hot pepper sauce if desired.

Baked Fish Fillets with Curry

Serves 4
Simple to prepare

4 (6-ounce) skinless lean white
    fish fillets
Dried basil or caraway seeds to
    taste or your choice of
    seasonings
Salt to taste

3 tablespoons white wine vinegar
6 tablespoons vegetable oil
Pinch of curry powder
Endive or other salad greens
⅓ cup finely diced tomato

Rinse fillets and pat dry with paper towels. Place in ungreased baking dish. Sprinkle fillets with basil, caraway seeds or your choice of seasonings. Season with salt. Cover dish with foil and bake at 375° for 6 to 8 minutes until fish is done. Check by cutting into the center of the thickest piece. Whisk together vinegar, oil and curry; pour into a small bowl. Arrange leaves of endive or other greens on 4 serving plates. Place baked fish to side of greens; garnish with tomatoes. Drizzle dressing over fish and greens at the table.

Note: 317 cal., 28 gm. protein, 22 gm. fat, 1 gm, carbohydrate, 81 mg. cholesterol, 181 mg. sodium.

Baked Curried Fish

Serves 5 to 6
126 calories per serving

1 cup sliced celery
2 small onions, thinly sliced
1 teaspoon curry powder
1 tablespoon butter or margarine

¼ cup skim milk
1½ pounds fresh or frozen fish
    fillets, thawed
¾ teaspoon salt (optional)

In a small covered saucepan cook celery, onion and curry in butter over medium heat for 8 to 10 minutes or until onion is tender-crisp, stirring occasionally. Remove from heat. Stir in milk. Place fish in a lightly greased 12x8x2-inch baking dish. Sprinkle with salt if desired. Spoon vegetables over fish. Bake, uncovered, at 350° for 25 minutes or until fish flakes easily with fork. Transfer to serving platter.

Sole with Orange Sauce

Serves 4
A delicate orange juice base

8 (3-ounce) or 4 (6-ounce) thin
  fillets of sole (or other lean
  white fish)
Salt to taste
½ teaspoon dried thyme
1 green onion, white and green
  parts separated and finely
  chopped

1 cup freshly squeezed orange
  juice
¼ teaspoon ground cinnamon
⅛ teaspoon ground ginger
Pinch of paprika
2 teaspoons cornstarch
2 tablespoons water

Orange wedges and parsley for garnish (optional). Rinse fillets and pat dry with paper towels. Season lightly with salt if desired. Lay fish on a flat surface, skin or dark side down. Sprinkle fish with thyme and white parts of onion. Roll up fillets from narrow end; secure with a toothpick. Place in a baking dish. Cover with aluminum foil. Bake at 375° for 12 to 20 minutes until fish turns from translucent to opaque. Meanwhile, in a small saucepan, combine orange juice, cinnamon, ginger and paprika. Bring to a boil over medium high heat. Lower heat and simmer. Blend cornstarch with water; add to orange juice. Cook, stirring, until thickened; remove from heat. When fish is done, lift from baking dish and drain on paper towels. Just before serving, stir green onion tops into orange sauce. Spoon sauce over fish. Garnish with orange wedges and parsley if desired.

Note: 165 cal., 28 gm. protein, 2 gm fat, 8 gm carbohydrates, 81 mg. cholesterol, 180 mg. sodium.

In 1779, the first town in the U.S. to be named in honor of
George Washington was Washington, Conn.

Tuna Casserole

Serves 4
Good served with ¼ cup mushroom sauce per serving

¼ cup chopped onion
¼ cup chopped green pepper
¼ cup chopped drained pimiento
½ cup water
2 cups lowfat cottage cheese

1 (7-ounce) can water packed
   tuna, drained
1 teaspoon mixed Italian herbs
4 egg whites, stiffly beaten

Cook vegetables until tender in water; drain well. Mix cottage cheese, tuna, vegetables and herbs thoroughly. Fold in beaten egg whites. Divide into 4 individual loaf pans or casseroles. Bake, uncovered, at 350° for 30 minutes. Drain before serving if excess liquid has accumulated during baking.

Sauce:
2 tablespoons butter or
   margarine, melted
2 teaspoons cornstarch
¾ cup skim milk

1½ ounces shredded mozzarella
   cheese
¼ cup canned mushroom
   pieces, drained

Melt butter; cool. Mix cornstarch in milk; add butter. Stir over low heat until thickened. Add cheese; stir until melted and smooth. Mix in mushrooms. Serve ¼ cup over each casserole.

Easy Lo-Cal Fish Fillets

Serves 2

1 cup whole grain cereal flakes,
   crushed
1 teaspoon garlic powder
1 tablespoon grated Parmesan
   cheese

¾ pound fresh fish fillets
   (haddock, flounder, sole)
½ cup plain lowfat yogurt

Combine crushed cereal, garlic powder and cheese. Put in pie plate and set aside. Dip fillets in yogurt and roll in above mixture until well coated. Bake in a single layer at 425° for 20 minutes or until flaky and crisp.

Crabmeat Stuffed Flounder

Serves 4
You'll not believe this is low-cal

2 tablespoons butter or margarine
¼ cup finely chopped celery
¼ cup finely chopped scallions
1 small clove garlic, minced
2 tablespoons lemon juice, divided
2 tablespoons dry sherry
¼ pound crabmeat or imitation crabmeat
⅓ cup plus 2 tablespoons breadcrumbs

3 tablespoons sour cream
1 tablespoon Worcestershire sauce
1 tablespoon fresh parsley, minced
1 teaspoon Dijon mustard
⅛ teaspoon salt
⅛ teaspoon pepper
4 flounder fillets (¼-pound each)
¼ cup dry white wine
¼ cup water
Paprika

In an 8-inch skillet heat the butter over medium high heat until bubbly and hot; add vegetables and saute, stirring frequently, until vegetables are soft, 2 to 3 minutes. Add 1 tablespoon lemon juice and sherry, stirring frequently for 1 minute. Transfer mixture to mixing bowl. Add crabmeat, breadcrumbs, sour cream, Worcestershire, parsley, mustard, salt and pepper, mixing until thoroughly combined. Spoon ¼ of the crabmeat mixture onto a fillet. Roll fish and transfer, seam side down, to a 1½-quart casserole. Pour wine and water and remaining lemon juice in casserole and sprinkle each roll with paprika. Cover and bake, basting occasionally with pan juices. Bake at 350° for 20 to 25 minutes until fish flakes when touched with a fork.

Note: 225 calories per serving, 25 g. protein, 6 g. fat, 11 g, carbohydrates, 56 mg calcium, 397 mg. sodium, 86 mg. cholesterol. From Weight Watchers Quick and Easy Cookbook.

In 1784, the first geographic map in the United States was printed in New Haven.

Hawaiian Baked Fish

Serves 4
160 calories each

1 pound fish fillets or steaks,
  thawed if frozen
¾ cup minced onion
1 cup minced celery
1 tablespoon butter or margarine

1½ teaspoons curry powder
¾ cup (6-ounce can) unsweetened
  pineapple juice
Salt and pepper to taste

Spray a non-stick baking dish well with vegetable cooking spray; arrange fish in a single layer. Combine onion, celery and butter in a small non-stick skillet. Cook and stir 5 minutes; stir in curry and juice. Season to taste. Bring to a boil then pour over the fillets. Bake, uncovered, at 350° about 15 to 20 minutes until fish flakes easily.

Sea Scallops with Pasta

Serves 12
375 calories per serving

1 pound sea scallops
1 tablespoon olive oil
1 bunch (6) scallions, sliced
1 pound spinach pasta, cooked
2 cups plain lowfat yogurt
1 cup clam broth

2 tablespoons minced fresh basil
  or fresh parsley
Salt and pepper to taste
1 (4-ounce) can water chestnuts
  (optional)

Slice scallops into thin coins; saute in oil for 1 minute. Add scallions; saute 1 minute. Drain pasta and return to pot. Stir in scallops and scallions. Thin yogurt with clam broth and stir into pasta. Heat on low until warmed through. Toss in fresh basil or parsley immediately before serving. Add salt and pepper to taste. Sprinkle with water chestnuts if desired.

Brussels Sprouts and Mandarin Oranges

Serves 4

2 cups fresh trimmed Brussels sprouts, halved or 1 (10-ounce) package frozen, thawed
1 tablespoon plus 1 teaspoon reduced-calorie soft margarine
1 packet reduced-sodium chicken broth mix
1 teaspoon mustard seed

½ cup coarsely chopped onion
1 clove garlic, minced
2 large mandarin oranges or tangerines, peeled and segmented or
1 (11-ounce) can mandarin oranges in natural juice, drained

In medium saucepan cook Brussels sprouts in ½ cup boiling water for 5 minutes, separating sprouts, if frozen, with wooden spoon; drain. In 12-inch non-stick skillet over high heat, melt margarine; stir in broth mix and mustard seed. Add Brussels sprouts, onion and garlic; cook 2 to 3 minutes, stirring frequently until lightly browned. Add orange segments; cook 1 minute, stirring.

Note: Each serving provides 1¼ veg ex., ½ fat ex., ½ fruit ex., 5 cal. opt. ex. Reprinted with permission from Weight Watchers Magazine, Copyright 1988.

Spinach Pesto

Serves 2
75 calories, 200 mg. sodium

1 cup cooked spinach
1 clove garlic
3 tablespoons grated Parmesan cheese

1 tablespoon lemon juice
1 tablespoon fresh chopped basil
3 tablespoons lowfat yogurt
Pepper to taste

Squeeze spinach dry. Puree in blender or food processor with remaining ingredients. Toss with pasta. Reheat if necessary. This sauce may also be spread over skinless chicken breasts before they are baked or mixed with rice for flavor.

Zucchini Casserole

Serves 8
Low-calorie

2 cups tomato juice
1 teaspoon oregano
½ teaspoon salt
¼ teaspoon pepper
1 teaspoon parsley flakes

3 cups sliced zucchini
1 large green pepper, sliced
1 large onion, sliced
1 cup shredded Cheddar cheese

Cook tomato juice until it thickens; add seasonings. Meanwhile, cook squash, green pepper and onion in water until tender; drain. In a 12x8x2-inch casserole layer zucchini mixture with sprinklings of cheese and tomato juice. Continue until casserole is ¾ full. Last layer should be cheese. Bake at 350° for 1 hour.

Aunt Bertha's Boiled Carrot Cake

Serves 9 to 12
Keeps well, great for freezing. My children's favorite birthday cake.

No eggs
1 cup coarsely grated carrots
1 cup raisins
1 cup water
1 cup sugar
2 tablespoons vegetable or
    safflower oil

1 teaspoon cinnamon
½ teaspoon ground cloves
2 cups all-purpose flour
1 teaspoon soda
½ cup broken walnuts

Combine first 7 ingredients in a saucepan and boil slowly for 8 minutes. Cool to room temperature. Add remaining ingredients; blend well. Bake in a greased 9-inch square pan at 350° for 45 minutes. Recipe may be doubled and baked in a 13x9x2-inch pan for 50 minutes.

Pineapple Cheese Cakes

Serves 2

1 (8-ounce) can crushed
  unsweetened pineapple,
  slightly drained
1 envelope unflavored gelatin
¼ cup boiling water

2 packages vanilla flavored
  shake mix
⅔ cup skim milk ricotta cheese
1½ tablespoons vanilla extract

Put crushed pineapple in blender, sprinkle gelatin over pineapple; let set 1 minute. Add water, process until smooth; add remaining ingredients blending until smooth. Pour into 6 paper-lined muffin cups. Put in refrigerator and chill overnight.

Fruit Crisp

Serves 4
Great harvest time dessert

1 cup sliced peaches
½ cup blueberries
1 sliced apple
1 tablespoon lemon juice
1 cup rolled oats, uncooked
2 tablespoons brown sugar,
  firmly packed

2 teaspoons fructose
⅔ cup non-fat dry milk powder
2 tablespoons plus 2 teaspoons
  reduced-calorie margarine,
  melted
1 teaspoon cinnamon

Place fruit in non-stick 9-inch pie pan. Sprinkle fruit with lemon juice. Combine remaining ingredients for topping until crumbly; sprinkle over fruit. Bake at 325° for 30 minutes. Top with whipped topping if desired.

Apple Strudel

Serves 10
75 calories per slice, 5 mg sodium, no cholesterol

5 phyllo leaves
2 apples, thinly sliced and cut
into ½-inch pieces
⅓ cup apple juice
½ cup water
½ teaspoon cinnamon

Dash of nutmeg
1 teaspoon brown sugar
substitute
1½ teaspoons cornstarch
1 tablespoon cold water
¼ cup raisins

Remove phyllo dough from freezer and place in refrigerator at least 8 hours prior to use. Leave unopened package at room temperature 2 to 4 hours. Place apples, juice, water, spices and brown sugar substitute in saucepan. Cook 10 to 15 minutes until apples are tender. Add cornstarch dissolved in water. Stir until thickened. Stir in raisins; let cool. Remove phyllo dough from package and lay on flat surface. Cover with plastic wrap to prevent air from drying out dough. Spray cookie sheet lightly with non-stick vegetable spray. Place 1 phyllo leaf on cookie sheet; spray dough lightly with vegetable spray. Repeat with remaining phyllo. Spread apple mix along 1 edge lengthwise and roll the dough up tightly, jellyroll-style. Spray top lightly. Bake, seam side down, at 375° for 15 to 20 minutes until golden brown. Cool and cut when cold on diagonal into 10 pieces. Remaining phyllo should be rerolled in waxed paper, sealed in plastic and refrigerated for 1 week or refrozen for 2 months. For variation substitute 1 (16-ounce) can unsweetened cherries, apricots or pineapple. Omit water and apple juice and substitute juice from can. Add 2 teaspoons sugar substitute.

Chocolate Candy Bar

Serves 1

½ medium banana
1 package chocolate shake mix

1 tablespoon peanut butter

Mash banana, add other ingredients and mix well. Shape into candy bar on plastic wrap or waxed paper, wrap and freeze overnight.

Spiced Cider Applesauce

Serves 6 to 8
Delicious for kids

2 pounds tart apples
⅔ cup cider
2 tablespoons lemon juice
2 teaspoons grated lemon rind

⅓ cup sugar
⅛ teaspoon salt
Cinnamon to taste

Peel, core and cut apples into ¼-inch thick wedges. In a saucepan combine apples with cider, lemon juice, lemon rind and bring to a boil over moderately high heat. Reduce heat and simmer for 15 minutes or until apples are tender. Add sugar and salt and break the apples into pieces with a fork. Add cinnamon to taste. Cook 5 minutes more and then allow to cool.

Green Tomato (Mock) Mincemeat

Yields 4 quarts

6 cups chopped apples
6 cups chopped green tomatoes
4 cups brown sugar, firmly
    packed
1¾ cups vinegar
3 cups raisins
1 tablespoon salt

1 tablespoon cinnamon
1 teaspoon cloves
¾ teaspoon allspice
¾ teaspoon mace
¾ teaspoon nutmeg
¾ teaspoon pepper
¾ cup butter or margarine

Combine all ingredients except butter in a large pot and gradually bring to a boil. Simmer gently for 3 hours. Add butter; simmer until butter is completely melted and mixed into mixture. Put into sterilized jars and seal.

Italian Meat Sauce

Yields about 6 cups

3 tablespoons vegetable oil
1 medium onion, chopped
2 cloves garlic, minced
1 pound ground beef
2 (6-ounce) cans tomato paste
4½ cups beef broth
¼ cup chopped parsley

1 teaspoon salt
1 teaspoon pepper
1 teaspoon crushed basil
1 teaspoon crushed oregano
1 bay leaf
¼ cup red or white wine

In Dutch oven combine oil, onion, garlic and meat. Cook until meat is browned and onion is tender. Skim off excess fat; add tomato paste, broth, parsley and seasonings. Simmer, uncovered, 2 to 3 hours or until sauce is thick. Stir occasionally. Add wine after sauce has cooked for at least 1 hour. Serve over hot spaghetti.

Mushroom Sauce

Serves 6
Great dish for vegetarians

1½ to 2 pounds fresh medium-
 sized mushrooms
3 tablespoons butter or margarine
1 (10¾-ounce) can chicken broth

1½ to 2 tablespoons all-purpose
 flour
2 tablespoons sour cream

Wash and slice mushrooms; saute in butter over high heat. Lower heat to simmer; pour off excess liquid when mushrooms are almost done and set aside, leaving a little liquid in pan. Fry mushrooms until golden brown. Add chicken broth. Sprinkle in flour and bring to a boil, stirring until lumps are dissolved. Add sour cream. Simmer, don't boil again. Serve with parsley potatoes and green salad.

Texas Weiners Sauce

Yields about 1 quart
Great for summer cook-out

2 pounds ground beef, cooked
   and drained
2 onions, diced
½ teaspoon garlic salt
½ teaspoon cumin
2 tablespoons chili powder

2 teaspoons paprika
1 (6-ounce) can tomato paste
3 cups water
1 teaspoon sweet basil leaves
Salt and pepper to taste

Combine all ingredients and simmer for 2 hours.

Beef Marinade

Yields about 1½ cups

5 ounces olive oil
2 ounces red wine
2 ounces Worcestershire sauce

2 ounces soy sauce
3 cloves garlic, minced
Lemon pepper to taste

Mix all ingredients in a glass bowl, cover and refrigerate. Use to marinate beef at least 5 hours or overnight before broiling.

Poultry Marinade

Yields about 2 cups

4 ounces orange juice
4 ounces lemon juice
4 ounces lime juice
3 ounces honey
¼ cup onion, chopped
2 ounces vegetable oil

Dijon mustard to taste
2 teaspoons rosemary
½ teaspoon coriander
½ teaspoon nutmeg
¼ teaspoon white pepper

Mix ingredients and chill for 3 or 4 days. Strain before using. Keep in refrigerator. Use to marinate chicken or turkey overnight before broiling.

Onion Barbecue Sauce

Yields 1 quart
May be frozen, thawed and refrozen

1 (1⅜-ounce) package onion soup
   mix
1½ cups water
½ cup vinegar
½ cup butter or margarine

¼ cup sugar
2 tablespoons prepared mustard
2 teaspoons salt (optional)
1 teaspoon pepper
1 cup catsup

Combine all ingredients except catsup; simmer 10 minutes. Add catsup, stir and heat. For spicier sauce, add ½ to 1 teaspoon chili powder.

Barbecue Sauce

Yields about 3 cups

1 cup pineapple juice
¾ cup catsup
¾ cup water
2 tablespoons vinegar
1 tablespoon salt

3 tablespoons brown sugar firmly
   packed
3 tablespoons chili powder
2 tablespoons Worcestershire
   sauce

Combine all ingredients. Use for pork or beef, spreading generously to start cooking and basting as necessary throughout cooking process.

Slow Cooker Pasta Sauce

Yields approximately 4 quarts
Freezes well

2¼ quarts fresh tomatoes, peeled
   and quartered
1½ teaspoons salt
½ teaspoon pepper

2 teaspoons Italian seasoning
30 ounces tomato paste
1½ cups cherry royal wine

Cook tomatoes, salt, pepper and Italian seasoning in slow cooker for 6 hours. Add remaining ingredients and cook for 3 hours more. Serve as is over pasta or add browned ground beef or Italian sausage for a meat sauce.

Sauce Á Spaghetti

Yields 8 to 9 cups
From a favorite restaurant in Canada

1 small onion, chopped
1½ pounds ground beef
1 teaspoon salt
1 teaspoon sugar
½ teaspoon chili power
½ teaspoon thyme
½ teaspoon oregano
2 tablespoons Worcestershire
  sauce

1 (46-ounce) can tomato juice
1 (12-ounce) can tomato paste
3 cloves garlic, finely minced
½ (12-ounce) bottle chili sauce
½ teaspoon pepper
¾ teaspoon red pepper
1 cup water
1 green pepper, chopped

Combine all ingredients except green pepper in large (6 to 8-quart) saucepot. Simmer 3 to 4 hours, uncovered. Add chopped green pepper last half hour of cooking. Serve with Parmesan cheese if desired.

Uncle Reggie's Super Steak Sauce

Serves 4 to 6
This originated from my uncle, P. Reginald Tucker in Bermuda

1½ cups Blue cheese, crumbled
4 tablespoons mayonnaise
1 tablespoon Worcestershire sauce

1 teaspoon dry mustard
Juice of ½ lemon

Place all ingredients in top of double boiler. Stir and blend over low heat. Place some on steak while broiling and the remainder may be placed on table for individual use. The recipe may be doubled. Also great as a dip for beef fondue.

Tarragon-Chive Mayonnaise

Yields 1 cup

1 egg
½ teaspoon Dijon mustard
¼ teaspoon salt
1 tablespoon fresh chives, minced
1 tablespoon fresh tarragon, minced

½ lemon rind, grated
½ small clove garlic, minced
2 tablespoons lemon juice
½ cup vegetable oil
½ cup olive oil

Place egg in blender and process for about 2 minutes until mixture is thick and sticky. Add mustard, salt, herbs, lemon rind, garlic and lemon juice and blend. With the machine still running, use a baster to add the oil drop by drop until over half the oil has been added and the mixture thickens. Add rest of oil in a steady stream.

In 1801, the first American cigars, known as "longnines," were made by Mrs. Prout of South Windsor.

Garlic Mayonnaise

Yields 1¾ cups

2 egg yolks
1½ teaspoons Dijon mustard
4 cloves garlic, minced
1 tablespoon tarragon vinegar
1 teaspoon salt

Freshly ground white pepper to taste
Dash of hot pepper sauce
1 to 1½ cups olive oil

Put first 6 ingredients in blender container. Blend at high speed for 30 seconds. Begin adding oil 1 drop at a time with a baster. After about ½ the oil has been added in this manner, the sauce will begin to thicken and the rest of the oil may then be added in a slow, steady stream.

Hot Fudge Sauce

Yields 2 cups
Served to hundreds of people at church suppers, in addition to being
the favorite of our family since 1953

½ cup butter or margarine
2 (1-ounce) squares chocolate
1½ cups sugar
½ cup cocoa

Pinch of salt (or none, if
   restricted)
1 cup evaporated milk
2 teaspoons vanilla

Melt butter and chocolate; mix together sugar, cocoa and salt. Stir all the
above together and add milk. Bring just to a boil; remove from heat immediately. Stir in vanilla. Serve hot or re-warmed. Rewarm by placing jar
in warm water. Doubles easily and well. Lasts well in refrigerator, if family
doesn't get to it first!

In 1876, the first cattle club to be formed (Guernsey Cattle)
was in Farmington.

Butterscotch Sauce

Yields approximately 3 cups
Easy

1 cup sugar
1 cup dark corn syrup
¼ teaspoon salt

1 cup heavy cream
1 teaspoon cornstarch
2 teaspoons milk

Cook sugar, syrup, salt and cream together in double boiler for 1 hour.
Add cornstarch mixed with milk and cook 3 more minutes. Serve hot or
cold. Keeps well in refrigerator or freezer.

End–of–The–Garden Relish

Yields 7 pints
A favorite of our family

1 quart chopped green tomatoes
1 quart chopped green peppers
1 quart chopped cabbage
1 pint chopped red peppers
1 pint chopped onions
½ cup kosher salt

1 quart cider vinegar
4 cups sugar
1½ teaspoons turmeric
1 tablespoon celery seeds
2 tablespoons mustard seeds

Combine vegetables with salt; let stand 3 to 4 hours. Drain, but do not rinse. Add to remaining ingredients in large pot. Bring to a boil. Fill hot jars. Process in hot water bath for 5 minutes.

Cranberry Salsa

Yields 2 cups
An unusual relish

1½ cups fresh cranberries
2 green onions, minced
1 small jalapeno pepper,
   minced
⅓ cup sugar

3 tablespoons fresh mint, minced
   or 1 tablespoon crushed dried
   mint
3 tablespoons fresh lime juice
¼ teaspoon ground ginger

Position knife blade in food processor bowl. Place cranberries in food chute; slice, applying light pressure with food pusher. Place cranberries in bowl; stir in remaining ingredients. Cover and chill 24 hours or up to 4 days.

Pickled Mushrooms

Yields 2 cups
Everybody loves this at a party

⅓ cup red wine vinegar
⅓ cup vegetable oil
1 small onion, thinly sliced and
    separated into rings
1 teaspoon salt
2 teaspoons dried parsley flakes

1 teaspoon prepared mustard
1 tablespoon brown sugar, firmly
    packed
2 (6-ounce) cans mushroom
    crowns, drained

In a small saucepan combine wine vinegar, oil, onion, salt, parsley flakes, mustard and brown sugar. Bring to a boil; add mushrooms and simmer 5 to 6 minutes. Chill in covered bowl for several hours, stirring occasionally; drain. Serve with cocktail picks for easy eating!

Pickled Beets

Yields 1 quart

2 cups sugar
2 cups water
2 cups vinegar
1 lemon, thinly sliced

1 tablespoon cinnamon
1 teaspoon cloves
1 teaspoon allspice
Beets, cooked

Bring sauce ingredients to a boil and cover beets; simmer 15 minutes. Seal in hot jars.

Tomato-Raspberry Jam

Yields 2 pints

4 cups tomatoes, peeled and
    finely chopped
2 cups sugar

½ teaspoon dry mustard
2 (3-ounce) packages raspberry
    flavor gelatin

Boil tomatoes for 15 minutes. Add remaining ingredients and boil 10 minutes more. Let cool. Put into jars. Keep refrigerated.

Quick Cranberry Chutney

Yields 2 cups
Served with roast turkey or leftover roast beef

1 (16-ounce) can whole-berry
   cranberry sauce
2 tablespoons frozen orange juice
   concentrate, undiluted
¼ cup finely chopped celery

¼ cup raisins
¼ cup chopped walnuts
2 tablespoons prepared
   horseradish

Combine all ingredients in saucepan; cook until heated through. Serve hot or cold.

Peach or Pear Chutney

Yields 1 quart
You may substitute apples if desired

1 quart peaches or pears, peeled
   and sliced
¼ cup raisins
¼ cup onion finely diced
½ cup brown sugar
   firmly packed
1 tablespoon mustard seed

½ tablespoon fresh ginger,
   minced
½ teaspoon salt
1 clove garlic, minced
1 teaspoon red pepper flakes
1 red pepper, diced
1 cup white wine vinegar

Combine all in a non-corrosive pot and cook slowly until thickened, about 40 minutes.

Note: This chutney goes especially well with roast pork or baked chicken. Just spoon some on during the last half of the cooking time.

Cranberry Conserve

Yields 3 to 4 cups

1 cup fresh cranberries
½ cup raisins
1 small apple, chopped
1 small clove garlic, minced
2 tablespoons slivered
  orange rind
1 medium onion, chopped
¾ cup orange juice

¼ cup cider vinegar
1 teaspoon rum extract
½ cup brown sugar, firmly
  packed
¼ teaspoon ground cinnamon
¼ teaspoon ground cloves
¼ teaspoon ground ginger

In a covered saucepan, bring all ingredients to a boil. Simmer, covered, stirring often to prevent sticking, about 10 to 15 minutes, until thickened. Refrigerate overnight, covered tightly to blend flavors, before serving.

In 1985, the largest crystal chandelier in America was unveiled at the Crystal Mall in Waterford.

Apricot Rhubarb Jam

Yields 5 to 6 pints

8 cups rhubarb finely chopped
4 cups sugar
1 (21-ounce) can apricot pie filling

1 (3-ounce) package orange flavor
gelatin

Combine rhubarb and sguar in a non-metal bowl and allow to stand overnight. Next morning, bring to a boil and simmer for 10 minutes. Add pie filling and bring to a boil again. Add gelatin and stir until dissolved. Place in jars and refrigerate or freeze.

Contributors

Linda Aakjar
Kathryn E. Abbott
Elaine Abrams
Jewel Abrams
Carolyn Adelman
Barbara Adler
Mrs. Daniel C. Ahlquist Jr.
Evelyn Anderson
Micki Andrews
The Ann Howard Cookery
Marion Annese
Shirley Appell
Rabbi Carl Astor
Cecile D. Auclair
Charlotte Austin
Patricia Backus
Iris Weissman Bailey
Mary Barnick
Bob Bartley
Priscilla Barton
Carole Bates
Mary Bates
Eileen Bauer
Emilia Behling
Elizabeth Behm
Cae Bengtson
Agnes Benson
Grace Benson
Gladys Berlowe
Lois Bernier
Dolores Berube
Laura Bialobrieski
Barbara Bidwell
Moppy Black
Lorraine Blake
Margaret Blake
Ruth T. Blake
Marion Bloomquist
Edith Bock
Karen Bogen
Leslie Bogen
Millie Bohannah
Eleonora Bohenko
Debora Bonaldo
Gerry Borgerson
Annette Bourdeau

Diane Bourdeau
Lilja Bradford
Pat Bragdon
Janet B. Breau
Lynda C. Breault
Jan Brennan
Joyce Brewster
Martha Briggs
Patricia Briguglio
Harriet Brown
Carol Browne
Marguerite Brungger
Bull's Bridge Inn
Katherine Bunk
Audrey Burke
Kay Burke
Inez L. Burne
Jane Butler
Sandra L. Cady
Yvette Cain
Christine Cameron
Jean E. Campbell
Ann Marie Candela
Jane Capecelatro
Eleanora Capone
Ann Kaleel Cappellina
John D. R. Cappellina
Captain Daniel Packer Inne
Anne Card
Beatrice D. Carillo
"Cheech" Carillo
Stacey Carretta
Nancy Carrington
Marian Casalino
Nancy N. Cassella
Carolyn Cavannaugh
Adrienne Cavarly
Dianne Cerruto
Carol Chambliss
Glenda-Risinger-Champagne
Mrs. Robert Charity
Karen C. Chorches
Yolanda Christadore
Florence Christian
Ann Cirillo
Elisa Civello

Beverly Clark
Shirley Classey
Hanna Clements
Betty Close
Marjorie L. Cluff
Hildred Coatney
Cobbs Mill Inn
Betty-May Coburn
Penny P. Cockerham
Ellen M. Coffey
Virginia Cohen
Helen L. Colella
Virginia Connell
Frances Cook
Jennie Cook
Christine Alesh Cooper
Josephine Corso
Esther S. Cotzen
Peg Coughlan
Carol Coviello
Judith Cowen
Gina A. Cox
Ruth M. Coyne
Doris D. Cramer
Carmela Crameri
Jennifer Cran
Marsha Creese
Janet G. Cresto
Gloria Cristaldi
Ruth Croker
Darcy Curran
Sona Current
Bette Kaleel Curtis
Mrs. Albina Z. Czapski
Henry Czarnecki
Sandra Dancosse
Peg Daniels
Virginia B. Darrow
Mary Ruth Daseke
Alice Davis
Arnold Dean
Mary Dean
Eleanor M. Decker
Tony DeFrancesco
Rita Ann D'Elia
Carol Denbleyker

Barbara Denza
Dorothy Deptula
Brenda L. Desrosiers
Brendalee Desrosiers
Darcy A. Desrosiers
Merritt N. Dexter Sr.
Audrey Dibbern
Dilworthtown Inn
Louise DiRuccio
Helen Dobson
Robert N. Dombroski
Ellen Donnarumma
Andrea Dooley
Thomas Dooley Jr.
Michele Dougherty
Mildred Drazen
Dorothy Dube
Marguerite Dumaine
Ann Dunn
Marion Edelstein
Eleanor Ellis
Beth Ellis
Mildred Ellis
Sarah M. Elsesser
Nancy Ely
Dorothy R. Endress
Jeanie England
Gail Epstein
Mildred Epstein
Angie Eraus
Audrey Eriksson
Virginia G. Erixson
Nelly E. Ermili
Annette Esposito
Angie Evans
Marie Everts
Eleanore W. Fabbri
Jeanne Farrell
Sheila Figarsky
Claire Finch
Lucille A. Fines
Nancy Finkenseller
Dorothea B. Fischer
Jessie Fitzpatrick
Mike Flis
Judi Floyd
Paul Flyer
Celia Fontaine
Nancy Foster
Amy Fox
Georgette Fragiacomo
Pauline Franzen
State Senator
　Judith G. Freedman
Freshfield's—A Country Bistro

Florence D. Frey
Josephine S. Fuchs
Gayle Gabrielli
Toni Gacka
Linda Gaffey
Jo-Ann Gallo
Mrs. George H. Gamble Jr.
Gloria Gancarz
Helen Gandelman
Arlene Gardopee
Elizabeth J. Geissler
Nica Georgetson
E. Giandino
Carolyn Gielda
Jean Gilpin
Linda Gilpin
Elaine Martin Golino
Edith Gorat
Peter Gorat
Janet Gordon
Ruth Gordon
Sylvia Gordon
Charlotte Gorman
Millie Graham
Kathy Granger
Lynn Grant
Lester Greene
Lois Greene
Dr. Alan Greenwald
Nettie Grella
Judith Grenier
Carol Gretemeyer
Joanne Gretemeyer
Diane Griffin
Mary S. Grimaldi
Ronnie Gordzicki
Carolyn Grosso
Doris Groves
H. Ruth Gunther
Margaret D. Hahne
Barbara Hammer
Shirley-Renkun Harkins
Kay Harrahan
Dorothy Hart
Irene Hasken
Mary Lou Hastings
Susie Heintzelman
Anne Herdic
Ann Marie Hernandez
Dr. Sara Herz
Brenda Higgins
Jackie Hill
Eleanor R. Hills
Marianne Hills
Beth Hillson

Joyce Hine
Beverly Holmes
Shirley Ann Holton
Anne Hornbergen
Georgi Hosking
Jan Chapman Huber
Judy Hughes
Rita Hughes
Rose Huilike
Judith Iacovelli
Rosalyn Infeld
Louis Isakson
Virginia B. Isakson
Brenda Wolak-James
Nancie Jankowski
Jared Cone House
Betty Jarvis
Shelley Jean
Louis Jelneck
Mary L. D. Jones
Dorinda A. Justus
Vi Kain
Cindy Kalindski
Norma Kalindski
Josephine Kaplan
Rhoda Kaplan
Teresa Karlak
Dick D. Kast
Jane Kast
Shirley Kelly
Concetta C. Kelman
Gisela C. Kemmling
Beverly Kennedy
Thomas Kennedy
Jan Kershner
Rosemary Kettelle
Charlene Kinelski
Dorothy Kinelski
Anne King
Lee Kirby
Judith Kluck
Melinda Kodz
Catherine Krick
Mark Kristoff
Darlene Krukar
Daniel G. Kucharski
Patricia M. Kuehnert
Ruth Kuk
Dorothy Lane
Janis Langner
Susan Landi
Anne Marie Landisi
Florence E. Landon
Joan LaRose
Shoshana Levinson

Irene Light
Joan Lindstrom
Catherine Lineham
Evelyn S. Lipton
Shirley Lirot
Joan D. Logervall
Helen Loman
Longleaf Plantation, Inc.
Aleta Looker
Anne Lopez
Geraldine Lord
Jerome Lord
Maryann Lord
Ellie Lowell
Deborah Lubitski
Barbara Luce
Judy Lupkay
Peggy Lutz
Jane Maccarone
Rosemary Macionus
Mary Lou Mack
Suzanne Macoy
Anita Maestas
Rosemary Malatesta
Kay Manger
Nancy Manger
Cathy Mantilla
Evelyn Marhefsky
Kay Marino
Nancy Hart Markgraf
Karen Markin
Eileen Marshall
Nancy Briggs Marshall
Grace Martin
Jeanne M. Martin
Jeanne V. Martin
Linda Martin
Daryl Marty
Dorothy Mastromonaco
Priscilla Mauro
Rosemary Maynihan
Bonita Mazzaferro
Frances Mazzeo
Pat McCarthy
Patricia McGrath
Thomas McGrath
Donna McGuinness
Diontha McMurrow
Mary Beth Melesko
Marge Mercury
Jan Meyer
David Miccinello
Anita Miller
Bonnie S. Miller
Edna Mae Miller

John Miller
Susan Milton
Dr. Ludmila Mitrevics
Nancy Modadlo
Ronald Mocadlo
Peg Molina
Barbara Monnaville
Patricia Moody
Audrey Moore
Irene Morgan
Alyce Morris
Ellen H. Morris
Gloria J. Mosley
Marguerite Movdino
Dorothy Murphy
Estelle Murray
Laura C. Mylchreest
Lorraine Nacsin
Pauline Nagy
Ann Perkins Nasin
Leora D. Natan
Margaret Naumann
Sharon Newkirk
Evelyn Newton
Connie Newtson
Dolores Nole
Jeannette Norton
Gloria Nuechterlein
Joyce O'Dea
Penny Ohnmeiss
Diane O'Keeffe
Old Babcock Tavern
Old Lyme Inn
Maryann Oliver
Audrey Ondayko
Nikki O'Neill
Bonnie Orintas
Phyllis Osias
Virginia Osterman
Carol Pagano
Patti Palattella
April Panagrossi
Thomas F. Pannone
Jennie T. Panos
Ruth Papp
Jean Parker
Virginia Parker
Janet Peckinpaugh
Susan Pedemonti
Donna Pelosi
Lois K. Penney
Phyllis Pepe
Josefa Perez
John A. Perkins
Elayne R. Perlstein

Pat Perry
Joanne Peters
Dianne Petry
Shirley Phelps
Charlotte Piggot
The Place Restaurant
Cleone Plunske
Ruth Podgwaite
Mollie Potoff
Judith K. Potter
Joan Pouliot
Barbara Powers
Mary Powers
Edith Praque
Deane Preuss
Eleanor Preuss
Sharon B. Preuss
Louise Pronovost
Judith M. Puhalski
Shirley K. Putnam
Eleanor Racette
Marie E. Rambush
Donna Randall
Lynn Rapsilber
Betty Goulet Reifers
Barbara Reilly
Cynthia Reznick
Robert D. Rhodes
Evelyn Ricci
Susan Richter
Mildred C. Riehard
Sandra L. Rijs
Mary Ellen Rivers
Charlotte Robe
Dorothy Roberts
Jo-Anne Roberts
Mrs. R. J. Robertson
Patricia M. Robinson
Pat Roche
Norma Rogin
Ruth Rosenbloom
Gary J. Ross D.M.D.
Annette Rouleau
Deborah Rouleau
Dottie Roux
Mrs. John G. Rowland
Marisa Roy
Bernice Daley Roys
Donna Ruane
Mary Ruby
Harriet G. Ruiret
Mary Ryan
Sue Ryker
Marilyn B. Sagor
Gloria Saharek

Joanne St. George
Arlene Salvati
Mary Sampley
Hilda Jane Samuels
Nydia Saros
JoAnn Scata
Linda Schermetzler
  (Covered Wagon Rest.)
Marie Schermetzler
Mike Schermetzler
  (Covered Wagon Rest.)
Yvonne Schipis
Phyllis Schondorf
Sally Schrumm
Christine Sechow
Eunice Senger
Judy Senkbeil
Shirley Sesto
Betty Shaw
M. Jay Shea
Mary A. Sheehan
Rita Sheets
Mari Shooks
Barbara Shugrue
Elinor Shumway
Ann Cunningham-Siggins
Jane Silberfeld
Lucy Simard
Dee Skovich
Chris Slate
Lillian Smith
Phyllis Smith
Terrie Smith
Valarie Smith
Laura Snell
Bonne Sornberger
Marilyn Spence
Janice Sprogell
Donald Stands
Connie Starsiak
Irma Stein
Katherine G. Stevenson
Marcia Stiehl
Mary R. Stone

Lyna L. Storrs
Robert M. Sulick
Margaret Sullivan
Renee Suprenant
Gert Sutcliffe
Eleanore Svehla
Kathleen C. Svetz
Mary Svetz
Lucille Sviridoff
Virginia Swan
Cynthia Swift
Linda Szegola
Ruth Tantony
Georgene H. Tapp
Elizabeth Tedesco
Mark Telford
Jan Tenney
Mary Anne Tessier
Michele Testani
Mary L. Thomson
Joanne Tichon
Melissa Timmerman
Kathrene M. Tobey
Joan Tobin
The Tolland Inn
Diane Tolokan
Paula Joan Toomey
Doris Torrey
Vicki Torsiello
Mary Totten
Lisa Traub
Leola Traver
James G. Trexler
Cindy Trice
Kristie Trice
Edie Tripp
Helen Tucker
Martha C. Udell
Melissa M. Vadas
Victoria G. Vaida
Irene VanHorn
Miriam Vannais
Renee Van Vlack
Carla Verderame

Marcia Veronneau
Marge Vissat
Susan Vitale
Ruth Voight
Margaret Volkman
Roberta Volkman
Grace A. Volkmann
Sue Volkmann
Nancy Lynn Wailonis
Peggy Weaver
Barbara Webb
Anne Weber
Weight Watchers Magazine
Hank Weintraub
Polly Weiss
Cathy Welch
Linda Bernhardt Wenger
Veronika Westbrook
Nina Whalen
Ruth R. Wheeler
Josie Whitney
Ginny Wickersham
Dr. Earl Wigodsky
Lee Wigodsky
Mary Wile
Pat Wilkes
Terry Wilmot
Rosemary Wilson
Elaine Glendenning Wood
Violet F. Woodman
Pam Woods
Pamela J. Woods
Karen Wright
Judith Yale
Hilda York
Barbara Zamer
Lyda Zentek
Linda Zifchak
Cindy Zorsky
Elizabeth Zucco
Ruth Zudekoff
Edna Zwack
Susan Zwich

Index

Connecticut Cooks III *is available at all unit offices of the American Cancer Society in Connecticut or send order form to:*
Connecticut Cooks III
American Cancer Society, 14 Village Lane, P. O. Box 410
Wallingford, Connecticut 06492

Please send _____copies of Connecticut Cooks III
at $11.95 per copy plus $1.25 per copy for
postage & handling: $_____
Enclosed is an additional donation of: $_____
                                          Total enclosed: $_____

Please print

SEND TO_____

STREET_____

CITY_____STATE_____ZIP_____

(   ) *Please enclose a gift card to read:*

_____

_____

Make check or money order payable to A.C.S. Cookbook

Also available at all unit offices: **Connecticut Cooks** and **Connecticut Cooks II.** Send orders to Connecticut Cooks or Connecticut Cooks II at the above address.

Please send _____copies of Connecticut Cooks
at $8.95 per copy plus $1.25 per copy for
postage and handling.

Please send _____of Connecticut Cooks II
at $9.95 plus $1.25 per copy for
postage and handling: $_____
Enclosed is an additional donation of: $_____
                                          Total enclosed: $_____

Please print

SEND TO_____

STREET_____

CITY_____STATE_____ZIP_____

(   ) *Please enclose a gift card to read:*

_____

_____

Make check or money order payable to A. C. S. Cookbook

Reorder Additional Copies